My Season on the Bench with the Runnin' and Gunnin' Phoenix Suns

SEVEN SECONDS OR LESS

Jack McCallum

A Touchstone Book
Published by Simon & Schuster
New York   London   Toronto   Sydney

To all those deserving players and coaches

who never made it this far

TOUCHSTONE
Rockefeller Center
1230 Avenue of the Americas
New York, NY 10020

This Touchstone Edition 2007

TOUCHSTONE and colophon are registered trademarks
of Simon & Schuster, Inc.

Designed by William Ruoto

Manufactured in the United States of America

10   9   8   7   6   5   4   3   2   1

Library of Congress Cataloging-in-Publication Data is available

ISBN-13: 978-0-7432-9811-7
ISBN-10:   0-7432-9811-X
ISBN-13: 978-0-7432-9813-1 (Pbk)
ISBN-10:   0-7432-9813-6 (Pbk)

For information regarding special discounts for bulk purchases,
please contact Simon & Schuster Special Sales at 1-800-456-6798
or business@simonandschuster.com.

THE 2005–2006 PHOENIX SUNS

MAIN CHARACTERS

Players

STEVE NASH—#13, point guard; franchise go-to guy in more ways than one; earned second straight MVP award during season; laid-back but as skilled at delivering well-timed insult as he is well-timed assist.

SHAWN MARION—#31, forward; nicknamed Matrix for special-effects playing style; had several big games in playoffs; has longest tenure with team; sometimes feels underappreciated.

RAJA BELL—#19, shooting guard; newcomer to team but instantly part of in-crowd; buddies with Nash from time together in Dallas; has combustible temper but good guy; became postseason folk hero.

BORIS DIAW (DEE-OW)—#3, center-forward; newcomer to team; hails from France; argumentative but upbeat; newcomer to team but change of scenery helped—won league's Most Improved Player award.

AMARE' STOUDEMIRE—#32, center, injured in preseason and played only three games; cast in role of shadowy superstar for most of season; team wasn't always sure he was working hard on rehab, but future fortunes are tied to his comeback.

LEANDRO BARBOSA—#10, combination guard; known to everyone as L.B.; hails from Brazil; one of the quickest players in the league.

TIM THOMAS—#8, forward, picked up on waivers late in season; relentlessly upbeat; hits big shots; doesn't exactly distinguish himself with hustle.

EDDIE HOUSE—#50, guard, newcomer; never stops talking and never

1

stops shooting; key for positive team chemistry, though struggled late in the season.

Coaches

MIKE D'ANTONI (DAN-TOE-NEE)—the head man; Coach of the Year previous season and finished second in 2005–06; has casual style of leadership but will show temper; playing and coaching legend in Italy; also became general manager late in season.

MARC IAVARONI (I-VA-RO-NEE)—D'Antoni's lead assistant; handles defensive strategy; won one NBA title as player; nobody works harder on film study but has a sense of humor.

ALVIN GENTRY—has more NBA coaching experience than anyone on the staff; a pro's pro with special knack for offense; keeps everyone loose with stories.

PHIL WEBER—gets down and dirty with players as clinician; prone to aphorisms; a bachelor whose Peter Pan lifestyle is the subject of gentle derision, as well as envy, among coaches.

DAN D'ANTONI—older brother of Mike by four years; first year on staff; playing legend at Marshall University; had kind of life they write country songs about but has settled down.

TODD QUINTER—lead scout so not around much until end of the season; his written observations are respected by the coaches; good guy whose high school hoops career was chronicled by author years ago for small Pennsylvania newspaper.

Front Office

JERRY COLANGELO—president and CEO and seminal figure in the organization; sold the team but still involved in big decisions; suffered a personal blow when son left franchise.

ROBERT SARVER—second on masthead but now running the show as managing partner; made his money in banking; brash and forward, but trying to learn the game.

BRYAN COLANGELO—son of Jerry; was general manager until he left to run Toronto Raptors in February after dispute with Sarver; widely respected around the league and not just for being Jerry's son.

DAVID GRIFFIN—promoted to veep of basketball operations after Colangelo left; savvy talent scout with photographic memory about prospects; also very funny.

JULIE FIE—head of public relations; been around so long she's comfortable traveling with mostly males; professional enough not to cheer but slyly pounds the table when things go wrong for Suns.

Staff

AARON NELSON—head athletic trainer; Steeler fan who rubbed it in after Super Bowl victory; quick-witted and acerbic enough to be a coach.

NOEL GILLESPIE—team video guru who sits in on every meeting and is like an assistant coach; he may have screwed up a clip during the season, but the author never saw it.

THE BACKSTORY

A few weeks before the 2005–06 NBA training camps began, I called Julie Fie, the Phoenix Suns' ace director of public relations, to propose a story idea for Sports Illustrated. *I would be with the team throughout training camp as an "assistant coach" and would then write a story about my experiences. (I may have even said "quote marks around assistant coach" during our conversation.)*

I was looking to do something different, something from the inside. In my twenty-five years at *SI,* which included two decades of following the NBA, I had covered everything from BASE jumping to the world championship of squash, but had never engaged in participatory journalism, unless you count having Shaquille O'Neal back his 350-pound ass into me to demonstrate how he doesn't commit offensive fouls.

Julie said she'd check with the authorities—general manager Bryan Colangelo and coach Mike D'Antoni—and get back to me.

I homed in on the Suns for a variety of reasons, not the least of which was Fie. I had known her for two decades and considered her one of the best in the business, not to mention someone who might actually think it was an idea that would fly. I automatically crossed out a couple dozen or so other PR directors who would either dismiss it out of hand or worked for a head coach who would rather push a mule cart down Broadway while wearing a thong than open a window into the inner workings of his team.

I also knew Colangelo and his father, Jerry, still the team's CEO and president. I knew D'Antoni and his assistant coaches, though not all that well, from interviewing them for a story I had written about the Suns during the previous season. I knew assistant coach Todd

5

Quinter well—I even wrote a few stories about him three decades ago when he was a high school basketball star in Nazareth, Pennsylvania—but, as the team's chief scout, he was away from the team much of the time. I knew Steve Nash and Shawn Marion, the team's veteran stars, though neither was what I would call a professional confidant. I thought they were good guys who might not mind a notebook-carrying dilettante; obviously, any such project would need the blessing of the team's superstars, tacit or otherwise.

The other reasons were purely pragmatic. First, the Suns were probably going to be good; unless a team is *profoundly* bad, like, say, the expansion New York Mets or the 2005–06 New York Knicks, it is almost always better to write about a winner. Winning teams are happy, happy teams talk, talk makes stories. Further, the Suns were coming off of a positively revolutionary season during which they had become one of the most entertaining shows in sports. D'Antoni, having spent most of his playing and coaching career in Italy, did not subscribe to the prevailing NBA wisdom that a fast-break team cannot succeed, and so he built a team around Nash that ran like hell and tossed up three-point shots like so much wedding confetti. And, though no one suggested that D'Antoni and his staff didn't work hard, they seemed to be serious about the idea of not taking themselves seriously. In short, they seemed like good guys to hang with.

Julie called back forty-eight hours later and said, "Buy a pair of sneakers. You're on the staff." So to speak.

There are certain stories that just work out, that through some weird alchemy present a combination of factors that trigger positive feelings in the reader. The preseason "assistant coach" story in *SI* was one of them. Judging from the letters, e-mails, and personal comments I received, people enjoyed the inside perspective, the lively interplay (especially the insults) among the coaches, the details of how players and coaches work together, what the coaches say about other teams, and the participatory/Walter Mitty aspect of the story, i.e., the outsider-amateur getting the chance to do what the insider-pro does. Along with allowing me total access to practices, meetings, and meals, the coaches let me participate in drills here and there. On the first day, Marion nailed me in the face as I held the ball during a shell drill, and I felt I belonged.

Soon after the story ran in *Sports Illustrated,* I was asked to expand it into a book. I had doubts as to whether it would work. As friendly and open as the coaches had been in early October, when workouts and scrimmages were held far from prying eyes, they were not about to allow me to muck up drills during the regular season. But perhaps they would once again grant me the same unfettered access and that would be the essence of the book. The publisher said, "Give it a try." I called D'Antoni and he said, "Sure." It was almost that simple.

I had written one "season-with" book *(Unfinished Business)* after spending a considerable part of the 1990–91 season with the Boston Celtics. I rode the team bus, collected stories from players such as Larry Bird and Kevin McHale, and just generally spent a lot of time hanging around. It was "inside" but not in any way, shape, or form like this would be. I didn't fly with the team when it went charter. Coach Chris Ford didn't invite me to coaches' meetings. I was not allowed into the locker room when the rest of the media wasn't there. I couldn't attend closed practices. So this would be an entirely different book.

When I showed up a couple of weeks into the regular season to begin my research, D'Antoni took, literally, ten seconds to brief the team on the colossal significance of my presence. "You remember Jack from the preseason," D'Antoni said at the beginning of an off-day practice. "He's going to be with us a lot of the time working on, I don't know, a book or something." That was it.

Rarely was I asked to keep something off-the-record. As the man in charge, D'Antoni would usually be the one to say, with a smile, "I'll kill you if this is in the book," or, more seriously, "Don't put this in." But considering the hours and hours I spent with the team from November to June, the requests were entirely reasonable. They came to trust me (I think) and further believed that (a) transparency is the best course, and (b) we don't say that many controversial things anyway.

The season turned out to be, in a word, memorable. It's the only word I can come up with. Going into the season, the Suns looked weaker on paper than they did last season because two starters, Quentin Richardson and, most significantly, Joe Johnson, had been traded. Their leading scorer, Amare' Stoudemire, went down with an injury in training camp and missed all but three games. Their supposed lone defensive presence, Kurt Thomas, missed the last two months of the regular season and played only a few garbage-time minutes in one playoff game. Their instant offense off the bench, Leandro Barbosa, missed twenty-five games with various injuries. Their fire-and-brimstone guard, Raja Bell, managed to get himself suspended for an elimination game against the Los Angeles Lakers. On it went.

But they always—*always*—seemed to have something in reserve. Just when it appeared that Nash had played himself into a state of utter fatigue, he would summon up some uncommon effort and hit a shot down the stretch. Just when it appeared that Marion was out of sorts and frustrated by having to guard bigger opponents, he would break loose and win a game almost by himself. And the franchise players were by no means the only source of miracles. Consider: During the playoffs, Phoenix got no fewer than three game-saving or game-winning shots from players (Bell, Tim Thomas, and Boris Diaw) who weren't even with the team last season.

More to the point, they did it their way. By returning to the "old" way of playing, they in fact did something very new. By going back, they moved the game forward. By looking to the past, when teams acted instead of reacted, they were revolutionary.

Truth be told, the Suns advanced further than I thought they would. When you're close to a team, you see not only their strengths but also their weaknesses, of which the Suns had many. You see the process at work, how long and difficult it is, how many minidramas have to play out, how many extraordinary moments have to be coaxed out of players, who, like everybody else on this planet, suffer crises of confidence from time to time. Off the court, the players and coaches were pretty ordinary guys; on it, they did some pretty extraordinary things.

The parameters of my access were simple: I went where the coaches did. I attended their meetings, accompanied them to practice, and sat in the coaches sections of the plane and the bus on road trips, usually next to Dan D'Antoni, the older brother Mike had brought aboard as an assistant. But for me, a journalist who for four decades has been on the outside looking in, nose pressed to the glass, it wasn't that simple suddenly becoming an insider.

I never walked through the Suns' training room, verboten to anyone except team personnel (more than once I saw a player's agent chased out of there), without feeling that I didn't belong, even though everyone welcomed me. I set all kinds of rules for myself. I wouldn't accept an employee pass, and, instead, spent a considerable amount of time snaking my way by any means possible into US Airways Center (which, before January 6, was known as America West Arena) for early-morning coaches' meetings. Yes, I ate the food on the team plane (but not too much), drank the bottled water in the coaches office, and plucked grapes from the pregame fruit plate. But I tried not to avail myself of the postgame buffet that sat, appetizingly, on a table in the locker room.

I went to great lengths to prevent my fellow journalists from seeing me step off a bus or get into a locker room before the prescribed press time. I literally dove for cover when NBA-TV filmed practices at which journalists were not supposed to be in attendance. I was able to insinuate myself behind the bench for many games but refused to adopt what Phil Weber, an assistant coach, calls "the State of the Union look" (white shirt, red tie) to help sell the idea to security guards and other arena personnel that I was actually a coach.

During the season, I wrote about the Suns for *Sports Illustrated* only once—a long piece about Steve Nash, in which he came across glowingly but no more so than if I hadn't been with the team. (I hope that's the case anyway.) When it came time to vote for end-of-the-season awards, I thought of recusing myself but finally decided I could vote fairly. I put Nash in third place (behind Detroit's Chauncey Billups and Cleveland's LeBron James) in the voting for MVP and put D'Antoni second behind San Antonio's Gregg Popovich for coach of the year. Nash won anyway. D'Antoni finished second, jokingly making the claim, whenever I was in earshot, that "one vote for Popovich spun the whole process upside down in some weird way," preventing him from winning for the second straight year.

I didn't hang out with the players much when the coaches weren't around. For one thing, it's not like their first thought was, "Man, we really want some fifty-six-year-old interloper dude going clubbing with us." But there is also a precise line of demarcation between players and coaches. You can't sit in on all the coaches meetings, then try to pass yourself off as some sort of special-exempt player. There were many times, however, when I would just sit in the locker room and listen to Eddie House's nonstop rap or chat with Shawn Marion, Kurt Thomas, James Jones, or Pat Burke about nothing at all. They are good people, and I enjoyed our conversations.

I had a good enough relationship with a couple players, Nash and Raja Bell in particular, that I could give them a gentle amount of grief, and they could certainly give it back. On the day the team photo was taken, the coaches insisted that I get into one just for posterity's sake, and, as I stood there, silently urging the photographer to hurry up and snap, Nash said, "Okay, be careful. The spy's in the picture." On the one occasion that I did pilfer a chicken finger from that postgame buffet, Nash caught me. "Jack, I hope you're paying for that," he said with a couple of other reporters around.

In the interest of full disclosure, I did two things that I wouldn't normally do as a journalist: I got Nash to autograph a jersey for a charity auction and Raja Bell to autograph for my sister-in-law. She thinks he's hot.

Going into the project, I was curious about one thing in particular—how do professional coaches deal with losing? I had coached an eighth-grade team for several years, and, though I don't consider myself a particularly competitive person, the losses would gnaw at my insides, keep me up nights, and have me on the phone for hours with my assistant coach trying to deconstruct what went wrong . . . with a bunch of thirteen- and fourteen-year-olds. What must it be like when the stakes are high? A basketball coach makes so many decisions during a game—substitutions, out-of-bounds plays, defensive alterations, time-outs—that any single one of them can have an impact on the result.

The answer turns out to be: The losses do indeed take a heavy toll. Coaches don't sleep well. They beat themselves up. They look terrible in the morning. They catch colds. They suck on candy. They drink too much caffeine. They snap at each other. Sometimes they order onion rings and French fries together. Then they come in the next day and do it again.

I flew back to Phoenix with the team after it had lost a 140–133 triple-overtime game to the Knicks in New York on January 2. The referees that night had suffered from a case of Madison Square Garden–itis. The Knicks shot fifty-four free throws compared to just sixteen for the Suns. Had Kurt Thomas not been called for a phantom foul with eight seconds left, the Suns would've won in regulation. It could hardly have been a more agonizing loss, especially since it came to an inferior team. Security at the private airstrip in Newark took forever. It was raining. The plane didn't take off until 1:15 a.m. Some players had brought along their families (they do that on a few road trips per year) and babies were wailing. I felt like wailing, too, and couldn't imagine how badly I would've felt had I been the one presiding over this godforsaken evening.

"Five hours of freakin' misery awaits," said D'Antoni as he boarded the plane. Then he and his assistants fired up their portable DVDs and watched the game, over and over and over, consigning themselves to their own personal small-screen hell.

Yet, no Suns coach—no coach I've ever known, in fact—wants to give up the life. The highs are too high. Though I never in any way, shape, or form considered myself a member of the team, I understood that feeling for the first time.

For at least seven months a year, NBA coaches spend as much as eighteen hours a day together. And the goal is to spend more—by advancing to the Western Conference finals, the Suns' coaches were together almost constantly from the second week of September until the first week of June. Part of the reason I was accepted into their fraternity, I theorize, was that I supplied relief, a diversion from the never-ending mission of *figuring it out,* a buffer when they got sick of each other.

They have no secrets. If one assistant dozes off on a plane or in the coaches' office, one of the others will pull out a cell phone and snap an unflattering photo of him. They rag each other endlessly about their packing "systems" on road trips and celebrate wildly when one or the other of them forgets socks or brings two different shoes. They shower and dress in locker rooms where space is at a premium and personal fashion peccadilloes become conversational fodder. Weber, for example, tucks his shirt into his undershorts, "a tip I picked up in *GQ*," he says. "Maybe it works in the magazine," says Dan D'Antoni, "but not in real life."

(AUTHOR'S NOTE: "D'Antoni" alone will refer to Mike D'Antoni.)

One day Weber and Dan told me how much pleasure they get out of watching Alvin Gentry take his morning vitamins because it is so difficult for him. I wanted to see it, so we spent fifteen minutes surreptitiously tailing Gentry around the training room as he juggled the pills in his hand and made the conversational rounds. Finally, he grimaced, put a pill on his tongue, took a long slug of water, and violently tilted his head back to get it down. We burst into laughter.

"Let me guess," he said, "you jackasses have been following me."

Studying a coaching staff would be rich material for an industrial psychologist. A delicate political game is played every day, even on staffs as close-knit as the Suns'. Coaches are by nature intensely competitive, their lives defined by the joy of winning and the agony of that alternative eventuality. But they have to find a way to get along, to consider each other's opinions yet make themselves heard in the eternal battle to gain traction within the organization. "There is an almost subconscious vying for attention," concedes Iavaroni. "You want to feel indispensable, you want your credit. But you have to subjugate that for the good of the team."

There is a distinct separation between the head coach and his assistants. Every day it is the head coach who must deal with the owner, the front office, the media, and the cold arithmetic of wins and losses. To the public, the most important person in the franchise is the star player; within the franchise, the most important person is the head coach. It's not even close. "You slide down two feet on that bench," says Gentry, who was once a head coach, "and you just *feel* the difference in pressure."

A head coach has to act like the boss, even a head coach with the easygoing and casual personality of D'Antoni. It might seem like a small matter, but in seven months with the team I never saw

D'Antoni, who is still in good shape, take a shot at the basket or do anything remotely connected to playing. Never. Before and after practice, I frequently shot around with the other assistants (I finished the season with a humiliating 3-13 H-O-R-S-E record against Iavaroni) and watched as they traded shots with and even got into some one-on-one work with the players. But D'Antoni was always the overseer. "Well, hell, why would I want to embarrass myself in front of guys who are the best players in the world?" he said when I asked him about it. My theory, though, is that he held off because, in some small way, it sets him apart. *This is my gym, my practice, my team.*

The theoretical role of the assistant is to give the head man enough information so that he can make his decisions, find his "comfort level," as Weber puts it. But an assistant has to sense when the head man has enough information and doesn't want to hear anything else. "I want every one of my coaches to say whatever the hell they want to say," says D'Antoni. "I want to hear everything. But if I don't follow what they say, I don't want to hear about it afterward." He rarely did. The Suns coaches move forward.

"Having been a head coach and an assistant," says Gentry, "I've seen it from both sides. It's tempting to just throw out suggestions aimlessly when something goes wrong. 'Hey, let's go trap this pick-and-roll.' But if you trap it and they throw it to somebody else and he hits a three, the assistant is not the one who has to explain it. That's on the head coach. That's why you just have to shut the hell up sometimes."

Countless teams have been ripped apart by assistants who curry favor with the star players or the general manager. "Getting your guy fired by backstabbing him," says Iavaroni, "is the most common way to get a head job." Over an entire season, I never saw one instance of that in Phoenix. That doesn't mean it didn't happen or won't happen, particularly if the team starts to lose. But I didn't see it. There were countless times when I was certain that one or a couple of the assistant coaches weren't in complete accord with D'Antoni's game-plan decision. But they never gave off a whiff of their doubt to the team. "Doug Collins used to have a saying when we were in Detroit," says Gentry. " 'Agree or disagree in the room, but, when the meeting's over, align.' We always align."

It was fascinating to watch the interaction of the coaches with each other and with D'Antoni, and he with them. Weber, for example, is below both Iavaroni (the designated lead assistant) and Gentry (the former head coach) on D'Antoni's pecking order, yet he is the assistant most likely to chat up D'Antoni immediately after a time-out is called. It's just Weber's personality. ("White Noise," Gentry calls him.) Iavaroni was schooled in a more formal process in Miami under Pat Riley. "I would never go right to Pat and say, 'Coach, I think we need to do this.' I would make a case with Stan Van Gundy [Riley's lead assistant]. And if Stan thought it was valid, then he would take it to Pat."

Iavaroni knows that D'Antoni doesn't share his insatiable appetite for video, so he reflexively semi-apologizes for it in advance. "I have a lot of clips here, Mike, so any time you want to stop me . . ." The assistants respect each other's territory. During a plane ride between Toronto and Detroit on April 1, Gentry, watching the replay of a game, catches Phoenix's quicksilver guard Leandro Barbosa jumping around on defense when he should just be guarding his man. He tells Dan D'Antoni about it, so that Dan, who had become more or less Barbosa's personal coach, could go back and discuss it with the player. Iavaroni, the de facto defensive coach, feels free to discuss that aspect of the game with any player. But if he happened to catch, say, a flaw in Boris Diaw's shooting, he would tell Weber about it, and Weber, Diaw's shooting coach, would be the one to bring it up.

If any of the assistants detected what they considered to be a major problem with the offense, they would certainly tell D'Antoni about it first, particularly if it involved Nash. Nash and D'Antoni are like quarterback and offensive coordinator. But D'Antoni respected the relationships—Iavaroni and the big men, Weber and Diaw, Dan and Barbosa—the assistants had with individual players, too. And D'Antoni would often count on Gentry, who has the gift for getting along with everyone, to talk to Marion or encourage one of the reserves who hadn't played much.

Part of my motivation for doing the original *SI* story was to demonstrate that NBA coaches do, in fact, coach. While football coaches are venerated for both their acumen and their organizational skills, and baseball managers are cast as mystics, able to turn around the course of a season simply by calling a pitchout, pro basketball coaches are victims of the worst kind of stereotyping. The average sports fan, even some NBA fans, believe that coaches roll out the balls, players pick them up and start firing, and that pretty much constitutes the essence of what the coach does, until one day he gets fired with a year or two still left on his contract. (Or, in the case of Larry Brown, four years with $40 million left.) To watch D'Antoni and his assistants disprove the flawed conventional thinking was a unique privilege.

Some readers may object to the occasional rough language, but this is what sports sounds like. There are faculty meetings, Boy Scout getaways, and, Lord knows, sportswriter bull sessions at which the language is ten times rougher than at a meeting of the Suns coaches or a locker room conversation among players. And if I had been looking to write about indecorous behavior on the road, I chose the wrong team, certainly the wrong coaching staff. Unless you call ordering both onion rings *and* French fries at Johnny Rocket's perverse—and you might—this was a strictly PG season.

Writing in the first person is an implicit act of narcissism, particularly when you are not the focus of the story. But the "I" voice does slip in once in a while and my only excuse is that it was unavoidable. Over time the book became an intensely personal experience, much more so than anything I've ever worked on. I witnessed more than half of the regular-season games and all except one of the playoff games live. That meant I spent quite a lot of time in "America's Sweatiest City," as Phoenix was declared by a publication called *LiveScience,* although from November to April it felt pretty damn good. I went on a dozen road trips and ate countless meals with the coaches. Night life was at a minimum, but Dan D'Antoni and I would share an adult beverage from time to time and solve most of the world's problems. When I wasn't with the team, I followed the Suns through the NBA-TV package, the Internet, and once, while en route to a New Year's Eve party, on satellite radio.

Around the league, I had to accept the joshing I got about my affiliation. P. J. Carlesimo, the San Antonio Spurs' assistant coach, saw me once and said, "Hey, there's the Suns' houseboy." I had no retort.

Family and friends eventually got a case of Suns stroke, too. Chris Stone, my editor at *SI,* had a lot of general NBA business to talk over with me but our conversations invariably began with Phoenix. "You pick up anything about their offense this week?" Chris might ask. Or, "Did Eddie House say anything funny?" My brother-in-law's wedding took place on the night of Game 7 of the playoff series against the Lakers, and I felt terrible about missing it. But when I reached the bride and groom by telephone to congratulate them, their first words were, "We saw the last part of the game in the bar at the reception. Awesome!" They may have had a glass of champagne or two by then.

Most emotionally invested was my wife, Donna, who in thirty years of marriage had never made a single comment about a player or game. One December morning when I was out in Phoenix, I awakened to find this e-mail message from her: "I think that Diaw's really going to be a player!" That's when I knew this was something different.

THE BACKSTORY

It was a fortuitous bonus that the season turned out infinitely more interesting than I thought it would. The postseason was so long and intriguing that the backbone of the book consists of those final six weeks of the season. And so we begin at the end.

—Jack McCallum
August 2006
Stone Harbor, N.J.

PROLOGUE

Phoenix, June 3, 2006 . . . .
GAME 6, WESTERN CONFERENCE FINALS
DALLAS 102, PHOENIX 93

It wasn't until the end—the very end—that Steve Nash truly failed. Through seventy-nine regular-season games (he missed three with injuries) and three enervating playoff series, twenty games, Nash had not always played superbly, but he had always played nobly, attempting to fulfill the myriad responsibilities he had as the Phoenix Suns' point guard and cocaptain. But now, when it was time for him to respond to a question from coach Mike D'Antoni . . .

Steve? You got anything?

The question hung in the air in a hushed Suns locker room in US Airways Center. Shawn Marion, the Suns' other cocaptain, a reluctant talker even in the best of times, had already offered a couple of the requisite banalities. *It was a great season. It was great playing with all you guys. Let's come back strong.* Platitudes, really, but nobody expected anything else. Platitudes are the lingua franca of sports, and, anyway, this was the time for platitudes. D'Antoni himself and Suns' owner Robert Sarver, two men accustomed to holding a stage, had already addressed the group and nothing they had said would ever find its way to *Bartlett's.*

D'Antoni: "All right, guys, unbelievable job. You guys gave everything you had and you should be proud."

Sarver: "I'm really proud of you guys, given the setbacks we had this year. You guys brought it every night and you won your division,

19

fifty-four games, took it all the way to here. But we're gonna be even better next year, come back hard, and you guys did a great job and thank you very much."

Actually, neither D'Antoni nor Sarver thought for a minute that *everyone had given everything they had*. But the Suns, collectively, achieved much more than anyone thought they would and, over the last eight weeks, had done it so dramatically. The Suns had finished the season with one word attached to them: *resilient*. So the message delivered by coach and owner, really, was the only one that made sense.

Steve? You got anything?

How many times during this eventful season—which included injuries, overtime nightmares, a fracture between ownership and front office, battles with referees, a couple of postseason miracles—had Nash dribbled himself into exhaustion, as he had in the dying moments of this season-ending loss to the Mavericks? How many times had he stood in the Suns' locker room, either before a game or at halftime, urging his teammates to get out early and warm up, preparation being one of the principal reasons for his unlikely rise to the top? How many times had he envisioned his Suns beating the Mavericks (the team that two summers ago had let him walk into free agency and into the eager arms of the Suns), the kind of sublime vengeance only a competitive athlete could understand?

Steve? You got anything?

How many times had Nash conversed with either D'Antoni or one of the Suns' other four assistant coaches about strategy, most of those talks predicated toward tweaking an offense that, over the past two seasons, had revolutionized the NBA, even as it left the franchise one agonizing step from a shot at a championship? How many practice jumpers had he launched, trying always to further refine a sweet stroke that was partly responsible for his rise to preeminence among the NBA's point guards?

Steve? You got anything?

For Nash, the season had been bittersweet, as every season is for players with unquenchable ambition and unrealized championship hopes. More sweet than bitter, to be sure. But frustration, doubt, and failure had been dogged companions from October to June, particularly for one so competitive as Nash. Win a second straight Most Valuable Player award . . . but deal with the doubters who say it should've gone to LeBron James, Kobe Bryant, or Dwyane Wade, players with more spectacular athleticism, as well as the whispers that his skin color (white) had something to do with the honor. Play well . . . but play always in pain, too—a congenitally creaky back, tight hamstrings, sore knees, wobbly ankles. Achieve so much as a team without an injured Amare' Stoudemire, an integral part of last year's team . . . but worry that Stoudemire's return next season will upset the delicate chemistry that had been built with new additions such as free-agent shooting guard Raja Bell and multipositioned Atlanta Hawks castoff Boris Diaw, benign additions to the locker room. Be happy for good pal and former Dallas teammate Dirk Nowitzki, whose outside shooting had helped throttle the Suns, and who was going to represent the West in the Finals . . . but be sad that Nowitzki, with whom he had twice broken bread during this Western Conference playoff, had beaten him to the big stage.

Steve? You got anything?

Since Nash arrived in Phoenix (the team that had originally drafted him in 1996 and for which he had played the first two seasons of his career before being traded to Dallas) in the summer of 2004, appearing at his introductory press conference in a pair of golf shoes (the only hard-soled kicks in his closet), he had become the face of the franchise, a face so popular that assistant coach Alvin Gentry once opened a box addressed to him to find a short note, a basketball, and an instant camera. "Could you please get Steve Nash to sign my ball and take a picture of him doing it?" was the plea.

There is not a face like it in all of American pro sports. Nash more closely resembles street urchin than street baller, hollow eyes, long nose, long, straight hair that he brushes away from his eyes and hooks behind his ears, sometimes in mid-play. Nash reads books, dabbles in lefty politics, has a BOYCOTT VEAL sticker plastered to his SUV, and tosses out a little Zen from time to time. "I don't like to build maps," he told me one day at practice after I had asked him if he has a favorite spot on the floor to shoot from. He's Canadian, too, giving him automatic legitimacy as a peace-loving anticapitalist. And so a certain counterculture ethos had settled in around Nash, and, by extension, the Suns.

But the idea of Nash as a symbol of something—the Indie Point Guard, the First Counterculture MVP—in fact obscures the central truth about him: He is first and foremost a gym rat. He doesn't fit in basketball around reading Karl Marx; he reads a little Marx and shoots a million jump shots. Only such a player could lead the D'Antoni revolution.

In the summers of his teen years, D'Antoni, the son of a celebrated high school coach in West Virginia and the younger brother of an outstanding player who is now on his coaching staff, played six hours a day. That included three hours of solitary ballhandling and shooting drills—the hard part that he loved—before three hours of playing pickup games at night. Lewis D'Antoni never pushed his youngest son or gave him much instruction—that came from older brother Dan—but he did free him from summer jobs so he could play ball. When D'Antoni got to Marshall University, he was the one who rounded up every member of his team in the off-season and bugged them about showing up at three o'clock for pickup ball in the gym.

Twenty years later, that's what Nash was doing at Santa Clara University. He and his buddies would be sitting around at night, chilling, talking sports, music, and women, and, when *SportsCenter* came on, that was the signal for Nash to get off his butt. "I felt uncomfortable being comfortable," says Nash. "I'd call the team manager, get the key to the gym, call some teammates, and go shoot for a couple hours."

The careers of player and coach hardly run parallel. Nash maximized his talents, hardened his body, toughened his mind, and, over the last two seasons, played point guard at a level at which only the pass-first greats of the game—Magic Johnson, Bob Cousy, John Stockton—were mentioned. D'Antoni, also a point guard, played in only 130 NBA games, and 50 more for the St. Louis Spirits of the old ABA, and always rued a certain lack of mental toughness, and a dubious outside touch, that kept him from really making it.

But in another time, perhaps, Nash would've been forced to follow the road less taken on which D'Antoni eventually traveled to basketball greatness. D'Antoni came into a league with only seventeen teams (there are thirty now) and precious few roster spots. He was a bit player for two seasons, went to the ABA briefly before the merger with the NBA, then came back with the San Antonio Spurs and got cut. A vision of his future pro basketball life passed before him—a career of splinters and garbage minutes and running the other team's offense during practices, and that was only if he *did* make it back with a team.

So D'Antoni, about whom there was nothing Italian except his surname, packed up and went to Italy to recharge his basketball batteries. He came back for one more try at the NBA, then abruptly left again, and made this break final. He then spent the next ten years blazing his name across European basketball, the Magic Johnson of Philips Milan, the most famous team in the Italian League. He didn't look or act anything like Nash—he has boyish features and a West Virginia aw-shucks approachable demeanor, none of that mysterious Canadian reticence—but, like Nash, he had that ineffable something known as *style*. Italy loved him. He loved Italy. And most of all he loved to play. His coach, Dan Peterson, coined the phrase *sputare sangue*—spit blood—to describe how he wanted his team to play. D'Antoni spat blood. Nash spits blood.

As much as they like and respect each other, and have interests outside of sports, basketball is the central—really the only—connection between D'Antoni and Nash. And when they came together for the first time in the 2004–05 season, the results were electric. Without Nash, the Suns had averaged 94.2 points during the 2003–04 season; with Nash running D'Antoni's offense, they averaged a league-best 110.4. The Suns had won twenty-nine games in 2003–04; with Nash running D'Antoni's offense, they won sixty-two. It was one of the most dramatic turnarounds in NBA history, engineered by a point guard from a hockey nation and a coach who had spent most of his professional life in a country known for pasta and ass-pinching.

When Stoudemire, who averaged almost twenty-seven points per game last season, went down with a knee injury in training camp last October, the supposition was the Suns could not possibly score at last season's clip. D'Antoni insisted they were going to average 110 points, nay, *needed* to average that to be successful. His stated goal was to win fifty games and make the playoffs. They won fifty-four and had the fourth-best record in the NBA. And they came close to 110, too, leading the league with 108.4 points per game and setting all-time records in three-point shots taken and made.

It wasn't as if D'Antoni had invented anything; rather, he had reimplemented a run-and-gun style that had been popular into the late 1980s. It is astonishing the degree to which the casual sports fan has it wrong about the NBA. As with the perception that coaching is little more than rolling out the balls, the casual fan perceives the NBA as a bunch of listless underachievers running around aimlessly, tossing up bad shots, ignoring the rudiments of dribbling and passing, and treating defense as if it were to be avoided like the chipped beef special at Denny's. In point of fact, quite the opposite was going on—too little running, too much stodgy offense, too many defensive schemes, an overcoached product that had removed much of the spontaneity of the game and put a premium on isolation alignments designed to get one player the ball and turn his four teammates into statues.

That's what D'Antoni wanted to change. And so he became the prophet for the new version of run-and-gun, and Nash was the apostle taking the message to the masses. *We have our best chance of scoring before the 24-second shot clock hits 17.* That means they wanted to get a shot up in seven seconds or less from the time they got the ball.

Steve? You got anything?

A dozen pairs of eyes swiveled toward Nash, who was standing in front of his corner locker. He was shirtless, wearing only a pair of black compression shorts. It looked for a moment like he was going to say something, but then you saw the blink of the eyes, the purse of the lips, and, finally, the quick shake of the head. He was crying, and, if he had a platitude to offer, he couldn't get it out. I looked over at one of the Suns' assistants, Alvin Gentry, who, having seen the pain and sadness in Nash, began tearing up himself. Then Nash walked toward D'Antoni and his teammates gathered around. They put their hands together and then it was time for the same ritual that ended every practice and every game. "SUNS!" Marion said. "ONE-TWO-THREE . . ." and everyone shouted "SUNS!"

Nash slung a towel around his neck and kept on going toward the training room, his home away from home, slapping a few teammates' hands along the way. He put his towel on a stool and climbed into the icy water, a procedure he follows religiously after every practice and game to reduce the swelling in chronically injured areas, which in Nash's case means a large percentage of his body. He winced slightly as he lowered himself into the tub.

The water temperature was fifty-three degrees. Like always.

CHAPTER ONE

[The Second Season]

Phoenix, April 21 . . . .

"The Suns are built for the regular season. Every series is going to be tough for them because when you live by your offensive three-point shooting, then any off-night you could lose a game."

It is generally believed, though not always elucidated, that NBA teams cannot suddenly change their essence when the playoffs come around. You are, to a large extent, what you have been for the previous eight months. But coaches and players are expected to offer the requisite chestnuts—We have a chance to turn this around. We're starting to peak right about now. It's time to make a fresh start—and broadcasters have to declare the official beginning to the Second Season.

After studying the Phoenix Suns at close range all season, I offer this projection about them:

Odds of beating the Los Angeles Lakers in the first round: 2–1.

Odds of beating either the Los Angeles Clippers or the Denver Nuggets in the second round: 5–2.

Odds of winning the Western Conference, probably by beating either the San Antonio Spurs and Dallas Mavericks, and making the Finals: 6–1.

Odds of winning the championship: 10–1.

Another thing that is generally believed—and *always* elucidated—is that fast-break teams like the Suns cannot go far in the playoffs. Tempo inevitably slows down, and that leaves transition teams playing an unfamiliar style. To the purveyors of that belief, which is a vast majority of NBA pundits, the fact that the Suns advanced all the way to the Western finals last season before losing to the San Antonio Spurs proves only that a fast-break team can't make it to the *Finals*. Had the Suns made the championship round and lost to the Detroit Pistons, the axiom would've presumably changed to: A fast-break team can't *win it all*.

Hearing that premise is one of the few things that will turn Mike D'Antoni's sunny disposition cloudy. (Another is a restaurant waiter mispronouncing *bruschetta* with a soft sound in the middle instead of the hard "K" sound, the way the Italians do it, "who, after all, only invented the damn thing.") The coach does not dispute statistics that indicate, yes, scoring usually does go down in the postseason. Nor does he doubt that competitive intensity, which is associated more with defense than offense, goes up significantly, also. But he doesn't see slow-down ball as inevitable. "Coaches hear it, start to believe it, then do it," says D'Antoni, "and it becomes a self-fulfilling prophecy. My point is, it doesn't *have* to be that way. It's not written in stone."

There is, to be sure, an extra buzz about this opening round, given the historical weight of the opponent. Though the Lakers finished in seventh place in the Western Conference, thereby drawing the second-place Suns, they had finished strongly, one of their final victories a 109–89 win over Phoenix on April 16 in Los Angeles. The Suns believe that the Lakers' transition defense is close to nonexistent and will provide an open highway for the Nash-led fast break, so this was the matchup they wanted. D'Antoni couldn't precisely orchestrate it—not in an eighty-two-game season—but the coach had benched Nash and Raja Bell for that late-season game, all but assuring a Laker win that would help them beat out the Sacramento Kings, who were in eighth place.

At the same time, the Suns assume that the Lakers, despite having lost three of four regular-season games to Phoenix and seven in a row before that victory on April 16, also wanted to play them. As hard as the Suns are to defend, there is the general impression that, perhaps, they will let you outscore them—that is more likely to happen in the fox-trot pace of the postseason—and, even if they don't, they won't beat you up physically. Since Kurt Thomas, the Suns' only interior player with a physical presence, went out with a stress fracture in his foot on February 22, the Suns had struggled to an 18-11 record and given up an average of 107.6 points per game, near the bottom in the NBA. Phoenix's further aversion to contact could be demonstrated by the fact that it set an NBA record for both fewest free throws made (14.5) and attempted (18.0). The Suns were deadly accurate from the line but didn't get there much.

Todd Quinter, the Suns' lead scout, feeds this perception in the fifty-page loose-leaf notebook he has prepared for the coaches before each playoff series. (He is already at work on one for the Los Angeles Clippers and Denver Nuggets, one of which Phoenix will be playing should it move on.) The book contains all relevant Lakers statistics, individual tendencies of the players, and even a pie-chart breakdown of the Lakers' offense. (They run "ISO's," which stand for isolations, 30 percent of the time, "side p/r," pick-and-rolls on one side of the court or the other, 22 percent of the time, etc.) To make sure the message gets across, Quinter writes:

> *While watching their last broadcast & postgame shows it was amazing to me how absolutely they dismissed us. They talked about getting home court advantage in the next round already like it was a done deal. For whatever reason their team and staff do not respect us at all!*

Phoenix has in fact become rather the popular upset pick among the scores of seers who lay out their playoff grids in newspapers and cyberspace. Ex–point guard Mark Jackson of ABC, former NBA coach Bill Fitch (picking for NBA.com), and David Dupree, *USA Today*'s respected NBA writer, all pick the Lakers. So does ESPN's Greg Anthony, a particular irritant for the Suns; during a memorable brawl with the New York Knicks several years ago, Anthony came off the bench in street clothes to attack Phoenix point guard Kevin Johnson from behind. "He's a Republican," Alvin Gentry says in dismissing Anthony.

A greater source of irritation is TNT commentator Charles Barkley, whose shadow looms over the franchise. (Insert weight joke here.) Barkley was the star of the 1992–93 team that made it to the Finals and lost in six games to Michael Jordan and the Chicago Bulls. He still lives in Phoenix but harbors some resentment toward the Suns, who traded him to Houston two seasons after that near-championship run. Barkley goes out of his way to praise Nash—"Man, I would've loved to have played with a point guard like Nash"—and even wrote a short essay for *Time* when the magazine picked Nash as one of its "100 Most Influential People." (You think essay, you think Charles Barkley.) But Barkley doesn't buy into the D'Antoni up-tempo style.

"The Suns are built for the regular season," says Barkley. "Every series is going to be tough for them because when you live by your offensive three-point shooting, then any off-night you could lose a game. I think the Suns are always going to struggle just because they don't rebound and they don't play good defense. The game always comes down to rebounding and defense. Your flaws don't show until you play a real good team. I think the Suns are too small to win it all."

The presence of Kobe Bryant adds to the buzz. With the possible exception of hockey, where a hot goalie can win a series himself, in no other sport does one superstar player make such a difference as basketball. Great players rarely win an entire series themselves, but they can win one or two individual games, and the Suns are hardly a mortal lock to begin with. The longer the series goes, the more Bryant can exert his considerable will upon it, especially considering that he averaged 42.5 points against Phoenix in four games during the regular season.

D'Antoni has his history with Bryant, too. Kobe grew up in Italy where his father, former NBA player Joe "Jellybean" Bryant, was enjoying an expatriate career. The star of Italian basketball at that time was none other than D'Antoni, the dashing Milan guard, who wore number 8. Lacking American role models, young Kobe wore 8 in honor of D'Antoni. Before most Suns-Laker games, Bryant stops by the Phoenix bench, and he and D'Antoni exchange a few pleasantries in Italian, which both speak fluently. (Bryant, though, has petitioned the league to allow him to change his number to 24 in the following season. It's no slight to D'Antoni, but, rather, Bryant's homage to what he considers his 24/7 work ethic.)

Raja Bell had his history with Bryant, too. Bell first gained a small measure of fame in the NBA when, as a member of the Philadelphia 76ers, he helped limit Bryant to 7-of-22 shooting in Game 1 of the 2001 NBA Finals. The Sixers won that game in L.A., 107–101, though the Lakers swept the next four to win the title. Early in the season, Bryant, reacting to what he considered Bell's overaggressiveness, elbowed Bell in the mouth and shoved him, drawing a technical foul. Later in the season, on April 7, with two weeks remaining in this regular season, Bryant had come to US Airways Arena and scored fifty-one against the Suns, the majority of them with Bell as his defender.

The game actually presented a template for how to conquer the Lakers—Bryant got his share, but his teammates never got involved, and the Suns won 107–96—but that gave Bell meager consolation. After saying all the right things to the press, Bell stood in front of his locker, doing well to contain the fury he felt inside. "Way to go, Rah-Rah," he said aloud. "You held him to fitty." (He deliberately used the street pronunciation of "fifty.") Eddie House and Brian Grant, two of the Suns always willing to lift a teammate up, were standing by.

"Rah-Rah, it was like B.G. said about that guy the night that Jordan went off on his ass," said House. "What was his name, B.G.?"

"Keith Atkins," said Grant, naming a former journeyman guard.

"Yeah," says House. "Keith Atkins says, 'Michael got sixty-nine on me, but he earned every one of 'em.'"

31

Plus, when Bryant was asked about the sometimes contentious scrums between him and Bell, Bryant scrunched up his face, as only Bryant can do, and said, with requisite contempt, "Raja Bell? I got bigger fish to fry than Raja Bell."

I asked Bell for his reaction. "I know exactly what he's doing," says Bell. "He's saying, 'How dare you mention his name in the same sentence as mine?' I understand that. That's how he thinks."

Bryant, meanwhile, has utterly dominated the preplayoff planning of the coaching staff, which is meeting, as is its custom, in the central office on the fourth floor of US Airways Center. A day earlier, the discussion had even turned physical when Dan D'Antoni suggested, half-kiddingly, that he could guard Bryant, or at least keep him off the baseline.

"You could guard Kobe?" Marc Iavaroni asked.

"Yep," said Dan.

"Well, what do you do if Kobe does . . . *this!*" said Iavaroni, lunging his six-foot-eight-inch, 240-pound body forward, inadvertently knocking D'Antoni off his feet and into a wall, as the other coaches collapsed in laughter.

As the defensive guru, Iavaroni is tasked with coming up with a plan. Plus, the Lakers are "his team." The assistants (with the exception of Dan, who is in his first year) divvy up the opponents during the year for careful scrutiny, and the Lakers belong to Iavaroni, meaning that he has already watched them on tape for countless hours. His intelligence will then be combined with Todd Quinter's more detailed scouting report.

It is, however, difficult to out-detail Iavaroni. His father was for many years the supervisor at Kennedy Airport, a man with an organizational mind who made sure the runways were kept clean, and the son has that kind of mind, too. He had a seven-year NBA career as a cerebral, overachieving forward and cut his coaching teeth on Pat Riley's uber-prepared staff in Miami. Phrases such as "Indiana's 42 Fist is our quick curl pinch" tumble easily out of his mouth. "I think even Marc would agree that, left to his own devices, he would spend more time in the room than any of us," says Gentry.

Like players, coaches have tendencies. Gentry tends to conjure up remedies and theories from his rich past, having been a head coach of three teams and an assistant under men like Larry Brown, Kevin Loughery, and Doug Collins. Weber is a relentlessly upbeat clinician and an unshakeable positive thinker who has read over four hundred books with titles like *Power vs. Force: The Hidden Determinants of Human Behavior* and written poems with lines like "So don't wallow in doubt or be crippled by fear/Take positive action and watch both disappear." He never has a bad day. Dan D'Antoni, Mike's older brother who joined the staff this season, coached high school ball in Myrtle Beach, South Carolina, for thirty years. Dan's default strategic position is: *Never mind all the X's and O's, let's just play harder than they do.* Iavaroni calls Dan, affectionately, "The Old Ball Coach."

D'Antoni's coaching instincts are closer to Dan's than to Iavaroni's. Early in the season D'Antoni had a dream in which he had to prepare an academic paper about the season. "But then I found out Marc had already finished his," says D'Antoni, "and I got all worried because I knew mine wouldn't be nearly as good." During a coaches meeting in December, D'Antoni said: "We need to play this lineup— Nash, Bell, House, Marion, and Diaw. Against the Clippers it was real nice; against New York it was real nice. We gotta have people who can make shots."

"But, Mike," said Iavaroni, "that lineup was only out there for a few minutes together."

"But if you watch the game," said D'Antoni, "you just get a better *feel* about it."

It was a constant dialectic between the head coach and his lead assistant: Iavaroni relies on tape and stats, D'Antoni on feel and flow. Art versus science. Quite often, after he has grouped his players into a certain offensive alignment, D'Antoni will say, "All right, from here, we just play basketball."

At the same time, D'Antoni has been around long enough to know that "just playing basketball" or "just playing harder" than the other team isn't enough. And so he relies heavily on Iavaroni's stats and ability to construct a defensive game plan. In preparing for the Lakers, Iavaroni wants to play more traditionally, less like an NBA team, and keep one defender on Bryant so he will be likely to take a lot of shots and freeze out his teammates.

"So the philosophy we use on Carmelo Anthony, Ray Allen, LeBron James, Kobe Bryant is, 'The more involved the superstar, the less involved his teammates,'" says Iavaroni. (When the coaches talk specific strategy about a player or team, they almost always bring in examples from other players and other teams.) "I know it's not real comfortable for us if Kobe is feeling it. But for every shot he makes, the other guys are saying, 'Oh, shit, Kobe's doing it all again.'"

D'Antoni sees some logic to that, but it makes him nervous. "I don't know why sometimes we just don't trap Kobe on pick-and-rolls," D'Antoni says. "Why give him a chance to really get off? Let's say we're going down the stretch and we're two points up. And now you can't turn Kobe off."

Iavaroni: "You can't turn Kobe off down the stretch anyway."

D'Antoni: "Yeah, but what I'm saying is that we might be up ten going down the stretch instead of two if we *didn't* let him get off. You lay back and let him score, which I understand at some level, but why not make him hit hard shots? I've never seen him get everyone involved whether you trap him or not."

Iavaroni: "I saw it on tape this year. A few times. He gets everyone involved and they create a team concept that has blossomed. If his teammates get the ball from him, they play with *his* balls." Iavaroni is so lost in thought that he doesn't even see the joke.

D'Antoni shrugs. He still has forty-eight hours to make the decision. During the endless hours of discussion about Bryant, it comes up often that he can score fifty points and the Suns could still win, as was the case in that April game. This drives Dan D'Antoni to distraction. As a former high school coach, he can't get his mind around the idea that an opponent, no matter how talented, can scorch you with fifty and everyone treats it as normal. "I don't think we should ever just say, 'Kobe can get fifty and we'll be all right,' " says Dan. "We should just say, 'We're gonna play our ass off on him, make him work and get on his ass.' "

Also worrisome are the inevitable defensive switches that will occur; good defenders like Bell and Shawn Marion have a hard enough time stopping Bryant without him running wild against the other Suns.

"I think it's death—*death!*—having Tim Thomas on Kobe," says Gentry. All agree except for Dan.

"We shouldn't be afraid of that," he says. "I expect Tim Thomas to play good defense. He's an NBA player."

"Could you reiterate that?" says Iavaroni with mock seriousness. "You *expect* Tim Thomas to play good defense? You are a trusting soul."

One thing everyone agrees with—it's not a good idea to show a bunch of video snippets of Bryant getting beneficial calls from the officials. "I don't want to mess with Raja's head, and I don't want to mess with Shawn's head," concludes Iavaroni.

The coaches are used to two sets of tapes anyway. They have a "coaches' tape," which contains lots of game footage and lots of mistakes made by the Suns, and a "players' tape," a heavily edited version that is shown at practice and almost never includes egregious errors by players. D'Antoni believes that embarrassment is a poor coaching tool. It is the job of video coordinator Noel Gillespie and his assistant, Jason March, to keep the tapes separate.

One other minor—but irritating—concern is Amare' Stoudemire. Back in October, before the season began, the Suns' superstar-in-the-making had gone down with what was first presumed to be a minor injury to his left knee but subsequently required surgery. Throughout the season, Stoudemire's physical condition had been the Subplot from Hell. He was supposed to come back in late February, but he didn't come back until late March. He was lackadaisical in his rehabilitation even as the Suns tried to sell the idea that he was diligent. By the time his left knee was pronounced fit for duty, his right knee had started to hurt. He came back anyway and played one promising game, one mediocre game, and one disastrous game before the Suns decided to deactivate him again. Then he got arthroscopic surgery on his right knee.

The knee injuries were one thing. But even when he was with the team, he wasn't quite *of* the team. For example, he had left at half-time of the team's April 17 game against the New Orleans Hornets, Fan Appreciation Night, which included a mandatory postgame flesh-press to thank the ticket buyers. (Similar blowoffs by Allen Iverson and Chris Webber in Philadelphia and Zach Randolph in Portland had produced headlines; Stoudemire got away with it.) D'Antoni had thought of telling Stoudemire to stay home during the postseason, or, at least, not having him travel with the team, but decided against it. None of Stoudemire's teammates would've jumped up to protest that move. Now, with the playoffs here, he wasn't always showing up when he should and wasn't always there even when he was there, concentration and intensity being two of Stoudemire's problems.

D'Antoni and assistant general manager David Griffin had thought that they were on the same page with Stoudemire regarding his plans for rehabilitation. They had all decided that Stoudemire would work diligently with the Suns' athletic trainers and try out the knee in the summer with the United States team that would meet for camp in Las Vegas in July, then travel to the Far East for an Olympic qualifier. Stoudemire seemed in accord with the plan, but then told reporters, "I don't think I can play for Team U.S.A. this summer."

And so the Subplot from Hell continues.

CHAPTER TWO

[*The Second Season*]

April 23 . . . .
GAME 1 OF LAKERS SERIES

"But it's the playoffs now, so, shit, I got to get something ready."

Eddie House stares at the big white greaseboard in the locker room on which Iavaroni has filled almost every inch with tips, reminders, slogans, and stratagems. One hour before tip-off, he is still writing. I ask House if this is the best board he's ever seen.

"Well, no disrespect because this is a good board," says Eddie, gesturing toward Iavaroni, "but, being completely honest, Stan Van Gundy had one hot board." House was with the Miami Heat when Van Gundy was Pat Riley's top assistant. (Riley later resigned as coach and elevated Van Gundy to replace him, only to take back the job, in December 2005, in a sort of reverse palace coup.)

Iavaroni, who had been a Heat assistant with Van Gundy under Riley from 1999 to 2002, agrees with House. He considers Van Gundy to be a board god, the Einstein and Picasso of marker. "Stan had a lot more to work with," says Iavaroni. "He had two boards, really, the top one-third of both filled with offense, the second third with defense, and the bottom third with general stuff." (Now that Van Gundy is gone, Riley has been known to erase and straighten characters that are slightly uneven.) "Someday," Iavaroni jokes, "I hope to give as good a board as Stan." The most important tip Iavaroni has written for this game is his instruction for low-post defense. *Active.*

Leveraged. Unpredictable. "I hope we're not too unpredictable," says Dan D'Antoni, looking at the board, "or we'll unpredict ourselves right out of this thing."

Mike D'Antoni, meanwhile, is in the players' lounge challenging the old-school-style video game. Against all logic, the fifty-five-year-old D'Antoni has the high score on the machine. Mike "Cowboy" Elliott, the Suns' assistant athletic trainer who is thirty years D'Antoni's junior, claims that his higher score was removed by a machine malfunction. "I think Mike pulled the plug," Cowboy says. (When pressed, D'Antoni will concede that Cowboy's score was higher but denies responsibility for its erasure.) D'Antoni says he picked up his video-game chops when he came to Italy. "I was alone in a strange land, and I had absolutely nothing to do except play video games," says D'Antoni. "And this machine is a lot like the one I played in Italy."

Phil Weber theorizes that the players feel relaxed that the head coach can often be found playing video games hours before a game. "It gives them a kind of ease," says Weber, who pays much more attention to the psychological game than any of the other coaches. (In fact, more than any person I've ever known.) "They see the head guy doing it and think, 'Maybe this game isn't all that important. It relaxes them.'"

Forty-three minutes before game time, two minutes after the press evacuated the locker room, the team breaks into two meetings. Iavaroni takes the centers and forwards (the "bigs"), and Weber, Gentry, and Dan D'Antoni talk to the guards and swingmen (the "wings"). D'Antoni remains in his office to fret alone and chew over what he's going to say to the entire group before he sends them onto the floor. Mostly, though, he just chews on popcorn.

The bigs meeting is invariably well organized, given the nature of centers and power forwards (stable and disciplined) and the purposeful bent of Iavaroni's mind. He and D'Antoni arrived together in Phoenix as assistant coaches, but it was always understood that D'Antoni was a little higher, first among equals, the likely next in the line of succession. With eight years as a head coach in Italy (where Iavaroni even played under him for five weeks) and one lockout-shortened season as the head man in Denver, D'Antoni had a track record.

In the off-season, Iavaroni had been a finalist for the head coaching position in Portland that the Trail Blazers eventually gave to Nate McMillan. He is generally considered head coaching timber. But he never acts, as far as I can see, like he's in competition with D'Antoni. Any tension that exists between them relates purely to their stylistic differences, not to Iavaroni's thought that he should be in charge. D'Antoni and Iavaroni (which sounds like a Milanese puppet show) have a bond, in fact, that none of the other coaches share. Both played in the NBA and both won championships, D'Antoni several times as a player and coach in Italy, Iavaroni with the Philadelphia 76ers in 1983. Both have been there at the highest levels of basketball, and that experience simply can't be taught.

Iavaroni plans each pregame bigs meeting down to the second, his minions sometimes moving from the video screen in the players' lounge to the big board in the locker room to another section of the locker room where various individual tips written on orange paper are taped to the wall. The whole thing comes off like a small military operation.

The wings meeting, by contrast, is a study in chaos, given the nature of guards and small forwards (squirrelly, hyperactive, independent). Weber does well to hold the players' attention at all. While Boris Diaw and Kurt Thomas stare stoically at Iavaroni's board and answer his snap-quiz questions, Nash, Bell, and House never stop moving. Bell grabs a cup of coffee. House leaves to use the restroom. Nash jiggles and jerks his body endlessly, wrapping a Thera-Band around his ankles and stutter-stepping across the floor, putting his hands on his hips and twisting his torso, lost in his own personal physiological voodoo. And the coaches can never be sure if Leandro Barbosa, the Brazilian-born speed demon who is being heavily counted on in the postseason, is comprehending anything. The highlight of the wings meetings comes at the end when they gather to-gether, and, after Weber says, "One-two-three," they all holler "WANGS!" stretching out the word for several seconds so it becomes "WAAAAAA-NGS." Quentin Richardson, a swingman who was traded to the New York Knicks in the off-season, started that tradi-tion the previous season.

Exactly how much players get out of the board sessions and scouting reports varies, of course, from player to player. D'Antoni claims that, when he was an assistant, he would occasionally write, "If you get this far, come see me" as the fourth or fifth tip on a report. And no one ever came. Most of the players shrug and say there is too much detail, and even the coaches admit some of the board is what they call a CYA (Cover Your Ass) defense mechanism. Surprisingly, though, no player whom I asked about it says that it's unnecessary.

Shawn Marion is a swing attendee, sometimes going with the bigs, sometimes with the wings. The joke is that he usually picks the wrong meeting, listening in on Iavaroni when he's playing small for-ward, chilling with the wings when his assignment is to guard the opposition's power forward. Marion is at the wings meeting on this night even though he will be defending primarily against Lamar Odom, a power forward. But Odom can also play on the perimeter, and, in all likelihood, Marion will also have to guard Bryant for sub-stantial minutes before the series is over. It is a tribute to Marion's versatility that, on most nights, he *needs* both perimeter and interior intelligence, though how much he absorbs is a mystery. "Shawn, you have to work Odom at both ends," says Weber. "He'll get flustered if you do that."

D'Antoni's pregame speech is straightforward and strategic, none of those this-is-the-first-step-on-a-long-journey proclama-tions. He doesn't subscribe much to them. "On Bryant side pick-and-rolls, we're going to trap them, okay?" says D'Antoni. The coaches have been talking about little else for the last forty-eight hours, and no doubt dreaming about how to defense Bryant while they toss and

turn at night, but this is the first time the directive has really been for-
malized for the players. "Also, don't go for pump fakes [a maneuver
used with particular dexterity by Bryant]," says D'Antoni. "In the low
post, do your work early and gold when you need to." ("Gold" is the
Suns' term for fronting an offensive player, thus discouraging a pass
from even being thrown.) D'Antoni's instructions have all been
sketched out, sometimes in great detail in the individual meetings,
but it is important for the whole team to hear them together. Now
there's a plan; now there's a team strategy.

One thing I'm waiting for is the return of Eddie House's pregame dance, which will take place right after the introduction of the
starting lineup, the exclamation point on the Suns' ritual of linking
arms and rocking from side to side. "I been holding back in the last
half of the season," says House. "Didn't want it to get stale. But it's the
playoffs now, so, shit, I got to get something ready."

D'Antoni sends the team out, the crowd goes crazy, the lights
darken as the Suns' starting lineup—Steve Nash and Raja Bell at
guard, Boris Diaw at center, Shawn Marion and Tim Thomas at forward—is announced, the Suns link arms ... and House finishes by
squirming around on his belly, doing the Worm. Game time.

The NBA has become a league of elaborate fraternization, every
game beginning with expressions of affection for the opponent, usually in the form of "shugs," those man-hugs that begin with a hand
clasp and end with a chest bump or a real squeeze. With trades, free
agency, myriad roster moves that have players changing jerseys at a
dizzying rate, plus an AAU and elite-summer-camp system that
throws players together at an early age, it is hard for a player not to
have had some kind of connection with his opponent. And most feel
compelled to demonstrate, tactilely, that brotherhood.

There is no such love shown between Kobe Bryant and Raja
Bell, however. They arrive at the scorer's table together and walk onto

the court without so much as a side glance at each other. This is *the* subplot to watch throughout the series. Bryant does not care much for Bell and certainly does not like the idea that Bell would be considered in any way, shape, or form a "Kobe stopper"; Bell, for his part, despises what he considers to be Bryant's arrogance and perfunctory dismissal of him as an athlete.

The Suns' get-it-and-go offense operates the way it should in the first quarter, putting up thirty-nine points. The problem is, the Lakers get twenty-nine themselves. Bryant is being trapped and doubled and chased out of his spots, but he makes the right pass out of trouble most of the time, and, when he gets space, releases his deadly accurate jump shot. There had been some internal debate that Marion should cover Bryant for stretches, if only to give the Laker superstar a different look, but D'Antoni has decided that Bell will have the primary responsibility. The coach has Raja ready to start the second period, in fact, but, when he notices that Bryant is getting a rest, he orders Bell back to the bench in favor of Barbosa. When Bryant returns, so does Bell.

The Lakers are playing well, and Phil Jackson is playing mind games. After two straight L.A. turnovers, the Laker coach asks referee Bernie Fryer to inspect the ball. He rolls it around in his hands a few times, then tosses it back. "Okay, Bernie," he says.

Around the league, there is a kind of benign resentment of Jackson, who has won nine championships as a coach. The media endlessly debates whether Jackson is just lucky (having had Michael Jordan for six titles in Chicago and both Shaquille O'Neal and Kobe for the other three in L.A.) or good, or some combination of the two, and even Jackson's peer group can't decide. Jackson's reliance on Zen teachings; his carefully cultivated intellectualism; his sly manipulation of the press; his romantic relationship with Jeannie Buss, the daughter of the Lakers' owner Jerry Buss; and, yes, his success and reported $9-million-per-year contract, all make him a logical target, not to mention, at six feet eight inches, an easily located one. Jackson seems determined to be looked on not as a coach, but, rather, as some sort of cosmic seer who uses basketball to communicate higher messages. In a gentle spoof of Jackson, D'Antoni had told the all-employees meeting the day before that he was reading *Zen for Dummies.*

Almost as if he's inviting further criticism, Jackson has taken to coaching from a large, high-backed chair, ergonomically suited to his aching back, hips, and God knows what else. (A former player who got by with guile and a willingness to swing an elbow or two, he appears to be a hundred years old when he gets up and starts walking. And in mid-ambulation, he suggests a skyscraper about to crash slowly to earth.) The chair puts Jackson literally above the crowd, which is where his peer group figures he sees himself anyway. Everyone refers to the chair, obviously, as the Throne. D'Antoni could have the health problems of Toulouse-Lautrec and would never sit in an ergonomic throne.

But the Suns' coaches respect Jackson's coaching chops. Several times over the last couple of days, a stark graphic has appeared on the television: Jackson is 14-0 in first-round series. "He's had great players," says D'Antoni, "but you don't win nine rings and do that well in the playoffs unless you know how to coach." Jackson always selects a ring to wear during the playoffs—this year it's the 2000 version, the first he won with the Lakers.

The Suns lead by 58–50 at halftime, but the atmosphere is tense. Nash, in particular, is being throttled on the perimeter by double-teaming. Kwame Brown is not much of a defender in the eyes of the Suns, but he's a big, agile body, and, when he comes out to help Smush Parker or whoever is guarding Nash, he is effective. The Suns can't get into their offense, and the game is tied 75–75 after three periods. Bryant isn't really killing the Suns, but Bell's offense is worse and Bryant has him in foul trouble with five. The fans try to help out as the inevitable "KO-BE SUCKS" erupts. You could pretty much go into any NBA arena outside of Los Angeles during the season and hear the same cheer.

But Tim Thomas bails out the Suns. At practice the day before, I watched him effortlessly put up three-pointers as Iavaroni tried to distract him. Thomas would get a pass, and Iavaroni would wave a hand in his face or fake a shot toward his nether regions, but Thomas would just smile and launch another, insouciance in a six-foot-ten-inch package. During games, Thomas has begun a ritual by which he waves his own hand directly in front of his face after he makes a jump shot, an indication that nothing can bother him. "I wish he'd take that hand and shove it up his ass," Alvin Gentry said, almost wistfully, after watching it on film a few dozen times. The gesture doesn't quite rise to the level of taunting. But it smacks of taunting. Of all the Suns, though, Thomas appears to be the most impervious to playoff pressure, which is good and bad. He is what Weber calls "a low-flame guy," coasting along at a certain speed, unable or unwilling to shift into a higher gear, but, on the other hand, maintaining almost an eerie calm.

In the end, Nash, playing a mediocre game by his standards, makes the big play. With 1:07 remaining and the Suns leading 98–95, Diaw rebounds a Bell miss and swings it to Nash in the right corner. As D'Antoni screams for his quarterback to bring it back out and kill some clock, Nash lets fly with a three-pointer that goes in, all but sewing up the win. D'Antoni looks skyward, grabs his heart and says, "Oh, shit."

After the game, Nash is told that D'Antoni wanted him to pull it out and get a new clock. "I couldn't hear him," says the point guard, who occasionally likes to good-naturedly stick it to his coach, "but I wasn't going to listen to him anyway."

Thomas, though, is unquestionably the player of the game. He finishes with twenty-two points, including four of five conversions on three-point shots, and also grabs fifteen defensive rebounds, one more than Odom. Bryant also has twenty-two points, his second lowest total since a game on December 23, and is castigated for his passivity; Thomas never seems to be anything *but* passive, yet, in this game, was the determining factor.

Thomas also gets props in the locker room for having raised a lump on Bryant's temple late in the game when the Laker star drove to the basket. Bell had been stopped by a pick, and, as Thomas and Diaw converged to help, Bryant got raked across the face. No call. Immediately after the game, Bryant stalked off the court, glaring at the officials, and later, in the locker room, Bryant showed reporters the lump. Thomas was then asked about it with the assumption that he would deny it. Protocol calls for a guilty party to deny everything, particularly during the playoffs. *He's crazy. I never touched him. If I did, it was incidental contact.* But Thomas just chuckles and says, "I definitely got away with fouling him."

D'Antoni's postgame speech is short. "We didn't play real well," says the coach. "We'll play better next time. Keep it on an even keel. We need fifteen more of these." (Sixteen postseason wins earns you a championship.) There is more a feeling of relief than triumph—the Suns now have a taste of how closely matched the teams might be, and everyone is vaguely wondering why they were not able to dominate a Game 1 at home, normally the surest of victories for a superior team.

"Well, that wasn't real easy, was it?" says Gentry, back in the coaches' office.

"I'm trying to remember the last time it *was* easy," says Iavaroni.

"Back in training camp?" I say.

D'Antoni shakes his head. "If you remember," he says, "it wasn't easy then either."

FULL TIME-OUT

October 7, 2005
TRAINING CAMP, TUCSON

Amare' Goes Down

Alvin Gentry is standing outside the Westin Hotel, waiting for his rental car to arrive from valet, when a distracted Suns' owner Robert Sarver comes wheeling around the circle, practically running over Gentry.

"That's okay, Robert," says Gentry with a smile. "Hit me. I always wanted to own an NBA team."

Sarver gets out of the car, looks at Gentry, and says, "Not today you don't."

Word has just come down that Amare' Stoudemire's left knee, which has kept him out of the last two days of drills, is much worse than anyone had originally thought, bad enough to require an operation. What it did to the Suns' plans for winning a championship was one thing. But it also opened up a schism between Sarver, who had just given Stoudemire a five-year $73-million contract extension, and the Suns' medical and training staffs, as well as between Stoudemire and the team. No one "blamed" him, of course, for having an injured knee. But there was the feeling that part of it was his fault, that the player had let it go too far.

In early August, Stoudemire had complained to Suns' athletic trainer Aaron Nelson about knee pain. But the club had trouble getting the notoriously unreliable Stoudemire to have it checked out. He canceled several appointments for MRI scans, and both Nelson and team orthopedist Thomas Carter, a highly respected surgeon, assumed the knee couldn't have been a major concern for the player. Athletes have aches and pains all the time and have a pretty good sense about which ones are serious. Sarver didn't even know that Stoudemire had been having knee pain.

Stoudemire finally had an MRI scan in mid-September, two weeks before camp began, and it revealed a small lesion in the knee.

The new deal that Stoudemire received had been a fait accompli since his breakout season in 2004–05. Rarely had one player elevated his game so dramatically, from 13.5 points per game as a rookie, to 20.6 the following season, to 26.0 with Nash dishing him the ball during the 2004–05 season. And he had done it so spectacularly, his rim-rattling dunks, sometimes from a standing, two-legged start, having become *SportsCenter* staples. Brian Grant, now with the Suns, said that the Los Angeles Lakers, for whom he played last season, called Stoudemire the Mad Hatter for his audacious, almost crazed eruptions of athleticism. Whether or not Stoudemire's rapid rise from Potential Star to Superstar was due to Nash's deft passing; D'Antoni's run-at-all-costs philosophy, which enabled the tireless Stoudemire to leave his opponents breathing his fumes; or the young man's own limitless athleticism seemed not to matter. He, Nash, and Marion would be the talented troika that would bring Phoenix the championship it had been looking for since Jerry Colangelo brought the franchise into the NBA in 1968.

And now that vision is on hold.

D'Antoni, Marc Iavaroni, and Phil Weber are pondering the Stoudemire news during the twenty-minute ride from the Westin to the University of Arizona. Alvin Gentry, Dan D'Antoni, Todd Quinter, and Noel Gillespie, the young video guru, ride in another car. These twice-daily trips have been, for me, one of the highlights of camp. Weber drives; D'Antoni rides shotgun; Iavaroni and I are in the back. A radio station sends out classic rock, just soft enough that we can criticize the tunes while at the same time singing along. Nonstop conversation, pierced with insults, is the real soundtrack.

But tonight there is a grim, anxious feeling. No Stoudemire for at least four months is the early medical prognosis. No twenty-six points a game for at least four months. No rim-rattling dunks for at least four months. D'Antoni, on whom the major responsibility falls to figure out how to compensate, says: "We just have to make the playoffs." It becomes his mantra. *We just have to make the playoffs.* Eighty-two games and six months lie ahead but *We just have to make the playoffs.*

"The injury is going to throw kind of a wet blanket over the entire town," says Iavaroni.

I ask D'Antoni how he plans to tell the team. He hasn't really thought about it.

"I'll probably talk to each of them individ . . . nah, I'll probably tell them together."

"Word spreads fast," says Iavaroni, "so they'll all know anyway."

D'Antoni chuckles when he thinks of Bryan Colangelo, the Suns' general manager, who drafted Stoudemire and who will undoubtedly be the one to deconstruct the entire situation—repeatedly—to Sarver. Owner and general manager have a tenuous relationship to begin with and this won't help it. "B's probably got his feet hanging over a cliff," says D'Antoni.

The coaches throw out tidbits about how to deal with the injury.

"Shawn's just gotta be a monster," says D'Antoni. "He has to get out there and get his shots. We have to get three-point shooting from our four spot [power forward]. He's gotta knock 'em down."

"We gotta get one more runner," says Weber. "One more guy to join the pack."

"I don't think there's a lot of real good fives [centers] walking around," says D'Antoni. "We more or less got who we got."

"Pat Burke can run," says Weber. "I just wish he'd start making his shot." Burke is a six-foot-eleven-inch, 250-pound left-hander who signed as a free agent in August. There hasn't been much thought about him . . . until now.

"Training camp four years ago in Miami, Mike, we heard about

Zo's kidney," says Iavaroni. "Pat Riley got 'em all together and we won 50 games. You can use it as a rallying cry." Iavaroni was speaking of his time in Miami when the Heat learned that star player Alonzo Mourning was retiring because of kidney disease. He later returned.

"I still think we can score 108, 109, or 110 points," says D'Antoni. That is the way he thinks: When trouble hits, outscore the opposition. When all else fails, amp up the offense. When that fails, amp it up again. "If we can hold up emotional-wise and endurance-wise, if Kurt Thomas stays healthy, if Brian Grant stays healthy, we can surprise a lot of people," says the coach.

We arrive at the University of Arizona's McKale Center just as the other coaches get there. "Well, Alvin, you coached the Clippers," says D'Antoni to Gentry, "what do we do now?"

D'Antoni has decided to tell the team collectively about Stoudemire. His speech is breezy and direct. "I guess most of you guys know about Amare'. Looks like the best it can be is that he's out a month. Or he could be out six months. So we don't know yet and won't until he has all his opinions in. So we just have to band together right now and get it done another way. I don't have any doubts whatsoever. Just make sure you take care of yourself. Get in your extra shooting, talk to Aaron right away if something comes up medically. Because you know what? We have to find a way to score 110 points. We have plenty here to do it, but we gotta find a different way than we did last year. So let's band together and go bust somebody's ass and get it done."

At each break in practice, the coaches gather together and discuss the Stoudemire injury, always facing the stark mathematical reality of replacing twenty-six points per game. (And the secret hope was that Stoudemire would up his average to near thirty without becoming more of a gunner.) Should Marion be more of a post-up player? Should Nash increase his scoring as he did in the previous season's playoffs when, against Dallas, he went for forty-nine points in a single game? Should they work on getting more offense out of Raja Bell, a shooting guard, who was brought in mostly for defense and overall toughness?

Practice is spirited but ragged, and the question hangs in the air: How do we get to 110 without Amare'?

A general atmosphere of optimism permeates the franchise on a surface level. Stoudemire's return date of "sometime around the All-Star Game," which is on February 18, is never confirmed by the medical staff (they know too much can happen) but it seems to be the going gospel anyway. The athlete is presented as a "tireless worker" who, as Nelson says, "would be down here all the time unless we watch him." Doc Carter says the defect in Stoudemire's knee is a centimeter, "which in the realm of things is very small."

But no matter what everyone says, dark thoughts creep in. Similar knee injuries, to NBA stars such as Penny Hardaway and Chris Webber, are dire precedents since neither player was the same after his procedure. And everyone wonders how Stoudemire will react to such a setback early in his career, one that calls for mental toughness. Stoudemire has come very far, very fast. But considering where he came from, doubts about where he is going are always present.

Yes, he is gifted with physical abilities that 99 percent of the world's population can only dream about—a six-foot-ten-inch body, strength, endurance, quickness, a thirty-six-inch vertical leap—but those gifts can't erase the heartache and shame he must've felt at least some of the time when he was growing up. There is so much that he missed, so many things that he'll never know.

His father, Hazell, died when he was twelve. He grew up hand-to-mouth poor, raised by his mother, Carrie, in a drug-infested neighborhood in Lake Wales, just south of Orlando. An older brother, Hazell Jr., ended up in prison on drug and sexual abuse charges. Amare' attended six high schools in five years. It would take two pages to cover Carrie Stoudemire's legal troubles—and should carry the caveat that at least some of the time she was trying to provide for her family—but they include arrests for drugs, prostitution, probation violation, and DUI.

Stoudemire seems almost desperate in his attempt to be a good person and has turned to scripture. He reads the Bible ("Proverbs," he said, "it's my favorite"), and the tattoos that compete for space on his body include Matthew 20:16 ("God bless the child") and the painting of Jesus and the footprints. ("That took four hours," he says, "and it hurt.") On the other hand, the tat that runs in script on his left arm bears a more secular message: "I was raised in this society and this is how you can expect me to be. I do what I want to do." He wrote that passage himself. And to a large extent, Stoudemire *does* do what he wants to do. If you rented a large ballroom and invited in all the professional athletes for whom self-absorption is the default sensibility, you wouldn't have room for a card table. But space would have to be found for Stoudemire. He wants the Suns to win, of course, but he needs to be the star.

Even last season, when he was tearing up the league, his teammates wondered about his commitment to team ball, and their affection for Stoudemire is not of a set piece. But there is a certain collective feeling that, hey, none of us made it here real easily, either, dude, so get your shit together. Marion had some of the same physical gifts, but he, too, overcame a hard life with a single mother who worked her hands to the bone trying to make it right for Shawn and his siblings. He told me one day that he almost never laces up a new pair of sneakers when he doesn't conjure up a memory of going to school in old hand-me-downs, "ratty, worn through, socks all wet, sneakers all wet, feet all wet." Eddie House grew up in a two-parent family, but nobody gave him anything, either. "I knew from early on that I needed a college scholarship to get anywhere," House says, "so I worked my butt off to get better at this game." Nash had domestic stability, but he had to work ten times harder—maybe a *hundred* times harder—than Stoudemire did. The odds on a normal-sized Canadian

Caucasian becoming a two-time MVP aren't even calculable. On it goes. No one gets a pass into the NBA.

But Stoudemire's nightmares with his mother go on. In July of 2004 she was charged with shoplifting more than $1,100 in clothes from a Neiman Marcus in Scottsdale. Some say that she is a good person at heart and that many of her mistakes were made while she was trying to dig out herself and her children from dire circumstances. That would be the first thing I would say about Amare', too—he's a good person. But he's still running hard from his past, and a man doesn't necessarily run any faster because he has a $73 million contract. Sometimes it slows him down.

CHAPTER THREE

[The Second Season]

Los Angeles, April 28 . . . .
SERIES TIED 1–1

"Around here, it's Steve this and Amare' that. What people forget is that I had to adjust my game to different people."

The friend Phil Weber has brought along to the morning coaches meeting in D'Antoni's suite in the Loews Santa Monica Hotel looks familiar. Weber introduces him as "Jim." It doesn't dawn on me who he is until Mike asks him what film projects he's been working on.

"I was gonna say, 'You look like the guy,' " I tell him, "except you *are* the guy." It's Jim Caviezel, the actor who played, most famously, Jesus in Mel Gibson's controversial *The Passion of the Christ*. He and Weber met years ago when Weber was working out players at UCLA and Caviezel was an avid pickup player.

"He gets that a lot," says Weber.

"I feel confident now," says Alvin Gentry. "Phil Jackson doesn't have Jesus sitting in his meeting."

"Phil's probably got some Eastern guy in a white robe," says Iavaroni. "Advantage, Suns."

The mood changes quickly. The Lakers' 99–93 win in Game 2 two nights earlier in Phoenix had put a dark cast on the series, the presence of the Son of God notwithstanding. Nash had played well with twenty-nine points, but, with the exception of Bell, who had twenty-three, everyone else pretty much disappeared, Shawn Marion most conspicuously. Marion had thirteen points (only two in the first half), while the man he was most responsible for checking, Odom, had an active game, making nine of his twelve shots.

A graver concern is that Marion has gone into the tank, or at least stuck one foot into it, partly because news has leaked out that Nash has won his second straight Most Valuable Player award. Marion legitimately likes Nash, and, at some level, recognizes his greatness. Marion never openly challenges Nash's primacy within the team and seems to have accepted his own role as a kind of vice president. When he is critical of the ways the Suns are playing, he generally leaves Nash out of it. "I could be under the basket by myself and don't nobody pass or want to push the ball," Marion complained to Paul Coro of the *Arizona Republic* late in December. "Steve's the only one pushing it. He can't do it by himself."

Still, Marion sees himself as every bit as valuable to the Suns as Nash, and, further, his people around him, in particular his agent, Dan Fegan, see him the same way. During the regular season, Fegan had lobbied with D'Antoni to include Marion in any MVP conversations with the press. Over the next couple of weeks, D'Antoni did exactly that. Yet voters, taking note of his limited ball-handling skills and inability to get off his own shot, don't see him that way at all—only one of 127 MVP voters had Marion in their top five.

His delicate psyche is never far from the coaching staff's collective mind. On the one hand, Marion is outwardly confident, cocky even, buying into that wonderful nickname, Matrix, given to him by TNT commentator Kenny Smith early in Marion's rookie year. The special-effects-driven movie was hot then, and "Matrix" was perfect for a player with an uncanny ability to suddenly materialize in the middle of a play (Marion seems to come from nowhere when he makes a steal, grabs a rebound or makes a quick cut to the basket) and leap from a standing start as if he's on a trampoline. Sometimes Marion refers to himself as the Matrix, as if he has bought into the idea that he is a superhero who defies normal physical laws. His team-mates call him "Trix."

On the other hand, Marion lives in a perpetual state of fear that he is being overlooked, underrespected, ignored, dissed, persecuted, singled out, patronized, whatever. He grew testy with Dan Bickley of the *Arizona Republic* when the columnist asked him about past playoff failures. (Specifically, his 7.8 points-per-game average when San Antonio's Bruce Bowen locked him up in last year's Western finals.) Back in January, Marion told reporters that, in regards to the Olympic team, "Jerry hadn't asked me." At that time, stories were beginning to filter out about which players Colangelo was inviting to the summer tryouts in Las Vegas. Marion was clearly upset; Colangelo was clearly stupefied and came over to resolve it at a practice session.

"Do you remember we talked about the Olympic team last May?" said Colangelo. "During the Dallas series?"

"I remember that," says Marion, "but, you know, I read about the formal interviews and stuff going on and we haven't done that."

"All right, Shawn, look at me," says Colangelo. "Are you in?"

"Yep," says Marion, breaking into a smile.

"Good." And they shake hands.

The Colangelos have always been strong supporters of Marion—it was Bryan who squelched any franchise talk of trading Marion (Sarver wanted to at least entertain the notion when he took over), and it was Bryan who gave him a contract that pays him $13.8 million this season and about $48.6 million through 2009. That is substantially more than Nash, who on his free-agent deal is getting $9.6 million this season and about $34.2 million through 2009. But Marion's view is that no matter how hard he tries, no matter how completely he fills up a box score with points, rebounds, steals, blocked shots, and assists (well, not assists), he cannot gain traction in an organization and a press corps bent on canonizing Nash and anointing Stoudemire as the next superstar.

Even when it works out for Marion . . . sometimes it doesn't work out. He went through a streak in late February when he was playing at a level equal to anyone in the league, and D'Antoni, speaking sincerely, carried it a step further, saying that "Shawn Marion, right now, is playing the game as well as anybody ever played it." Marion had scored thirty points and grabbed fifteen rebounds in four consecutive games when D'Antoni, unaware that he was going for five straight, a milestone never previously reached by any Phoenix player, took him out of a safely won game against Milwaukee. When he realized it, D'Antoni hurried him back in. It was awkward, for Marion and both teams, and he missed two shots and one of two free throws to fall one point short.

All this angst gives Marion a certain joylessness from time to time. He really is a good person who should enjoy the game and life a little more than he does. Before a game in New York on January 2, Alvin Gentry was lying on a bench in the locker room, felled by the flu, complaining that he needed something to fill his stomach. As Eddie House waved a bag of greasy chicken fingers over Gentry's nose, Marion said, "See, Alvin, that's what you get when you take three Viagra in one night." Even Gentry laughed.

The day after a home game against the Cleveland Cavaliers on January 14, one the Suns had won 115–106, I asked Marion for his thoughts on the game. "Man," he said, "I don't know what it looked like for you guys. But it was a fun, fun game to be in, you know what I mean?" I did know what he meant. It had been a fun game, an outstanding game, and I was glad that Marion felt that joy. Maybe he feels it more than he shows. A more tender Marion moment came in early February, when, before practice, he suddenly blurted out to his teammates, "I want to thank you all for treating my family nice when they were out here." Marion is extremely close to his mother, Elaine, who was just fourteen when she gave birth to Shawn and his fraternal twin, Shawnett. Two children followed, and Elaine worked two jobs to raise her children. "She did everything for me," says Marion, who does not speak of his father other than to say that he was "recently released from prison." Whenever D'Antoni gets exasperated with Marion, he usually ends up saying: "But Shawn is such a good guy at heart. A really good guy."

There is also a charming naiveté about Marion. He chows down on Hamburger Helper and doesn't care who knows about it. He's an avid cartoon watcher. He's a little, well, thrifty. He favors Holiday Inn Express when traveling on his own dime. One day we were having a conversation about the advantages of having kids close together and Marion pointed to what he considered the key factor—the savings on baby clothes. During his annual pilgrimage to Friedman's, the Atlanta shoe store that caters to large-footed jocks, Marion spent thousands of dollars, then complained about the $17 it cost to mail them. One day last year, one of the trainers was thumbing through a luxury car magazine and musing about making a six-figure auto purchase.

"Why don't you just buy it?" asked Marion.

"Shawn, how much money you think I make?"

"I don't know," said Marion. "Two, three hundred thousand?"

(That is reminiscent of the comment made by Darius Miles, a young player for the Portland Trail Blazers, after he heard that a player had been fined $300,000. "My mother would have to work over a year to make that kind of money," said Miles.)

The question is: Does Marion have a point about being treated unfairly?

A minor one, perhaps.

"I mean, damn, I'm doing things in this league nobody else is doing," Marion had told me a couple of days before the Laker series began. "Come on, now give me my respect. I'm not no big man. I'm a basketball player out here doing things at my size that no one else is doing."

Marion has his defenders around the league. "You can say what you want about Nash and Stoudemire, both great players," Indiana Pacers coach Rick Carlisle said during the season, "but Shawn Marion's ability to run the floor at breakneck speed forces you to play their game. He's more important than anybody knows. If you don't run with him, he goes ahead and dunks it. Or somebody has to pick him up who shouldn't be guarding him, like a guard, and that leaves the three-point line open."

Marion's constant complaint is that, at a lean six-foot-seven inches and 215 pounds, he is frequently asked to defend against players who are much taller, wider, and more physical. (And though he doesn't mention it—but is probably thinking it—the Suns sometimes have to hide Nash on defense.) Marion desperately wants to be known as a "3," a small forward, generally the most athletic player on a team, rather than a "4," a power forward, generally a bigger and slower player. What the coaches want to communicate to Marion is that going against bigger players, filling the power forward spot, is precisely what has *made* him an All-Star. He can use his speed, quickness, and leaping ability to leave other fours in the dust, whereas, against the typical small forward, some of his athleticism would be negated.

I ask Marion if he's happy in Phoenix. He says he is. He even feels that it was "my destiny to be here." While playing in a junior college tournament in Mesa, Arizona, a decade ago, Marion took a side trip to watch the Suns play and got a chance to take one shot on the court. "It was a three-pointer," says Marion, still smiling at the memory, "and it went in. First NBA three-point shot I ever took. I thought, 'This is where I want to be.'" He was elated when the Suns made him the ninth pick of the 1999 draft.

"But, still, there are certain things I can control, certain things I can't," he says. "The things I'm doing now are the things I've been doing since I've been here, before anybody got here." It hurts him that he has never been The Man in Phoenix. Jason Kidd was The Man, then Stephon Marbury was The Man, then Nash became The Man the moment he showed up in the summer of 2004. There have always been other Hamlets, while Marion has been consigned to the role of Rosencrantz or Guildenstern. Worse, Stoudemire, before his injury, seemed to have settled into Second Man status behind Nash, leaving Marion as the Third Wheel. After he was selected as an All-

Star reserve, Marion said, "Ever since I've been in Phoenix, I tried to make myself the face of the Suns on and off the court. That's what it's all about." But he is not the face of the Suns. Nash and D'Antoni are the dual faces, and, whenever Marion's face appears, Stoudemire's is likely to, also. That drives him crazy. He appreciates Nash and gets along with him, but he doesn't feel the same about Stoudemire.

"Around here, it's Steve this and Amare' that," says Marion. "What people forget is that I had to adjust my game to different people. I had J-Kidd. I had Steph. Now I have Steve. All of them are different. I made the adjustments. You got to give me credit now. Don't overlook that.

"The other thing is, people judge players on points. And I think that's wrong." That is obviously directed toward Stoudemire.

During the season, Marion was angry that his likeness didn't appear among the huge bobblehead dolls in the Suns' team store in the arena—the featured ones, of course, were of Nash and Stoudemire. During a couple of regular-season games, a drum line of young men performed during time-outs, all wearing replica jerseys of either Nash or Stoudemire. No Marion. He noticed. It sounds trivial to be complaining about that kind of stuff, particularly when you're compensated as a maximum player, but Marion had a point. There is Stoudemire, not even active, clowning around on the bench, and there is Marion trying to defend Lamar Odom, and yet Stoudemire gets all the love from the drum line. For all the bravado and posturing in the NBA, it is a breeding ground for insecurity.

Marion is also distressed that he doesn't have more of a national profile, both on and off the court. Stoudemire, in street clothes, got more All-Star fan votes than Marion did this season. Marion's main endorsement is with the Room Store in Phoenix, a deal that supplies him with furniture for his mansion in Scottsdale, and the commercial Marion did for the store loops endlessly on local television. He isn't one of Nike's main men, but he does have a signature sneaker, and his swoosh commercial—which was quite good; it showed Marion dominating a pickup game while wearing a weighted vest—ran often during the regular season on national TV. None of the Suns, in fact, Nash and Stoudemire included, are big-time endorsement figures.

Feeling dissed is a common malady in the NBA; the issue is, how does a player react to it? Marion, when feeling undervalued, sometimes gets inspired and sometimes goes into a funk, which is what the staff doesn't want to happen in the remaining games of the series. Two Marion problems had emerged from Game 2. The first is that he wanted to stay, in Iavaroni's words, "hooked" to Lamar Odom. "A certain situation came up in a huddle and I said, 'Okay, Shawn, just switch,'" says Iavaroni. "And he says, 'No, I want to stay on him.'" That is a frequent problem coaches face when trying to communicate the importance of team defense and shared responsibility. A player might come off his man to double-team or trap another player—Marion is adept at that part of the game when motivated—but then get ripped in the press if his man scores a lot of points.

The coaches also have to figure out how to get Marion running on every play, on every turn from defense to offense. Matrix in full flight is the Suns' most potent weapon. But Marion, who averaged forty minutes per game during the regular season (five more than Nash), argues that he can't always run if he's under the defensive basket wrestling with giants. Marion is fond of mentioning that D'Antoni rarely calls a set play for him, and that he needs to get his points "in the flow of the game," as he said after the depressing Game 2 loss. This ignores the fact that the Diaw-to-Marion backdoor lob is probably the "settest" play in the Suns' arsenal.

There are other worries, or, rather, just a kind of undefined, general one. The Suns didn't play well, really, in either of the two games. Their offense, in fact, has really not played well since they scored seventy-two points in the second half to thump Sacramento in a statement game on April 11. Bryant has not yet taken over, which he might decide to do at home in the Staples Center, and the Suns perhaps won't be able to weather it. Each coach deals with the uncertainty in his own way, Iavaroni digging into his personal vault of defensive schemes, D'Antoni latching on to his personal credo that "We're not scoring because we're not pushing," Dan insisting that it's all about effort and will. "I don't think we came out in Game 2 and played like you should in a playoff game," he says. "We didn't come out and say, 'Fuck you.'"

"That's it," says Iavaroni, endlessly searching for the perfect phrase to tell the team. "We have to get back the fuck-you factor."

As the morning shootaround gets underway at the Staples Center, Marion spies Jim Caviezel, sitting courtside.

"Hey, I know you," he says, shyly.

"I'm an actor," says Caviezel.

Marion smiles. "I'm an actor, too."

"Yes, he is," says Iavaroni. "And in the role of the Matrix . . ."

"I loved you in that," says Caviezel.

Marion positively beams. Most athletes quickly learn now to adopt a superior attitude to the public at large, but they still turn into little kids in the presence of movie stars. Stoudemire, on hand as a spectator, edges over to Caviezel during practice and talks to him for fifteen minutes, no doubt positioning himself as a future action hero. "Black Jesus meets White Jesus," says Iavaroni. (Stoudemire has a "Black Jesus" tat on his neck.)

During the film session, Gentry, the pro's pro, sits by Marion, clarifying points from time to time, but mainly just letting him know that the coaching staff is still behind him.

Later, at a restaurant near the hotel, Jesus doesn't make the check disappear, but he does buy lunch.

It's thirty minutes before game time at the Staples Center and nobody looks overly nervous. Perhaps it's an act. In trying to figure out

61

what mentality they should adopt, the Suns finally decided upon "loose," having concluded after Game 2 that they had, according to Eddie House, "lost that carefree attitude they had during the season." Gentry emerges from the wings meeting, doing the that's-right-I'm-bad walk that Richard Pryor and Gene Wilder did in *Stir Crazy*. Stoudemire, who was born in Lake Wales, Florida, and whose favorite team is Florida State, and James Jones, who graduated from the University of Miami, are engaged in a spirited debate over which school has sent the superior talent to the NFL, going through it on a position-by-position basis. If Stoudemire is able to devote half that degree of attention to the rudiments of defense, the Suns will be a much superior team next season.

D'Antoni's main message is to be offensive-minded:

"Okay, guys, catch and shoot. Catch and drive. Dribble-ats. Spread the floor. Attack, Spread the floor. They do have a habit of touching the ball and messing with it. [He means that after the Lakers score they sometimes catch the ball or bat it away to keep the Suns from quick-breaking.] We'll try to bring it to the refs' attention, but you should just grab it and get running. Okay, Noel."

That is the signal for Noel Gillespie to turn on the video. Last season D'Antoni came upon the ploy of ending every pregame session with a minute or so of high-octane Suns' offense. Every possession ends in a basket. The players watch raptly. They can never get enough of their own success.

"This is when we're at our best," says D'Antoni as the video runs, "when we're changing ends on the fly. They have no answer for it. Kwame is awful. Odom's a very average defender. Vujacic [backup point guard Sasha Vujacic] can't guard anybody. And Bryant in the open floor takes chances that aren't good. Let's go get 'em."

The coaches retreat to the small office. Like many arenas around the NBA, the Staples Center devoted little money to the visitor's dressing room. Suddenly, from out in the hallway, comes the voice of Nash.

"NINETEEN ON THE CLICKETY!"

The "clickety" is Nash's word for the clock that clicks off the time until tip-off. Lately, he has taken to loudly shouting out the minutes, screaming it in fact, partly as a joke but also to get his teammates to follow him onto the court to warm up. Those sports movies in which a team comes charging out of the dressing room together? It doesn't work that way in the NBA. Players drift out in drips and drabs and finally congregate outside the door where they then shout out some sort of war chant and trot onto the floor.

"There's four on the clickety," says Weber to the other coaches. "We better get going."

The game could hardly begin worse for the Suns. In the first minute, Luke Walton knocks Tim Thomas to the floor as he drives, picking up a flagrant foul. Thomas glares at Walton for a moment, and, predictably, several players move toward the action under the basket. From outside the pack, Bryant pushes Diaw, who falls into Smush Parker. Eddie F. Rush, a veteran referee, calls a technical on Diaw.

"Eddie, Eddie, did you see it?" D'Antoni pleads with Rush. "Boris never pushes anybody. He didn't do it. He got pushed."

"I saw what I saw," Rush tells him.

"But did you see the push?" D'Antoni says.

"I saw what I saw."

A few minutes later, Diaw is hit with the obligatory three-second defensive call, which results in an automatic technical foul shot. It's like a little beeper from the league office goes off during the first period of every game, reminding officials to make the call, after which they will ignore the defensive three-second call the rest of the way since virtually none of the spectators—and only half of the players—understand it.

In the third quarter, Bell gets elbowed by Kwame Brown, and, in an ensuing scrum, Diaw falls. Brown is whistled for a technical foul. But then Brown stands over Diaw, his crotch somewhere over Diaw's midsection, and glares down at him. Perhaps Brown is still trying to prove something to his coach; earlier in the season, Jackson had called him a "sissy." Jackson said he didn't mean it like it sounded, but it resonated for Brown, who had been called a "faggot" by Michael Jordan, who drafted him when he was a Washington Wizards executive, then torched him when he was a Wizards player.

Brown's action is exactly the kind of thug behavior the NBA is trying to curtail, but no technical foul is called. Nash moves toward the action, and, in the process, pushes away Vujacic's arm. Bryant then trots over to Nash and they jaw at each other. Later in the third period, Bryant is called for a foul on a blocked shot attempt and, irritated, walks away, lifting his jersey over his head in front of another veteran referee, Bill Spooner. Spooner tells him, "Put your jersey down."

Clearly, L.A. is trying to punk a team it considers punk-able. The Lakers never really run away and hide, but they seem in control, calm even. When Bell is whistled for fouling Bryant with 4:18 left, he explodes in anger and draws a technical foul. Then D'Antoni, rushing to support him, gets one, also, the second and third T's the Suns have received. Leandro Barbosa's layup brings Phoenix to within 92–90 with 3:28 left, but Walton and Parker score consecutive baskets and the Lakers go on to win 99–92.

It is the nightmare scenario presented by Iavaroni. Bryant scored only seven points, but every other starter was in double figures. Kobe played the role of Prospero, directing everything, seeing all, being all, and acting quite superior about it all. D'Antoni decides on a psychological ploy, telling the media that Bell has done a great job subduing Kobe. Perhaps that will rile up the Laker and precipitate a shooting spree that will freeze out his teammates.

But with a 2–1 series deficit and Game 4 on the road, reality has set in: The Suns are two losses from an ignominious first-round exit.

CHAPTER FOUR

[The Second Season]

Los Angeles, April 29 . . . .
LAKERS LEAD SERIES 2–1

"If you get a reputation as a punk-ass team—and that's what we are right now—it's one of the worst things that can happen."

It's 7:30 a.m., and Steve Nash can't sleep. He leaves his wife, Alejandra, and adorable twin daughters, Lola and Bella, upstairs, grabs a towel, and heads downstairs, where he runs into D'Antoni. It goes without saying that the coach hadn't slept either. He rolled around for most of the night, pizza and diet soda in his gut from a postgame video review, the horror of a 2–1 deficit on his mind, anger building about what he perceives as inept officiating. So the two of them relax in the back lobby of the Loews Hotel in Santa Monica, the still, blue waters of the Pacific visible through the wide picture windows behind them. Nash had been on his way for an ocean dip, in fact, when he encountered D'Antoni. Nash figured the ocean wouldn't be any colder than his daily restorative ice bath and would afford him time to think. Anyway, he's Canadian.

They are comfortable with each other, as comfortable as player can be with coach. Without talking about it, they understand what one has done for the other, Nash getting a coach who will let him dribble-probe, D'Antoni getting a point guard who can implement his unselfish, play-quick system. They even joke around with each other, which doesn't happen much given the delicate psyches that prevail in pro sports. A couple of times during the season, after Nash had a big scoring first quarter then turned to his inevitable role of distributor, he would throw a jersey across the locker room in mock anger after the game. "Frickin' D'Antoni got me out of my game!" When Nash was named Canada's athlete of the year, D'Antoni said to him, "That's a great honor, Steve. Did you beat out one of those curling guys who sweep the ice?"

Player and coach talk for a half hour about a lot of things, neither of them coming to any definitive conclusions about the series outside of the reality that the Suns have to get tougher. They are getting bullied, pushed around, maybe even intimidated by the Lakers. Nash will admit to being a little tired and concedes that he is having a hard time getting around Kwame Brown when a pick-and-roll produces a switch.

"We have to keep diving," says Nash. When the Suns' offense is at its best, there is constant movement off the ball. Nash dribbles and probes, probes and dribbles, and the other Suns make quick cuts—dives—to the basket. What sometimes happens, though, is that his teammates stand around and watch him, like it's a halftime exhibition, and if Nash can't get by his man, the offense stagnates. It's not always the fault of the others, though. If Nash is stopped far from the basket, and two taller defenders are putting up a wall around him, he simply cannot see over them. Players can dive all they want, but it will be for naught. Still, it's a percentage game, as Nash sees it. He considers his greatest strength to be finding open men while he's dribbling, but it's mandatory that he find them on the move.

At the end of the conversation, Nash asks D'Antoni, with a charming earnestness: "You don't believe in those conspiracy theories, do you?" Conspiracy theories in the NBA are nothing new. Pro basketball has always had such a tenuous hold on the American public that there is the perception in some quarters that the league must, well, *guide* the fortunes of the postseason into the most attractive matchups. And the only way to guide is through the officiating. The most attractive matchups are always about personalities, and, while the hard-core NBA fan is likely to appreciate the Suns as much as any team—the up-tempo play, the unselfishness, the ball distribution, the lightning-quick air strikes of the Matrix, the creative abilities of Nash—the casual fan thirsts for Kobe Bryant, a *personality*. The farther the Lakers advance in the playoffs, the more Bryant; the more Bryant, the higher the TV ratings. And if the Lakers could somehow emerge as the Western Conference champion, and the Miami Heat could come out of the East, the Finals would amount to a reality show pitting Bryant against Shaquille O'Neal, onetime Laker teammates who are now adversaries. America would *understand* that.

"Nah, I don't believe that, Steve," says D'Antoni. "We'll get some whistles tomorrow night. We'll go spank 'em, get this thing tied up, get home and get right."

Robert Sarver is waiting with the assistants in front of D'Antoni's suite. Even after their one-hour postgame video review, the coaches had been up for much of the night. Weber fell asleep sitting up, awakening to find that his pen had drawn a jagged line through his notes. Iavaroni is almost apologetic as he confesses that he had done a poor job of analysis. "I was too emotionally invested last night," he says. "I felt like I was dying after that game. I'll do better this morning." Sarver had gotten only a little more sleep but he is fired up.

"This L.A. bullshit has got to stop," said the owner. Right before the tip-off of last night's game he was incensed to see actress/director Penny Marshall, a long-time NBA fan, near the Suns' huddle, talking to some of the players. "I already told Tucker [team security director Kevin Tucker] that that bullshit stops on Sunday. This is war!" To no one in particular, he says, of the Lakers: "I hate those guys."

The time has come for toughness. Or, at least, tough talk. As the coaches once again review Game 3—it doesn't look any more palatable than it did seven hours earlier—they alternate between being furious at the officiating and furious at how placidly their players have been in dealing with the Lakers' aggressiveness. Aside from Nash getting into it briefly with Bryant, the Suns have been cast in the role of Curly, the Stooge who gets fingered in the eye and conked on the head and accepts it all.

"I tell you what," says Gentry, "if you get a reputation as a punk-ass team—and that's what we are right now—it's one of the worst things that can happen."

On screen, there's a scramble for a loose ball late in the game, and the Lakers pounce on it. Gentry becomes animated.

"After all that happened, don't you just . . ."

"I think you drive his fucking head into the ground," says D'Antoni.

"Thank you," says Gentry.

"Whose head are you talking about?" I ask.

"Any of their heads," says Gentry. "Obviously, Raja would do it. But they know he's watching them."

Indeed, a couple weeks earlier, Bell had been awakened by a call from the NBA, warning him that he would be closely watched in the playoffs for prior acts of aggression. Such warnings are not unprecedented, and the NBA considers them to be a favor. The Suns prefer to think of Bell as being on "double secret probation," as the brothers of Delta House were in *Animal House*.

Sarver relishes this kind of talk. He was never much of a basket-ball player—his sports are tennis and golf—but his no-nonsense business personality and general feistiness suggest the kind of bulldog who would knock his opponent down, then step on him as he headed back in the other direction.

"So, in other words, if a guy has a layup, instead of just patting him on the back, you should knock him down so he can't make it?" asks Sarver, warming to the subject.

The problem is, as the coaches explain, with the exception of Bell and Kurt Thomas (who is on the shelf with a foot injury), the Suns are not naughty by nature.

"Eighteen years in the NBA and I can tell you this: It's either in you or it's not," says Gentry.

"So you can't just appoint somebody to do it?" asks Sarver, sounding disappointed.

"No," says Gentry. "If we were going to do it, we would've done it last night after Kwame stood over Boris, punking him. We wouldn't have had to say anything. Next time down it goes into Kwame and he laid it in for a three-point play, that right there, somebody would've taken him down. Raja would've done it, but he knows they're watching. Coaches don't have to tell you to do those things, you just do them."

"In all fairness to us," says Sarver, "we knew we had a certain lack of toughness last year and we addressed it. We got Raja. We got Kurt, who should be in there. Amare' should be in there."

Sarver's presence is not taken as unusual or discomfiting by the coaches. It might've been last year when he was just learning the ropes and seemed to have a knack for saying and doing the wrong thing, such as flapping his arms like a chicken at the San Antonio bench when Spurs coach Gregg Popovich decided to rest an injured Tim Duncan. But now it seems like he's honestly trying to learn the game.

But his curve is stiff. Jerry Colangelo, the man against whom Sarver will be eternally compared, was unique as an owner in that he was a player, a coach, a general manager, and a scout. Colangelo also chaired the NBA's competition and rules committee for many years. "The game itself," Colangelo says, "is everything to me." The game is not everything to Robert Sarver and never will be. The important thing is that he not suddenly start recommending lineup changes or suggesting defenses to apply on Kobe.

"You know what?" says Gentry. "If we have Amare' in this series, he rolls down the lane, gets the ball, dunks on Kwame Brown's head, and next thing you know Kwame Brown is sitting over there on that bench."

There is also the problem of *how* to fire someone up. Should a coach get in Marion's face and scream at him that he *must* knock down Odom? Would that be effective? There is a reaction to every action. Sarver is transfixed by this, stupefied by the coaches' attention to psychological detail. He lets them know that by his high-pitched laugh.

"Hey, Robert, in this business you have to be careful," says Iavaroni. "A guy will go into an absolute funk if he feels you're beating him up."

"It's the exact opposite of how the regular business world works," says Sarver. "You try to be sensitive to the people who make the least money because they're not getting paid necessarily to do it right. But the guy who's making three, four hundred grand, he's the guy you come down with the hammer on."

"Does he have a five-year guaranteed contract?" asks Iavaroni with a smile.

Sarver laughs. "Hey, I'm not saying it's wrong. I'm just saying it's bizarre. Okay, hang in there, guys."

There is a feeling of quiet desperation in the room. Down 2–1 on the road. Make a drastic change on offense or defense? Iavaroni returns to the theme with which he began the series: Get Kobe shooting, which will get the others watching.

"I know this is a little drastic," says Iavaroni, "but hear me out. How about if we just one-swipe Kobe and let him shoot." "One-swipe" is exactly what it sounds like—a second defender would come over toward Bryant, take a swipe at the ball to (perhaps) discourage penetration, but then return to his man. It would not be a double-team or a trap.

Mike shakes his head. "I'm not there, Marc."

"I'm just searching a little bit," says Iavaroni.

"Well, I don't know whether we should be searching," says D'Antoni. "We should tighten up things, sure, but I think we should get better at what we're doing."

You can tell Iavaroni doesn't agree, but he concedes. "I just want to win the next game," says Iavaroni, "and we're all smart enough to realize that the next game pretty much decides the series."

"No, I'm not there, either," says D'Antoni. "I know what you're saying, but I'm not there. We lose tomorrow? Okay, we win at home. We gotta win the sixth game here. That's it. That's what it comes down to. I understand being down three-to-one is hard. But let's keep doing what we're doing. Give ourselves a chance to win. Give ourselves a chance to get it done. Keep doing what we're doing. I'm not sure we're that far away. We were there last night, as hard as it was to lose. We had our shots to beat them. We had our opportunities."

The room is quiet for a moment. Then D'Antoni speaks again. "I don't think there is a big, grand solution. I just think we have to do a better job of doing what we're doing. We're there. We're there."

I'm not sure D'Antoni really believes it, or keeps saying it just to convince himself. But he is convinced that superior teams win not by panicking or changing schemes but by holding the line and doing what they do best. He decides that the afternoon practice will be simple and will reflect none of the angst being poured out in this morning meeting. "We'll talk about bringing up the ball quickly and being more decisive on offense," says D'Antoni. "Defensively, our schemes are exactly where they need to be. We'll talk about tightening them up and not over-helping."

Comic relief, fortuitously, is supplied when the coaches come to the third-quarter play where Diaw is knocked down and Brown stands over him. The play had brought coaches from both benches onto the court, and, at the side of the frame, here comes Phil Jackson, ambling into view, with his peculiar, pain-ridden, side-to-side gait.

"Look!" says Mike. "It's the Penguin!"

Penguin sounds fill the room for the next minute. That and laughter, which is desperately needed.

CHAPTER FIVE

[The Second Season]

Los Angeles, April 29 . . . .

"After I finished talking to Stu, I think my blood pressure hit three hundred."

The Suns bus to practice at a middle school in Santa Monica, a facility frequently used by teams when they don't want to make the long downtown drive to the Staples Center. No one would know that this is a team in crisis. None of the uncertainty about what to change and how to play and who to guard with whom comes up. D'Antoni gathers them around and says:

"This is something we talked about earlier. You lose one and you never think you're going to win again; you win one, you never think you're going to lose again. We do have to win three games, but we only have to do it one at a time. We can do that starting at 12:30 tomorrow. We win that game and all of a sudden we're coming back with the edge.

"Okay, we lose this game, we go back to Phoenix and win a game, and, again, the pressure's on them. We have to have the mind-set, one possession at a time, one game at a time. Don't let the outside stuff, don't let the papers, don't let anything distract you."

Snippets of the game are shown on the portable video system that Noel Gillespie lugs around on the road in a gigantic orange case. (It looks like something a magician would carry; everyone calls it "Noel's Lady.") The coaches had just spent an hour bemoaning the number of times that the Suns failed to make the extra pass or failed to get a better shot, but they choose only one to show—a play where Marion has both Bell and Barbosa wide-open but instead launches a three-pointer. D'Antoni says, "Be cognizant of the fact that there are times we can swing it."

Practice is short and crisp. The media comes in, looking for a fresh angle on the Suns' obituary that is almost ready to be written, but finds a loose team rather than a desperate one. It could've been the day before a meaningless game against the Charlotte Bobcats in December. Nash shoots alone at one basket while Dan D'Antoni bangs his ear. Phil Weber works with Diaw on his shooting, the Frenchman frowning every time the coach sends him to a new spot but eventually complying. Diaw likes to demand an extra shot when he gets started; instead of a "mulligan," a word that does not exist in French, he calls it a "hooligan." Kurt Thomas is playing a shooting game with Kevin Tucker, the Suns' security man, who played college ball at Northern Arizona. A buzz has begun about the possibility of Thomas returning from his foot injury—everyone in the Suns' camp would pay a week's salary to have Thomas come in and bust Kwame Brown in the chops—but D'Antoni considers it a long shot. "I haven't shot a ball in nine weeks," says Thomas to Tucker, "and I still kicked your ass."

Vinny Del Negro, the Suns' radio analyst and a former NBA player, works with Barbosa on his shooting. Pat Burke and Nikoloz Tskitishvili, "Skita" to everyone, play a spirited one-on-one game. As the playoffs go on, and the likelihood of the eighth through twelfth players actually getting into a game decreases, the ferocity of the scrubs' postpractice battles intensifies. Stoudemire, a pick sticking out from his hair, studies his BlackBerry and relates to James Jones the selections from the ongoing NFL draft.

Eddie House approaches D'Antoni. He isn't sure he should do it, but the coach always seems open to suggestions.

"You know, the bench was a big part of what we did all season," House tells him. "Don't forget about us now." In last night's game, the top six—Nash, Marion, Diaw, Bell, Tim Thomas, and Barbosa—all played thirty or more minutes. Bell played forty-five. But James Jones got in for only eight minutes and House played for only five.

"I appreciate that, Eddie, I really do," says Mike. "And I'm going to think about it. We'll need you down the road. But I have a hard time playing you and Steve together because of how physical they are." What he didn't add was: *We're not cutting Steve's minutes, and we're worried about your ability to handle the ball under pressure.*

Back in the winter months, House had been playing so well that he was an early candidate for the Sixth Man award. He was D'Antoni's torch, instant offense off the bench. One game in particular, against the Denver Nuggets at home on December 2, sums up his contributions. He made five jumpers in a row to pull the Suns out of trouble. On one play the ball was barely in his hands before he got his quick 1–2 pitty-pat steps down and shot it in rhythm. It was the game-clinching three-pointer from the right wing, and, as the Nuggets called time-out to cool him off, House sat down, received high-fives all around, and said, "Fuck those motherfuckers." That is classic Eddie House. *Fuck those motherfuckers.* On at least a half-dozen occasions, his bravado had carried the Suns in those early months; House and his teammates loved it when Noel Gillespie found the scouting report of an opposing team that said this about House: *Won't shoot it unless he has it in his hands.*

But, now, with the playoff noose tightening, Eddie House is just another stray scrounging for scraps.

On the way out of the gym, Gentry sidles up to Boris and says, "Well, another day, another franc." Stoudemire asks, "What's that? Like a French dollar?" Diaw shakes his head as only the French can. "It is the other way around," he tells Stoudemire. "The dollar is the French franc. The franc was around for five hundred years before the dollar." Stoudemire considers this.

· · ·

For D'Antoni, the real business of the day—and it is unpleasant business—is calling Stu Jackson, the NBA's director of operations. Jackson, a former player, coach, and general manager, is charged with everything relating to the game itself. During the season, for all intents and purposes, that task boils down to handling team complaints about referees, meting out punishments to players and coaches for technical fouls and flagrant fouls, and—deep below the radar—fining officials for bad calls. While the league announces every dollar taken from a player or coach for bitching about the officials, referee fines are kept in-house.

Any fair-minded individual would have to concede that Jackson has a difficult job, akin to listening to the complaints about the czar from a mob of pissed-off peasants during the Russian Revolution. Jackson's predecessor in the job, by the way, was Rod Thorn, a West Virginian who is now the general manager of the New Jersey Nets. Thorn is a basketball legend in the Mountain State. He followed Jerry West to the state university and was given West's number 44. Four years after Thorn graduated, Mike D'Antoni, a six-foot-three-inch playmaking guard from the mining town of Mullens, was recruited with the understanding that he would wear 44 and continue the line. But D'Antoni opted to play at the state's "other" university, Marshall, where brother Dan had forged a fine career. (West Virginia University recently retired 44 in West's name only, which, as D'Antoni says, "The dumb asses should've done in the first place.")

There is little personal bond between D'Antoni and Jackson, which is how it should be. The worst thing that could happen to Jackson would be the perception that he favors one team over another. On the other hand, the idea that Jackson is an impartial observer is ridiculous. Jackson works for the czar and lives in the palace. He's the Big Chief of the Referees. Asking for judicial relief from Jackson is not unlike the Kafkaesque feeling a college student has when he appeals a suspension handed down by the administration, only to find that the appeals court is the same one that handed out the suspension. Anyway, officials' calls are not reversible in board-rooms. Except for questions about a shot beating the clock, which the refs can review at courtside, calls are set in stone the moment a whistle is blown. The reason coaches and GMs call Jackson to complain, beyond the fact that venting is good for the soul and the blood pressure, is to set the stage for the next game. *Watch out for this.* That is particularly important, obviously, during a protracted playoff series.

Earlier in the season, Jackson happened to be in Phoenix when the Suns lost an agonizing 103–101 game to the Minnesota Timberwolves—the Suns protested that a goaltend should've been called against Kevin Garnett in the final seconds. D'Antoni came into the office, kicked his chair (which sent the height adjustment lever flying), then whipped off his sport coat and heaved it against the wall. "The good news," he said later, "was I managed to lay off the plasma TV." The Suns protested to Jackson, who promised to review the play (though it wouldn't do any good anyway). The next day Jackson came back with his verdict: "Had there been another half-turn on the ball before Garnett blocked it, it would've been a goaltend." Alvin Gentry, who has impeccable comedic timing, said, "They also found a second shooter on the grassy knoll."

D'Antoni places the call to Jackson in the early afternoon. He gets Jackson's answering machine, but Jackson is good about returning calls. D'Antoni states his case:

—The game started badly when Luke Walton flagrantly fouled Tim Thomas, and Diaw was mistakenly called for a technical on the ensuing group grope around the basket. The Suns did nothing and received the same penalty as the Lakers.

—After being hit with a technical for throwing an elbow, Kwame Brown stood over Diaw and glared down at him, essentially putting his crotch over Diaw's face. He should've been assessed another technical and ejected.

—Bryant walked right by referee Bill Spooner and put his jersey over his head to protest a call. That should've been a technical.

—And in a general sense, the Lakers, a much more physical team, are manhandling our players, on and off the ball. Yet, in last night's game, Phoenix shot seventeen free throws and the Lakers shot twenty-three.

At five p.m. D'Antoni comes downstairs, bound for the annual media dinner hosted by public relations chief Julie Fie. No players attend, but D'Antoni has given his commitment. He wishes he hadn't. He looks ashen and shaken. He has a half-smile plastered on his face, but it's one of those dangerous, I-might-kill-somebody smiles. D'Antoni talks animatedly to his brother, then to Gentry. Then he comes over and explains what Jackson said when he called back.

"Stu said he looked at everything and, at the end of the day, he says he's assessing Raja a flagrant-one [the lightest of the flagrant fouls] for a play that happened with four minutes to go in the third period," he says.

"I don't remember the play," I say.

"A rebound gets tapped out, Raja turns and starts to run and Kwame Brown grabs him and holds him for a second, so Raja rips his hand away and his hand hits Kwame in the mouth. That's it. I had to look for the play myself."

"Why would that be a flagrant-one?"

"Stu said that it's the kind of thing that escalates into a fight. He said he even talked to David Stern [the commissioner] about it. He said Raja and Kwame became 'intertwined.' I pointed out that Kwame grabbed him, and that's not the real definition of 'intertwined.'

"Then I went back to the first play and said, 'You're telling me that what Raja did, reacting to a foul that should've been called, is more dangerous than Kobe pushing Boris into the fray?' Stu says, 'I understand that one. We're rescinding the technical on Boris. [Meaning Diaw will not have to pay $1,000, or whatever that is in francs, the standard technical-foul fine.]'

"So let me get this straight. Luke Walton tackles our guy. Kwame

Brown elbows a guy, then puts his crotch over somebody's face. Kobe Bryant lifts his jersey over his head. And I'm walking into my locker room tomorrow and telling my guys that, after all that, they get one technical and one flagrant, and we get one flagrant and three technicals. That's what you got for me? Because I'll tell you right now what the player reaction will be: We're getting screwed. I just want to make sure you're okay with your decision."

D'Antoni says Jackson told him: "I understand you're upset. But that's the decision."

Jackson has his own interpretation of all this, of course. Luke Walton committed a flagrant foul and it was called. Somebody went sprawling in a pack, and the ref did the best job he could to determine who was guilty of a technical; the technical itself cannot be rescinded but the attached fine has been. Not calling technicals on Brown and Bryant are judgment calls. Hitting Bell with a flagrant-one stops a potentially explosive situation; Bell had been previously warned not to be an aggressor. And as for the free-throw discrepancy, well, the refs are calling them the way they see them. Lots of times—maybe even most times—the more aggressive team will get to the foul line more often. There you have it.

The Lakers would have their own interpretation of all this, too: The Suns are whining, and we have them in our hip pocket.

D'Antoni attends the media dinner, almost in a daze. "After I finished talking to Stu," he says, "I think my blood pressure hit three hundred." I urge him to have a glass of red wine instead of his usual Diet Coke. He relates the story of the Jackson phone call to Sarver and Del Negro. He has another glass of wine and a good meal. By the time he takes a cab back to the hotel, he says that, while he hasn't forgotten the spirit-sapping phone call, he is now focused on tomorrow's game.

"These are the times that try men's souls," he says.

"Thomas Paine," I say.

"No," says D'Antoni. "I'm pretty sure it's Phil Jackson."

CHAPTER SIX

[The Second Season]

Los Angeles, April 30 . . . .
LAKERS LEAD SERIES 2–1

"We better have enough edge that it doesn't come down to one shot and number 8 has the ball in his hands."

The quiet of the pregame locker room is spoiled by a cameraman who, while taking a close-up of Eddie House, trips over a bench and falls. "It's NBA-TV, ladies and gentleman," intones Pat Burke. "We're bringing you a live shot of Eddie House's balls."

Burke, a communications major at Auburn, is a very funny guy, though he's gotten a little less humorous and a lot more bitter with the disappearance of his playing time as the season has gone on.

Robert Sarver enters. He is fired up, more fired up, it seems, than the handful of players who are quietly getting dressed.

"Fuck L.A.," he announces. "Fuck Kobe. Fuck these fans. Fuck the refs. Fuck everything. We beat these guys like a drum three times during the season. Let's go out there and kick fucking ass."

A few players murmur assent. Kurt Thomas is talking to his girlfriend on a cellphone. Who was that? she asks.

"Oh, that was our owner," answers Thomas.

Before the game, Paul Coro, the Suns' beat reporter for the *Arizona Republic,* asks Bell for his reaction to the added flagrant 1 he had received from the league office on the play that few people remember.

"I don't know what you're talking about," says Bell.

D'Antoni had decided not to inform Bell until after the game but forgot to mention that to Coro. Bell shrugs it off. "Guess that mean's they're still watching me," he says.

Iavaroni gathers the bigs together for their meeting. He believes it's the most important meeting of the year, a Game 4 on the enemy court with your team down.

"I wanna tell you a story," he begins. "I don't do it much. It's my first preseason game as a rookie with the 76ers. Nineteen eighty-three. We're playing the Celtics. I'm guarding Larry Bird. I get it inside, turn, and he fouls me. So Bird says to Dennis Johnson, "We got us a bitch here." I turn to D.J. and say, 'Can't he play this bitch without fouling?'

"Well, I got into Bird's head. I could see it and I could hear it. He did nothing but talk the rest of the half, trying to get back at me. And he didn't do that well. But in the second half he just comes out and plays. Somebody tells me later that he scored the first twenty points of the half himself.

"Moral of the story? He was best when he was all business. He wasn't talking. He was concentrating his energies on playing. That's what we have to do today. Take care of business."

Iavaroni calls on Kurt Thomas, as he often does in the bigs meeting. (When Thomas played for Dallas in the 1997–98 season, Don Nelson made him an assistant coach during the time he was injured.) "Kurt," says Iavaroni, "you're one of the best, if not *the* best, post defender I ever saw. Tell us some of the things you kept in your mind when you think about playing a guy one-on-one."

"Stay low," answers Thomas. "Stay centered. Keep your balance. And you have to hit him first once in a while. Don't be afraid to throw in a cheap shot. Hit him with an elbow. Let him know you're there."

That might've been more information than Iavaroni was looking for. But he moves on. "Kwame Brown," says Iavaroni, "is just a big fucking guy who doesn't move much. But you have to adapt to play him. It's origin of the species. Anyone ever hear of a guy named Charles Darwin? You gotta adapt."

D'Antoni is normally a strategist in the general sense. The Suns don't have a lot of set plays, but they do have that philosophy of keeping the ball moving, so he generally just reminds them to use every offensive weapon at their disposal. But tonight he drifts toward the mind game.

"Every possession play with your heart and your mind," he says. "Ignore the refs. Don't let them get into your head. It falls on us. It's not about them. It's not about the Lakers. It's about us. It's about whether we can get it done."

Out on the court, meanwhile, Sarver is putting his fuck-L.A. mind-set into action. He sidles up to Norman Pattiz, the founder of the Westwood One Radio Network and one of those irritating Laker superfans who sit near the bench and scream at any opposing player who happens by that area. Sarver says to him, "You ever touch one of my players again, you'll have me to deal with." Sarver thought he had noticed Pattiz getting into the face of Tim Thomas during Game 3.

"You're an asshole," says Pattiz dismissively.

"I may be an asshole," says Sarver, "but you better understand—you'll have me to deal with."

The game is even through most of the first half, which ends in a 41–41 tie. But it's the kind of *even* that favors the Lakers—the slow tempo, the shaky shooting, the physical play, and, most of all, the fact that Bryant missed eleven minutes of action after getting his third foul. That was the time to capitalize, and the Suns couldn't do it, having been outscored 16–15. It was like getting beat by just the Pips at a talent show.

But the Suns finally wake up in the second half, Marion in particular. They battle for loose balls, turn Parker and Luke Walton into nonfactors, and no longer seem intimidated by Kwame Brown. Nash goes out for his prescribed rest late in the third period, but his problematic back tightens up and he sits out the first couple minutes of the fourth quarter. Still, the Suns stay in control. A trio of dagger three-point shots by Devean George, a perennial Laker underachiever; some emotional play by Sasha Vujacic, who looks like he's going to burst into tears at every call that goes against him ("You suck," Bell calmly informed Vujacic during Game 2); and the overall brilliance of Bryant keep the Lakers close. But with 5:41 left, Bryant forces a shot between two defenders, and, in the ensuing time-out, Lamar Odom remains on the court, pouting, staring at Kobe. The Suns lead 81–73. This is the Iavaroni model: Kobe is trying to take over the game and his supporting cast is angry at him. The *Good Ship Laker* has been turned into *Family Feud*.

But then two straight atrocious calls go against the Suns. Marion cleanly blocks a Bryant shot, but referee Sean Corbin calls a foul. On the previous play, Bryant had "mother-fucked" Corbin, complaining about a noncall—the F-word in some form will usually get you a technical—and the Suns view this as a makeup. On the Lakers' next possession, Odom, in a post-up position, gets the ball and simply barrels over Marion, makes the basket, and, incredibly, gets a foul call, too. He completes the three-point play and, worse, the foul is Marion's sixth, sending him to the bench. He had been the one who had held the Suns together in the second half with fourteen points and seven rebounds.

The one-two punch puts the Lakers back in the game, but, still, the Suns show fortitude and reseize control. With twelve seconds left they lead 90–85. John Black, the Lakers' director of public relations, asks me if I'll be back in L.A. for Game 6; this one is essentially over. I leave my press seat and squeeze in between Dan D'Antoni and Todd Quinter on the Suns' bench. Walking in with the team is the only way I can get access to the locker room before the rest of the press corps.

"This is okay, right?" I ask them.

They look at me nervously but don't say anything.

At that moment, the Lakers inbound the ball, and Smush Parker, the third option on the play, an erratic marksman who had missed his first twelve shots of the game, hits a three-pointer with Nash right in his face to cut the lead to 90–88. D'Antoni and Quinter look at me as if I'd brought with me a case of the Black Plague. The Suns take time-out to plan an inbounds play, D'Antoni giving responsibility for Diaw to get it to Nash. A statistic that has haunted the Suns all season must be in the minds of a few of them: In regular-season games decided by seven points or fewer, the Suns are 0-7. It is hopeless to figure out the logic of that, given the reality of Nash, the ultimate heady quarter-back and one of the best foul-shooters in the league.

This play goes badly right away. The Lakers swarm Nash, and Diaw looks anxious. Nash keeps moving toward the pass, trying to shake Parker, and slips just as he receives the pass. Parker is right on top of him and steals the ball. Parker taps it to George, who gets it to Bryant, who takes a few high-speed dribbles and puts up a high-arcing, high-degree-of-difficult layup over the outstretched arm of Diaw. It goes in. Tie game 90–90. I return to my press seat without a word, taking the Plague with me.

D'Antoni designs a brilliant inbounds play that all but frees James Jones for a layup, but he is held by at least two Laker defend-ers—in those situations, fouls are rarely called—and can't get off a clean shot. Overtime.

Momentum had clearly switched to the Lakers, but the Suns play with guts in the extra period, and when Nash, gritting his teeth in pain (his back had started to hurt him), hits a three-pointer, they lead 98–95 with forty-nine seconds left. The Suns get the ball back but, with the shot clock going down, Bell shoots an air ball. What Phoenix needed was something that would've at least drawn iron, bounced around, killed some clock. But it gives the Lakers a dead-ball situation.

Afraid to foul, the Suns allow Bryant an open lane to the hoop and he scores a layup with 11.7 seconds left to draw the Lakers within one, 98–97. The Suns' plan is obvious: Get it to Nash, one of the surest dribblers and free-throw shooters on the planet. They elect not to take a time-out and inbound from under the Lakers' basket. Probably better that way. More room for Nash to operate.

Nash begins dribbling under pressure and heads toward midcourt, veering left all the while. As it becomes evident he's going to run into a crowd, Diaw calls and motions for a time-out. Nash hollers for one, too, but can't make a hand gesture because he's concentrating too much on his dribble. He gets jostled as Lamar Odom and Luke Walton close in on him. Referees Bennett Salvatore and Kenny Mauer peer in at the play but don't call anything until, finally, Salvatore motions for a jump ball. Walton against Nash.

Brian Grant insists that he heard Diaw calling for a time-out from the bench, which is across the court. The coaches are incensed that the Suns weren't given the time-out or a foul wasn't called. Of the three possible calls in that situation, a jump ball is by far the rarest.

But jump ball it is. The six-foot-eight-inch Walton has the edge on the six-foot-two-inch Nash, and, predictably, taps it back to Bryant with about six seconds to go. It is so predictable that even the press corps wonders why more Phoenix defenders are not grouped around Bryant. He dribbles toward the Laker basket and even then is not as swarmed as he should be. Diaw is closest to him, just as he was on the layup, and, as Bryant goes up for a jumper, I can hear Alvin Gentry's words from the Friday night postgame video review: *I tell you, we better have enough edge that it doesn't come down to one shot and number 8 has the ball in his hands.*

With perfect rotation, the ball goes in, and the home crowd goes nuts. Lakers win 99–98. The moment is instantly sanctified as one of the greatest in Staples Center history, right up there with the Robert Horry jumper that beat the Sacramento Kings in Game 6 of the 2002 Western finals. The Randy Newman song blares: *I love L.A.! I love L.A.!*

The Lakers and their fans are still in wild celebration as the Suns troop funereally to their dressing room. The coaches gather outside, as they always do, but no one has anything substantive to offer. D'Antoni stands with his head down for a full two minutes, and, when it's time to address the team, he has almost nothing to say. "We're going home, guys. We'll get 'em there. A lot of stuff happened. Try to forget about it."

Leandro Barbosa emerges from the shower, a stricken look on his boyish, open face. "Did . . . you . . . ever . . . see . . . anything . . . like . . . that?" he asks, almost as if he's in shock.

"Can't say that I have, L.B.," I say.

Dan D'Antoni switches off his cell phone as he walks slowly from the dressing room to the tunnel, where the team bus is waiting to take them to the airport and on to Phoenix. "I feel like a hundred years old," he says, limping, a badly swollen Achilles tendon turning every step into agony. "I'm smart enough to tune out all the experts," he says. "See, Mike's gotta deal with them all." His brother leans against the bus, cell phone to his ear.

The plane ride back to Phoenix would be more forlorn if not for the presence of the wives and children. The normal suspects— Marion, Bell, Kurt Thomas, House, Tucker, and Mike "Cowboy" El-liott, the assistant trainer—play poker. Nash feels like a line from "Old Man River"—body all achin' and racked with pain—but he enter-tains his twins. He *thinks* he was fouled and he *believes* he should've gotten a time-out, but he *knows* he should not have dribbled toward the midcourt sideline, either. That's the Dead Zone. The coaches vent about the referee calls—it seems they got nothing but a solid diet of bad whistles in L.A.—but they also know that the turnover on the Diaw-to-Nash inbounds play was the result of sloppy execution, and that the defense should've done a smarter job of blanketing Bryant on the tip play.

The plane ride is short and nobody even bothers turning on his video machine to review the game. Too painful. Eight months together and this is absolutely the lowest point. A television replay streams, with no audio, across the two screens in the front of the play, at one point flashing a stark graphic: Of the 160 teams that have been behind 3-1 in a playoff series, only seven have come back to win the series.

Back home, before D'Antoni turns in, he fields two phone calls. The first is from Duke coach Mike Krzyzewski, under whom D'Antoni will be an assistant this summer on the United States Olympic team. They had gotten together late in the season and hit it off.

"I'll see you soon," Krzyzewski said. Jerry Colangelo, the executive director of USA Basketball, has scheduled meetings for the Olympic coaches in Phoenix beginning on May 7, the following Saturday, also the date of a Game 7 should there be one.

"I just hope we're still playing," says D'Antoni.

Then Sarver calls with a simple message. "Kiss your wife, forget about the game, and get some sleep." D'Antoni accomplishes the first, fails miserably on the last two.

CHAPTER SEVEN

[The Second Season]

Phoenix, May 1 . . . .
LAKERS LEAD SERIES 3–1

"We're gonna have to come back here, play as hard as hell, beat their ass, and then watch the pressure go back on them. This ain't even close to being over."

Nash is the first one in the practice gym, which is not unusual. I ask him if he watched a replay of the game.

"I never do," he says. "I just went home and beat myself up. I got to sleep okay, but I woke up at 4 and couldn't get back. I got up and played with my daughters."

"Now that it's past, what bothered you the most about the jump-ball play?" I ask.

"That they didn't call the time-out," he says. "They could've called a foul. But, the time-out, I mean, Boris was screaming it. I was saying it, too, but I was concentrating on the dribble. But the refs had to have heard Boris."

Bell, meanwhile, has come down and is shooting with Weber at another basket. He is fixated on Bryant.

"What gets me is that, all of a sudden, everybody loves him again," says Bell. "And he is just not a great guy."

The remarks resonate. When Bryant scored eighty-one points against the Toronto Raptors in January, I wrote a story about it and subsequently received a couple dozen e-mails and letters criticizing me for celebrating him. They referred to Bryant's notorious rape case in Colorado (the charges were dropped), his arrogant on-court manner, or both. I didn't make any value judgments about Bryant in the story; I was writing about an athlete who had done something transcendent, which is part of my job. But when an athlete earns headlines for his exploits, there is the perception that he is being canonized as a human being. And that perception sticks in the craw of those who don't like the athlete in question.

The 3–1 deficit notwithstanding, Bell feels good about the defensive work he has done on Bryant. The Game 4 buzzer beater wasn't Bell's fault, and Bell has held Bryant in check to a greater degree than the Suns could've hoped for.

"I'm not sure I can play him any better," Bell says.

"Yes, you can," says Weber. "You're gonna play him even better in Game 5." Weber, Mr. Positive Thinker, says it with emphasis. And Bell smiles.

"Good, Phil," says Bell, "I'm glad to hear you say that. I'm gonna keep that in my mind."

The challenge for everyone, players and coaches, is to forget the horror of yesterday's game, the reality of the 3–1 deficit and the seeming mountain of calls that have gone against them and figure out what has to be done to get back in the series. The Suns just haven't played well against a team they consider to be inferior. Nash's dribble toward the corner of midcourt was un-Nash-like—he should've kept it in the middle of the floor. Iavaroni wonders, half-kiddingly, if the Suns shouldn't have tried to beat the Lakers in that late regular-season game, and maybe taken it easy in a game six days earlier against the Sacramento Kings, so that the Lakers and Kings would've flip-flopped positions. "Well, right now," says Gentry, "the Kings would be beating the dogshit out of us worse."

The feeling of malaise comes also from a general distaste for the Lakers. During a morning trip to Starbucks, at least a dozen people approached D'Antoni and told him they appreciated how the Suns had reacted to the unfortunate chain of events in Games 3 and 4. "They saw it," says D'Antoni. "Kobe's lifting up his jersey and showing his chest and doing all that stuff, and Steve is just saying, 'Well, we blew it.' At least, we're taking the high road anyway."

As the Suns see it, the Lakers trek along the low road. Bryant is arrogant. Brown is just a big body with nothing behind it. Smush Parker was a Sun for a couple of weeks last season, and no one rued his departure. Lamar Odom is just too damn big and long. Luke Walton seems like a nice guy, and his father, Bill, is a humorous announcer, but he laid out Thomas in Game 3 and triggered a miserable chain of L.A. events that ended with the nightmarish jump-ball call and the Kobe jumper. Sasha Vujacic (pronounced VU-ja-seech) is an all-universe whiner with an unpronounceable surname. Over the last week Dan D'Antoni has variously tortured it as "Vooasick," "Voojacheech," and, finally "Vooacheck." "Apparently," says Mike, "Danny thinks he's John Havlicek's younger brother." It is comparable to Dan's fused pronunciations of the surnames of Cleveland center Zydrunas Ilgauskas and Philadelphia forward Andrew Iguodala as "Inkadacus," "Ingadalis" or "Iladala." Whenever he becomes tongue-tied on a nickname, Weber says, "First day with a new mouth, Danny?"

Plus, Phil Jackson sits on a throne.

Plus, who the hell likes purple and gold?

Plus, the Lakers are kicking their ass.

There is concern among the coaches about Tim Thomas, who, after his terrific Game 1 performance, has not been much of a factor. Thomas is what is known around the league as "a ball stopper," a player who, having received a pass, holds it or dribbles it, looking for his own shot and killing a lot of clock in the process. If Thomas's shot is on, or if he can break down or successfully post up his defender, as he was able to do in Game 1, he's a valuable asset; if not, he suffocates the offense. Ball stoppers are less of a problem in standard NBA attacks that call for isolation plays, but they are disastrous to a ball-moving team such as the Suns.

When the Suns contacted Thomas, one of those ultra-talented players who in eight previous NBA seasons had never come close to fulfilling his golden promise, he was sitting back in his home in suburban Philadelphia. Thomas had been traded from the New York Knicks to the Chicago Bulls in the preseason, but, when he arrived in Chicago, he and coach Scott Skiles were at immediate loggerheads. Skiles is one of those no-nonsense run-the-stairs-for-me type of guys; Thomas is one of those I'd-rather-take-the-elevator-and-maybe-stop-and-get-a-frappucino-along-the-way type of guys. So Skiles, in a move that was strange even by the standards of disciplinarian coaches, told him to pack up, go home and take his $13.5 million salary with him. Thomas spent the winter working out at Villanova and said he enjoyed being with his family for all the major winter holidays. Honest, that's what he said.

When Thomas came out of Paterson Catholic High School in New Jersey in 1996, he and a kid from Lower Merion, name of Kobe Bryant, were the top scholastic players in the country. Bryant opted for the NBA. Thomas, recruited by virtually every school in the country, enrolled at Villanova, which had added the carrot of hiring his uncle as an assistant coach. Thomas stayed on the Main Line for just one year—that was pretty much the understanding going in—after which the New Jersey Nets made him the seventh pick in the 1997 draft. It is astonishing how top universities make such deals and no one calls them on it. And with the NBA having raised the draft-eligibility age, there will be even more one-year college attendees. Thomas was one of the first.

Thomas said that Skiles never gave him a chance. Skiles said that Thomas was out of shape and had an attitude problem. Thomas's demeanor is not the problem for D'Antoni, but he does wonder if he has become a bad fit for the offense. "Maybe I fell into the trap of having to get bigger and stronger and loused up our offense a little bit," says D'Antoni. But the bottom line for the Suns in acquiring

Thomas was the bottom line: They are stuck for only $290,000, the prorated veteran minimum, while the Bulls are paying the rest of his comically extravagant contract. Phoenix almost couldn't afford *not* to get him, particularly with the injuries to Stoudemire and Kurt Thomas. "Pretty good rental, huh?" Iavaroni would say after Thomas had a good game. Perhaps he can be one again.

Earlier in the day, at the coaches meeting, D'Antoni had asked suddenly. "What's that porno actress's name? Del Rio? What's her first name?" It was a strange question coming from a man who had shown no previous interest in the bone-and-moan industry. Plus, he named an actress who was popular more than a decade ago.

"You gotta do better than that," says Gentry. "Go with Jenna Jameson. More recognizable. Local connection. And I guaran-damn-tee you most of our guys have seen her work."

When D'Antoni calls the team together, I say to Iavaroni: "I don't know what Mike's got planned with the porno actress, but I bet he doesn't end up using it."

"I don't know about that," says Iavaroni. "It's getting near the end of the season. You gotta use everything you got."

"All right, guys, everybody cool?" D'Antoni begins, his usual salutation. "I'm sure everybody has talked about it, rehashed it. It is what it is. Not the best thing in the world, but we gotta take something out of it. We busted their ass a couple of times and we're gonna come back and do it now. We know we can.

"We all know we're getting screwed more than Jenna Jameson . . ."—there is a titter in the gym, possibly because D'Antoni sounds so uncomfortable making the reference, possibly for other reasons—"anyway . . . I forgot what I was going to say . . . but, we're gonna have to come back here, play as hard as hell, beat their ass, and then watch the pressure go back on them. This ain't even close to being over."

I watch for signs of insincerity. Every coach has those moments when he has to out-and-out lie to his team—*Fellas, we're down forty but that's not so bad . . .* —but D'Antoni really seems to believe the Suns can come back.

"You know, you guys have gained a lot in this. The way you've handled it without going off. Public opinion is on your side. I've already had people come up to me and say how well you've handled it. The media is all over it, so let them do the talking for you. We're just going to play basketball."

Then D'Antoni moves to his and Bell's favorite subject.

"They're talking about Kobe and how great it is that he's playing with the team. Well, isn't that what you're supposed to do? Now he's the savior because he's playing that way? He's no god. He does what he's supposed to be doing, which is what we learned in kindergarten. Share the ball and play. And that's what we do better than they do. That's what we're going to do tomorrow night and get back in this thing. Everybody cool?"

The coaches usually immediately disperse after practice— they've already been together for five hours by that time—but they find themselves together in the locker-room office where D'Antoni mentions his concern about Nash's playing time. The book on Nash—and a major reason Dallas Mavericks owner Mark Cuban let him get away to Phoenix—is that he plays so hard he wears down late in the season. "If I keep him in, he gets tired," says D'Antoni, "but if I take him out, he gets stiff. He really felt it on Sunday."

"I think you have to play him almost the whole second half," says Gentry. "But you rest him like a minute or forty seconds before the time-out [the designated TV time-out] and that gives you like three minutes of rest for him."

"I hate to play without Steve at this stage of the season, but he needs some rest," says D'Antoni, thinking aloud. "I mean, I love Eddie House, and I'd like to get him in there and in the process rest Steve. But Eddie just can't get his shot off against these guys."

"I agree with you," says Gentry. "But, man, back when Eddie was shooting, we had something, didn't we?"

FULL TIME-OUT

December 15, 2005
BATON ROUGE, LA

Of Shooting Games, Tickets, and the Raiders: Eddie's in the House

The Suns' postpractice shooting games feature a revolving cast of characters, but Eddie House, "Edward Shooter Hands" as Raja Bell has taken to calling him, is almost always one of them. He usually wins. One day I asked Bell if he had ever taken any of the House money.

"Don't go there," he said in mock anger. "Get out of my face with those Eddie questions."

House has a stockpile of shots, many of which he accompanies with his own commentary.

"There's Magic Johnson across the lane, the little baby hook . . . GOOD!" House says, as he replicates Magic Johnson's junior skyhook that beat the Boston Celtics in Boston Garden in Game 4 of the 1987 NBA Finals. House then trots to the sideline, where he collects imaginary high-fives from teammates.

He also has "my three-sixty," in which he twirls completely around and releases a jump shot, and another turnaround in which he takes one dribble, spins, and puts up a left-handed hook. The argument today is whether Bell is allowed to take two dribbles before shooting.

"The important thing," argues Bell, "is the shot itself, not the dribble shit."

"That ain't right," says House. "It's a whole thing I got going, and you're trying to variate my shit." To make his point, House appeals to bystanders. He grabs a ball and performs his shot, finishing it up with a loud "Ah-Ha" as he makes the move.

"What, I gotta say the 'Ah-Ha,' too?" asks Bell.

93

"No," says House, shaking his head, "that's the crowd responding to my shit. Ah! Ha!"

December 16
BATON ROUGE, LA

A few players are sorting tickets for tonight's game against the New Orleans Hornets (who are playing several home games in Baton Rouge due to damage from Hurricane Katrina) as House looks on. I ask him if he buys many tickets for family and friends.

"Not too much anymore," says House, "because you know what happens? You buy them and leave them at the window and then the game starts and they don't show up and you're checking the stands and losing your concentration." House ponders this. "I mean, you can look for your parents in the crowd and shit," he continues, "but you can't be looking for specific motherfuckers."

"Specific motherfuckers" becomes the phrase of the week.

The pregame chatter is monopolized by talk of the NFL, which is moving into playoff season. It started when Nash says, "I don't think Terry Bradshaw is among the top twenty quarterbacks in history." Nash doesn't really care much about the subject, but there are two certified Steeler crazies in the locker room—Ohio native Jimmy Jackson and athletic trainer Aaron Nelson—and Nash knows he can get a rise out of them. Of course, Eddie House, who was born and raised in Richmond, California, hard by Oakland, wants to talk about his team, the Raiders.

"What about the Snake, Kenny Stabler?" says House. "You gotta have him high in that top twenty. Partied all night, showed up Sunday, got the job done. You got to get motherfuckin' points for that."

"We were talking about Bradshaw," says Nelson. "We weren't talking about the Raiders."

"Well, I'm talking about the Raiders," says House.

"All I know," says Jimmy Jackson, who is getting treatment from Mike Elliott, "is that the Steelers got the better franchise overall."

"First of all," says House, "why are you getting into the conversation when you're over there all isolated and shit with your headphones on?"

"I been listening the whole time," says Jackson, "just waiting to jump in and rebuttal your ass."

"Bottom line," says House, "our winning percentage is better than your winning percentage. And I'll put a thou-wow on that shit."

"Thou-wow" becomes the second phrase of the week. And he's correct about Oakland having a better all-time winning percentage.

December 28
WASHINGTON, DC

At shootaround, Alvin Gentry swishes a half-court shot, rather his specialty, to defeat House in a shooting game. Gentry runs forward, falls to his knees and says, "In the words of Brandi Chastain . . ." then strips off his shirt.

House looks over and says, "Yeah? You got titties like her, too, Alvin."

Hours later, before the game against the Wizards, the talk turns, inevitably, to the NFL again. Now, House is talking about the combine at which teams test the athleticism of college stars.

"They make a big deal about running a four-point-four," says House, talking about forty-yard dash times, "and I know I could run a four-four. You watch me tonight going to the corner. It'll be four-four shit."

"I could run that, too," says Amare' Stoudemire, who is along on the road trip though he is still out with the knee injury.

"How about nobody in this room even runs a four-*five*," says Nash. There is respectful silence for a moment—Nash doesn't often join in group bull sessions and he is presumed to have a more logical mind than anyone else.

"You telling me I can't run faster than a defensive tackle?" House says finally.

"You know a defensive tackle who can do a four-four?" asks Nash.

"There's a couple of them," says House.

"Maybe some freaks," answers Nash. "And if they can, then they're faster than you."

"How about Shawn?" chimes in D'Antoni. "Could he do a four-four?"

(An hour later, with the Suns losing to the Wizards at halftime and walking the ball up, D'Antoni derisively brings up the conversation. "Before the game we're talking about times in the forty? Shit, you have to clock us with a calendar.")

"Shawn's the one guy who could worry me," says Nash. "And L.B." (Barbosa, suffering from a sprained left knee, is not on the trip.)

But House isn't finished. "I'm telling you, I'm feeling four-four shit. You're gonna see it tonight."

That night, he misses six of his seven shots in the Suns' 104–99 victory. None of his forays down the court look very four-fourish.

December 30
CHARLOTTE, NC

House's lowest moment in the NBA came when Charlotte Bobcats coach Bernie Bickerstaff called him into his office in December 2004 and basically told him, "We don't think you're an NBA player." The Bobcats were picking up Kareem Rush, and House was told he'd be sitting behind him. Way behind him. So, House asked to be waived.

On this night in Charlotte, House is unusually serious before the game though he professes to have no special thoughts of vengeance. He scores twenty-six points, including twelve in a decisive five-minute span, as the Suns win 110–100. After one field goal, House runs back on defense, pounding his chest, glancing ever so subtly at Bickerstaff on the Charlotte bench.

After the game, Bickerstaff is asked about House. "He can make shots," says Bickerstaff, "and he sure has a strong chest."

January 2, 2006
NEW YORK, NY

House has so much shtick and seemingly so much self-confidence that it's hard to believe how many times he has been cut. There are hundreds of players like him in the NBA, high school and college stars (he still shares with UCLA's Kareem Abdul-Jabbar, then Lew Alcindor, the Pac-10 record for points scored in a single game when he got sixty-one for Arizona State against Cal in 2000) who scratch around, make a roster and live the life, but who exist in a perpetual state of anxiety. Since House was drafted in 2000, he has been unwanted by not only the Bobcats but also the Heat, L.A. Clippers, Milwaukee Bucks, and Sacramento Kings. And though he's been, to this point, everything the Suns could've wanted, he has no assurance that he will be back next season, even though his guaranteed salary of $932,000 is low.

"I thought I was sticking out in Sacramento," House says before the game. "It's tough when somebody tells you they don't want you."

He pulls out a bible and reads a passage.

"What is it?" I ask him.

"Jeremiah 29:11," he answers.

"What's it say?" I ask.

"Look it up," he says. "Maybe you'll learn something."

Later I do: *"For I know the plans I have for you,"* declares the Lord, *"plans to prosper you and not to harm you, plans to give you hope and a future."*

CHAPTER EIGHT

[The Second Season]

Phoenix, May 2 . . . .
LAKERS LEAD SERIES 3-1

"Go be a bitch then. I'll forgive you in the morning."

**When I walk into the morning coaches meeting,
everybody's first words are: Did you see the paper?**

Someone had e-mailed a photo of the controversial Game 4 jump-ball call to the *Arizona Republic*. It was placed on page two of the sports section. Never mind whether a foul should've been called or a time-out granted—it shows Luke Walton's foot squarely on, and in fact well over, the out-of-bounds line. Walton was the one who tied up Nash, which he could not have legally done from a position out of bounds. The photo also shows referees Bennett Salvatore and Kenny Mauer looking squarely at the play. It's impossible to conclude whether or not they can see Walton's foot, of course, but they are in perfect position to have seen it.

By morning's end, someone in Suns Nation has obtained a wider-angle version of the photo, added his or her own captions, and sent it into cyberspace. Diaw is shown running toward Nash, his mouth open, yelling.

NOT CALLING TIME-OUT reads the caption. The one above Nash reads PROFOUND SENSE OF DÉJÀ VU. The caption next to referee Salvatore reads FEELS NOTHING BECAUSE HE OBVIOUSLY SOLD HIS SOUL TO THE DEVIL (STERN). Actually, the funniest captions on the photo are next to actor David Arquette, a courtside Laker fan (STILL AMAZED HE GOT COURTNEY COX TO MARRY HIM) and a background Laker Girl (HOPING THE LAKERS SCORE A TOUCHDOWN).

Another story this morning is about the $10,000 fine that had been assessed Denver Nuggets forward Reggie Evans for grabbing the testicles of Los Angeles Clipper center Chris Kaman from behind (or, as Eddie House puts it, "right up through his ass") during a scramble for a rebound. "That's the NBA," says Gentry. "You get fined ten grand for grabbing a guy's balls and ten grand for wearing your shorts too long."

From time to time the coaches go out of their way to compliment a job done by a particular referee. Iavaroni is most likely to do it, and, occasionally, he will even take the side of an official when the coaches are reviewing a call they thought was particularly heinous. (That takes guts.) During an agonizing 139–137 triple overtime loss in Denver on January 10, Iavaroni leapt off the bench to protest a blocking call on Nash that he thought should've been a charge on the Nuggets. Joe Forte, a veteran ref, came over to the bench and said to him, "First of all, you split your pants. Second, you gotta calm down." It was true—Iavaroni was trying to get by with a pair of suit pants that had a small rip in the crotch. "I just respected the calm way Joe handled it," said Iavaroni.

But most of the time the Suns feel as if they get screwed by the zebras more than their opponents do. And every other team feels the same way. The state of refereeing is always a hot topic during the playoffs. Jermaine O'Neal of the Indiana Pacers and Shaquille O'Neal of the Miami Heat have already been fined for blasting refs. Commissioner David Stern is asked about the officiating during an impromptu news conference at the Pacers-Nets series. Stern estimates that officials make the wrong call about five percent of the time. "Right now," says David Griffin, "we're getting ninety-five percent of the five percent."

. . .

It's four hours before tip-off, and D'Antoni is a mess. "I tell you, I haven't been right since I found out Raja got hit with an extra flagrant," he says. "That was three days ago. I know I should get it out of my head, but I can't." He fills these nervous pregame hours tinkering with matchups and listening to his iTunes, in particular a song by the artist Pink called "Dear Mr. President," an excoriating indictment of the Bush administration.

Political discussions come up with some regularity among the coaches. D'Antoni, Iavaroni, and Gentry are fervently anti-Bush. Under pressure, Phil Weber once admitted that he voted for Bush, and D'Antoni has never let him forget it. Dan D'Antoni tends more toward a form of libertarianism. Their political views parallel the brothers' feelings about religion. Mike and wife, Laurel, attend church together when it's possible but adhere to a liberal view of Christianity in which the church gets involved in social causes. Dan believes that all organized religions are, at root, hypocritical, in line with his political conviction that "both the Republicans and Democrats will steal you blind." The elder D'Antoni even voted for Perot back in 1992. "Danny was so eager not to get a Democrat or Republican," says Mike, "that he voted for a nut."

In the training room, meanwhile, Nash has ordered assistant trainer Mike Elliott and assistant equipment manager Jay Gaspar into the ice bath as a show of faith. Elliott and Gaspar lower themselves in, looking miserable. "Suns in seven," says Aaron Nelson, working on Nash's back.

Word comes down a couple hours before the game that Kwame Brown is being investigated for a sexual assault that allegedly happened after Game 3 in Los Angeles. Reporters who meet the Laker bus for comment are greeted only by stony silence. Brown has already released a statement denying culpability. When word reaches the Suns' locker room about the story, D'Antoni asks, "Was the assault on Boris Diaw?"

The Suns come out to wild applause and the sight of the Gorilla, their inventive mascot, holding a sign that reads MISSION POSSIBLE. They seem energized and loose, beneficiaries of that magical potion known as home-court advantage. Teams in every sport do better at home, but the advantage is more pronounced in basketball; during the regular season, home teams had won about sixty percent of the time.

There are the predictable reasons. The environs are more familiar. A player slept in his own bed, ate his favorite food, drove to the arena in his favorite car, parked in his favorite spot, got good-luck messages from his favorite people around the arena. The locker room feels familiar, the pregame coffee and energy drinks are familiar, the fruit plate is familiar. This is his kingdom and, once again, he is king.

Once on the court, he gets a lift from the fans, the dance team, the banners, the messages on the video board. More than any sport, basketball (at any level) is subject to the vicissitudes of momentum, emotional ebb and flow. The fans are a factor. They are closer to the action, more organic to the flow of play. The roar in a football stadium might be literally louder than in a basketball arena, but it sure as hell doesn't *sound* louder to the players. Sound is distilled by the vastness of the stadium; it *reverberates* in a basketball arena.

Then, too, though referees and the league office would deny it, home teams generally get more favorable calls than visiting teams. How could they not? Referees are human. Lamar Odom ducks a shoulder and knocks Marion to the floor in Los Angeles. Foul on Marion. The same play in Phoenix? Offensive foul or a no-call. A few veteran referees—Steve Javie and Joey Crawford being the two most notable—are known for giving visiting teams a good whistle, some-

101

times all but daring the home fans to get on them. But, overall, a home team gets the majority of close ones. Put it all together, and it's home-court advantage.

Bell and Bryant walk onto the court without so much as a glance at each other. All around them is hand-slapping and good-lucking (though it does seem more subdued than usual), but their subplot of hand-to-hand combat was long ago established. *I hate you, you hate me, let's not pretend we don't hate each other.* It's actually refreshing.

The Suns jump out to a 7–0 lead. When they get up 15–5, D'Antoni feels comfortable enough to give Diaw a rest, but the Lakers get back in the game. The coach learns quickly that on this night he has to keep Diaw on the court. Diaw seems to be playing at warp speed, while Kwame Brown, perhaps distracted by the assault investigation, appears slow. The Suns outscore the Lakers 40–20 with Diaw on the court in the first half but get outscored 27–16 when he's not. Diaw converts the Suns' final eleven points of the second quarter to give them a 56–47 lead at halftime.

One of his baskets in that stretch is a resounding dunk from the wing on a fast break. Whenever Diaw finishes with a flush, it's worth at least a basket-and-a-half to the Suns. Stoudemire's injury eliminated not only twenty-six points a game but also most of the shock-and-awe component of the Phoenix attack. For an offensive-minded team, the Stoudemire-less Suns get precious few *SportsCenter* moments. Marion's Matrix moves are electrifying but there haven't been enough of them. Watching Nash weave his way through a minefield of defenders and deliver an eyes-in-the-back-of-his-head pass to a cutter is stuff for the basketball purist; crowds prefer the Stoudemire Cirque du Soleil aerials, and they can be more of a mood lifter and game changer for the team.

Diaw is a reluctant dunker, and, further, often passes out to a jump shooter when he's in position to dunk, perhaps the first center in the history of the game to even think about doing that. That pass-first mentality is a big part of what makes him unique, but there are times that the Suns wish he would just rip down the rim.

The lead reaches 73–56 midway through the third period, as a couple of Lakers glance over at Jackson to see if he wants a time-out. The be-throned coach gazes stoically into space. *Work it out yourselves, fellas.* The lead reaches 84–60 late in the third. The Suns can't let this one get away, can they? Of course they can. The Suns have shown the capacity to blow leads all season, which frustrates their fans but is understandable at some level. Since they shoot the ball quickly, there are more possessions per game for both teams. During the season Phoenix gave up a league-leading 87.09 field goal attempts per game, almost five more than second-place Denver, which also plays up-tempo. One of the keys to the Suns' success was that their defensive field goal percentage, 45.4, wasn't bad (and would've been much better had Kurt Thomas not gotten injured). Giving up a lot of shots *and* allowing the other team to make them is a prescription for disaster.

Even so, the greater the number of possessions, the more chances for the opponent to start making baskets and rallying, and, conversely, for the Suns to start missing and leaking oil. Which is exactly what happens. L.A. converts back-to-back three-point shots to close the third, then scores on five consecutive possessions to open the fourth. The crowd is getting nervous. From his courtside seat, Robert Sarver motions for the scoreboard operator to replay on the big screen any close calls that go against the Suns.

The game is getting chippy. Bell and Bryant had already drawn double technicals in the first half for jostling each other off the ball, and now they are fighting for every inch on every possession, an individual ground skirmish framed within the larger battle. The Suns have contended all series long that Bryant is a master cheap-shot artist, albeit a slick one. When he pump-fakes or shoots, he frequently manages to land an elbow on or about Bell's face. The contact takes place lower, too. Bryant comes down and rams his hip against Bell's hips. Bell pushes back, sticks his foot inside Bryant's base, tripping him up. *I hate you, you hate me, let's not pretend we don't hate each other.* Focusing on the two of them would've been a great opportunity for an isolated camera—the game within the game. When Bell complains to a referee near the Laker bench that Bryant was not whistled for an elbow, he hears a comment from Phil Jackson that includes the words "deserve it." Bell has to restrain himself from going at Jackson.

With 7:33 left in the game, the Suns fighting to sustain a double-digit advantage, and Bryant holding the ball near the free-throw line, Bell suddenly puts his left arm around Bryant's neck and horse-collars him toward the floor. As Bryant begins his descent, Bell gives a kind of what-the-fuck push with his right arm, too, as if gravity weren't sufficient to have done the job. The play is nothing short of stunning. It would've been comprehensible had they been locked up in some way, or if Bell had done it in retaliation for something overt that had happened on a previous possession. But it comes out of nowhere.

Nash, angry that his backcourt buddy has snapped, angry that the Lakers are rallying, angry about the whole combative atmosphere of this whole confounding series—this is not his kind of ball—walks over to referee Leon Wood, a former NBA player, and says, "It's you guys who caused this."

Wood is taken aback. "Not me," he says.

"You let things get out of hand," says Nash. "And this is what happens." He didn't mean Wood individually; he meant the referees collectively, including those in Games 3 and 4 in L.A.

Bell is, of course, ejected. And Bryant, as is his wont, hits a three-pointer on the next possession and the Suns lead only 93–83 with 7:17 to go. The season is in the balance, Raja Bell is in the locker room, and Kobe Bryant is on a roll.

But, then, suddenly, the Suns find the touch again. It comes, it goes; it comes, it goes. It comes. Leandro Barbosa hits a monstrous three-pointer, then Shawn Marion comes down and launches another three. Marion's unusual-looking long-distance shot, released one-handed—the Matrix goes retro—seems to reach the ceiling before it begins its slow descent. It should be accompanied by one of those air-raid whistles and a shout of "IN-COMING!" from the scoreboard. Marion gets furious when he is asked about his unorthodox shot. He feels, in that defensive way of his, that his form is being used to disrespect his game, which is not the case. It's just a source of fascination for the onlooker. There is no predicting whether a Marion three-pointer will (a) sail over the basket, as it sometimes does when he shoots it from the corner, (b) fail to reach its target, as it sometimes does from anywhere, or (c) settle blessedly into the basket, not unusual since he is a career thirty-five percent three-point shooter, a good number for someone whose marksmanship is so suspect.

This one goes in. The Suns go on to score six more points before the Lakers get a basket, and it's over.

With 3:11 left and the issue decided, Bryant complains to Wood about a call and draws a second technical and automatic ejection. Wood gets no love from either side for the call. The Lakers figure that he did it in response to Nash's complaining, and the Suns figure that he took a stand too late. Bryant smirks as he leaves the court, shaking his head, and the enmity toward the NBA's most talented player pours down upon him. KO-BE SUCKS! KO-BE SUCKS!

As time winds down on the 114–97 win, Alvin Gentry finally gives voice to something he had been holding in the entire game. "Danny," he says to Dan D'Antoni. "you got on two different shoes." Gentry had noticed it early in the game but didn't want to mention it as long as the outcome was in doubt. "I just kept praying, 'Please let us win so I can bust him, please let us win so I can bust him,' " says Gentry. He alerts the bench and Stoudemire shakes his head. "Damn, Coach Dan," he says, "you can't be wearing a lizard on one foot and a gator on the other."

The Suns are ecstatic with the win, of course, but a sense of uncertainty immediately sets in. They try to sell the idea that the pressure is back on the Lakers, but Game 6 is in Los Angeles, and Bell, already on double secret probation and maybe even on double-double secret probation, will almost certainly be suspended.

Julie Fie convinces Bell that he should go to the interview room and fall on the sword. She has a vague worry that Raja will soliloquize about Bryant's defects as a human being, but, she figures, he's a smart guy who can be a diplomat when so required.

As Bell gets dressed, Tim Thomas says, with a big smile, "Don't be a bitch to the media now."

"They tell me that's my only chance," says Raja.

"I understand," says Thomas. "Go be a bitch then. I'll forgive you in the morning."

Almost lost in the hubbub about Bell is the play of Diaw, who finishes just one assist shy of a triple-double—twenty-five points (including 11-of-11 from the free-throw line) and ten rebounds. "Boris Jordan" they call him in the locker room.

"I don't know where we'd be without that kid," says Gentry. "From where he started to where he is now? It's one of the most amazing things I've ever seen, I can tell you that."

FULL TIME-OUT

October 9, 2005
TRAINING CAMP, TUCSON

Getting to Know the Frenchman

As befitting someone with a curious mind and disposable income, Boris Diaw got the news that he had been traded to the Phoenix Suns while on safari in Africa. To put it generously, Diaw was an after-thought in the acrimonious deal that sent Joe Johnson, a mainstay starter during the 2004–05 renaissance season, to Atlanta. General manager Bryan Colangelo thought Diaw was good and assistant GM Dave Griffin thought he was *real* good, but almost no one else in the Suns' organization even knew him. "Who's the Russian?" asked Al-van Adams, a Suns' legend as a player and now the arena manager, when he heard about the trade last August.

Diaw had averaged 4.8 points, 2.6 rebounds, and 2.3 assists in Atlanta, a team that finished with a 13-69 record, worst in the league. Colangelo and Griffin insist that Diaw never got the opportunity to demonstrate his versatility in Atlanta. The coaches don't know enough about Diaw to confirm that, reserve players on cellar-dwelling teams commanding little time in scouting reports. At the very least, he has innate athletic ability. His Senegalese father, Issa Diaw, was once an outstanding high jumper. His mother, Elisabeth Riffiod, is considered one of France's all-time great women basketball players. Diaw the Younger can do a lot of things, but, sometimes in the NBA, that is a negative. A player needs a position. The Suns coaches are less wedded to that concept than most teams, but even they can't quite decide what Diaw is. Backup point guard, which is what he played (more or less) with Atlanta? Small forward? Power forward? He's six-feet-eight—can he guard some of the smaller centers?

Whatever, the coaches are sure of one thing: They desperately miss Johnson, who had been a free agent at the end of last season. Owner Robert Sarver did not see Johnson in quite the same light as the coaches. Sarver saw a fourth wheel who was not nearly as important to the Suns' future as Steve Nash, Amare' Stoudemire, or Shawn Marion, certainly not with a big-dollar deal with Stoudemire in the works. Sarver was willing to offer Johnson a six-year deal worth $75 million. That sounds generous, but in the NBA, as in the Fortune 500 world, worth is skewed and relative. The Hawks, looking to rebuild behind Johnson, offered $70 million, front-loading $19 million of it. Sarver wasn't ready to make that kind of commitment and said, "Work out a trade."

Even the coaches weren't absolutely sure Johnson was worth that money. But they knew they had lost a six-foot-seven-inch warrior who guards multiple positions, runs tirelessly (Johnson is among the perennial leaders in minutes played), and creates his own shot in the half-court. "One thing we can't replace," says Phil Weber, "is Joe's ability to get into the lane and take over parts of the game."

Nash, Marion, and Stoudemire had been penciled in as starters from the beginning of camp, of course, with Kurt Thomas (center) and Raja Bell (shooting guard) probably joining them. Behind them were a lot of question marks, of which Diaw was one. Personnel matters had gotten even more complicated, however, when it became known that Stoudemire would probably require knee surgery.

Now the rotation gets murky, the inevitable ripple effect caused by an injury to a prime player. Someone has to replace Stoudemire in the starting lineup, and that someone would've been a sixth or seventh man, so now that someone has to take the new starter's minutes, and someone has to take the other someone's minutes, and next thing you know a couple of guys are playing more minutes than they should. Extended minutes reveal deficiencies.

"If we can get twenty-four minutes with Shawn at four, and

twenty-four with Kurt Thomas or Brian Grant, we'll be fine," says D'Antoni. "That gives me time to play James Jones, Eddie House, Boris Diaw, or whoever. But can we play eleven guys? Ten guys? Hell, nine guys?" There are many responsibilities that separate a head coach from his assistants, but none starker than the burden of playing time. Assistants suggest substitution patterns and offer opinions on which players have earned extra minutes. But the head coach pulls the trigger, and D'Antoni has begun worrying about playing time from the first moment of camp.

"A lot of it is on Brian Grant, and whether he can keep up," says Dan D'Antoni. Grant is a cagey thirty-three-year-old veteran who signed a free agent contract with the Suns in the off-season. Even with bad knees, Grant is a bargain for the Suns, who are paying him $1.7 million, although he's into the Lakers for $14.5 million (and $15.6 million the following year), the result of a huge deal he originally signed with the Portland Trail Blazers.

"Pat Burke is going to be the eleventh man," says D'Antoni. "Nothing against him, but somebody's gotta be. Now, between Boris Diaw, Eddie House, L.B., and Brian Grant, one of those four have to be number ten."

"In my mind it's going to be B.G.," says Dan. "I watched that clear-out and they were blowing by him. He had no chance. And it wasn't because he was tired. He's in good shape."

"Brian Grant is competing against Eddie and L.B. for minutes," says D'Antoni, "even though he's not their position."

"He's competing against style," says Dan.

"Well, what everyone is playing against is how good Boris Diaw plays in our system," says D'Antoni. "Can he be a legit backup power forward?"

"What I worry about, with Boris, is his attitude," says Alvin Gentry. "He just doesn't seem to want to learn."

"Boris is in your head, Coach," says Iavaroni, smiling.

"Damn right he is," answers Gentry.

"Look, it's tough in two-a-days," says Iavaroni. "Let's get back to Phoenix and work with him."

"You try to get Boris to do anything in practice he doesn't want to do, and it's tough," says Dan.

"Put it this way," says Weber, "you have to have *discussions* with Boris." Weber has already started working with Diaw on his jump shot. Though Diaw is never likely to become a three-point shooter, the Suns would like to see him become a perimeter threat. Diaw seems to have his own ideas on shooting drills, and most everything else. Which is perhaps to be expected from someone whose full name is Boris Babacar Diaw-Riffiod. It sounds like he should have "Marquis" in front of his name. But if anyone can break him down, it's Weber, a tireless clinician.

"I know I shouldn't say anything to Boris," says Gentry. "I mean, he won a whole thirteen games last year in Atlanta. What did we win, sixty-two?"

For all of that, there is something likable about Diaw. There is the suggestion of arrogance about him—"I do not date American women," he says, "I *have* them"—but also the suggestion of class and refinement. And he is unfailingly upbeat with a word of greeting for everyone. "How are you doo-EENG?" Diaw says to whomever he sees, a refreshing change from the American *howyadoin*. And Diaw's sing-songy "thank you"—which sounds like "sank youuuu!"—is already being replicated around the locker room. Eddie House has been caught practicing it.

But, all in all, Diaw looks like a problem for D'Antoni on whom the distribution of minutes, as well as the burden of owner and fan expectation after sixty-two wins in the previous season, falls. And he will be trying to accomplish all that without Stoudemire (for at least four months), three-point threat Quentin Richardson (who went to the Knicks so the Suns could add Kurt Thomas for interior strength), and Joe Johnson. And *with* a joyfully cantankerous, or cantankerously joyful question mark from France named Boris Diaw. "Boris is probably just good enough to get us all fired," concludes D'Antoni.

At this early checkpoint, then, Boris Diaw is one step above a "whoever," a certified attitude problem, a possible backup power forward, a possible tenth man, and a possible coach killer. Good thing the front office likes him.

CHAPTER NINE

[The Second Season]

May 3 . . . .
LAKERS LEAD SERIES 3–2

"Do I know this guy? I don't know this guy. I might've said one word to this guy. I don't know this kid."

Jerry Colangelo brought the Suns into the NBA in 1968. He coached them, general-managed them, scouted for them, and owned them, and, two years after selling the team to Robert Sarver, is still chairman and CEO. Beyond that, Colangelo is rather the Godfather of the NBA, and not just because he is a tough Italian. Over the years, he is the one who makes the secret deals and knows where all the bodies are buried, strictly in the figurative sense. Over the last two decades, as David Stern has expanded his power to become the commissioner of commissioners, Colangelo is the only team executive who has consistently had Stern's ear.

Colangelo's place in the Suns' hierarchy is now tenuous. His son, Bryan, left his job as general manager after a midseason dispute with Sarver, and now Sarver and Colangelo circle each other warily, like two panthers angling for space in the same small cage. But Jerry is still the top figure on the franchise flow chart (his contract as chairman/CEO runs until June of 2007), and, when Jerry speaks, Suns Nation listens. And it was decided immediately after Game 5 that Jerry should make the call to Stu Jackson to plead the case for Raja Bell.

"Here's how I laid it out," Colangelo tells D'Antoni. "I told him he kind of owes us one. Three miscues [no foul call, no time-out call, Walton out-of-bounds] cost us Game 4. 'Do you think that was important, Stu? Losing a game we should've won and going down 3–1?' Then there was the technical not called on Kwame Brown when he stood over our guy and glared at him. The stray elbows. The Kobe theatrics with pulling the jersey over his head when a technical wasn't called either." As a last resort, Colangelo also suggested to Jackson: "If you have to suspend Bell, why not make it for two games at the beginning of next season?"

Even with Colangelo at bat, everyone in the Suns' organization knows this: There is positively, absolutely no chance that Raja Bell—a marked man even before the playoffs started—won't be suspended. "Johnnie Cochran couldn't get him off," concludes Alvin Gentry at the morning coaches meeting.

"Johnnie's dead," says Phil Weber.

"So's Raja," says Gentry.

Though no one will concede the point, Colangelo's preemptive lobbying is as much about discouraging Jackson from suspending Bell for *two* games, a distinct possibility. The coaches study the photo of the clotheslining that appears on page one of the *Arizona Republic.* There is no abundance of love for Kobe Bryant within the Suns' franchise, but everyone admits there are legitimate grounds for indictment. "I tell you guys, Kobe could have gotten really hurt there," says Gentry. "The league can't allow that."

At 9 a.m., athletic trainer Aaron Nelson calls up to the coaches room. "NBA security just asked for Raja's number," reports Nelson. The hammer will be coming down soon.

"What I worry about is from this one angle it just looks like Raja is rearing back and throwing the forearm, like a punch," says Dave Griffin.

"Maybe because he kind of was?" I add helpfully.

"And then they put it on page one for all the world to see," says Gentry.

I feel obligated to speak up for my newspaper brethren. "Any newspaper that didn't put that photo on page one wouldn't be doing its job."

"Oh, I'm not saying that," says Gentry. "I would've put it on page one, too, if I was the editor."

The task now is to strategize with the assumption that Leandro Barbosa will be starting in place of Bell. Having Barbosa in the starting lineup makes the Suns even more, well, Suns-like. Barbosa is perhaps the fastest player in the league with the ball, Philadelphia's Allen Iverson and Dallas's Devin Harris being his only competitors. Despite an orthodox, almost two-handed release on his jump shot, he is an excellent three-point shooter, having finished the season with a .444 percentage on three-point shots, best on the team and third best in the league. He has a six-foot-ten-inch wingspan that enables him to get off shots in heavy traffic. In short, he is a better offensive player than Bell.

But L.B. is not nearly as good a defender. Bell has been a rock defensively, fundamentally sound, and, above all, tough. The Suns use part of their accrued fine money to pay fifty bucks for every charging foul drawn, and Bell had picked up $3,650 during the season for drawing seventy-three, best in the league. There's a saying around the league that "the more money you make, the less you take a charge," but that doesn't apply to Bell. After finally getting a good contract— the Suns gave him $23.8 million over five years, a free-agent deal that at least one pundit termed the worst of the summer—Bell threw his body around like a Hollywood stuntman. Oddly, he became known as both a tough guy and a flopper, i.e., a player who exaggerates contact and falls backward or down with the exuberance of a stage actor. As to the latter, Bell prefers to say that he is merely "emphasizing a call that should be made."

Barbosa, slightly built at six-foot-three and 188 pounds, gets pushed around. He has much to learn about positioning and plays too much with his hands, reaching out and grabbing, a personal foul waiting to happen. Barbosa is not a bad defender by any means—he is quick, willing, and tough-minded—but in Game 6, another elimination challenge, he will be asked to check the game's best player.

There is really no alternative plan, though. Marion could guard Bryant, but that would force Diaw into guarding Marion's man, Lamar Odom, and the Suns don't like that matchup. The biggest worry for the coaches is that Barbosa will be unable to gold Bryant, i.e., front him to discourage an entry pass, a stratagem that Bell has been using effectively. The Suns know that their double-teams on Bryant have to be more forceful than they were with Bell on the court.

"L.B.'s got to know when he can deny him and when he can't," says Dan D'Antoni, "but most of all he has to realize that it's not the end of the world when he does score."

There is no doubt that Barbosa will take the challenge, for no one works more diligently at improving. That fact, his boyish innocence, his occasional torturing of the English language ("Nobody was believing myself at that time" is his way of saying that he surprised a lot of people around the NBA), his sincere love for his family back in Brazil, and about a dozen other things make Barbosa the most beloved player on the team.

In one of the golden school-trip moments, I can still see Barbosa in the back of the bus as it headed for the airport in Toronto on the morning of April 1 after a win over the Raptors the night before. A spontaneous chorus of "O Canada" broke out, and Barbosa, with a big smile on his face, waved his arms like a conductor. He wasn't singing, probably because he had no idea what the words were—he was just smiling and conducting. He had grown up a poor kid in São Paulo, Brazil, learning the game from his older brother, Arturo, a taskmaster who used to whack him with a stick when he made the wrong move during ball-handling drills. A small scar runs along the base of Barbosa's left thumb bears memory to their workouts. And there he was conducting "O Canada" in an NBA bus.

"If you don't like L.B.," says Dan D'Antoni, who has become

Barbosa's personal coach, assigned by his brother to that task early in the season, "there's something wrong with *you.*"

Nash is out shooting early on the practice court when Bell, somewhat sheepishly, walks in. "There he is!" shouts Nash, as if announcing the appearance of a rock star. Bell waves and smiles, though he is a little embarrassed. By any logical reckoning, Bell's flagrant foul on Bryant was a brainless act. It occurred when the outcome was still in the balance, Bell was not retaliating to contact (indeed, Bryant was alone in the middle of the court; it was akin to a mugging), and, moreover, he was jeopardizing the entire series. Yet there is universal support for Bell within the team. The coaches love Bell not just for his competitiveness but also for his loyalty. Shortly after he signed his free-agent contract, the Suns went after another free agent, Michael Finley, and, though signing Finley would've meant less playing time for Bell, he was among those who went on Finley's "recruiting trip." (Finley eventually signed with San Antonio.)

The support for Bell is predictable on one level: He who does not stand up for a teammate in time of need is a traitor. But there is also the fact that throughout the season and in this series, the Suns are always the team that is considered soft, always the team that gets pushed around. Bell himself had noted that weeks earlier, during halftime of a game in Sacramento on April 11, one of the more memorable nights of the year. The Suns trailed the Kings by 68–51 and appeared to be mailing it in at every position. Including coach. D'Antoni had been down on himself for failing to ignite his team, which, having all but mathematically clinched second place in the Western Conference, seemed to be drifting along, content with the world, failing to build playoff momentum. At the break, D'Antoni went at the team, but then Bell asked to speak, and his words, delivered calmly but forcefully, were the ones that made the difference.

"Right now they think we're their 'hos," Bell said. "And I want to tell you something: I ain't nobody's 'ho. There comes a time when we gotta go out there and change what people think of us because, right now, people think of us as pussies. I'm going to do it right now. This half."

And the Suns responded with their best concentrated play of the season. Eight of them scored at least nine points apiece. They made 71 percent of their shots. They scored seventy-two points. They weren't nobody's 'ho. They won going away, 123–110, against a home team that had won six of its previous seven games. That game helped reposition the Suns, in their own minds, as a championship contender.

I wander over to Bell and ask if he has heard from the league.

"Not yet," he says, "but I expect I will."

Then I ask, with all due care, "So, um, why did you do it?" It seems better than, *What the hell were you thinking?*

Bell shakes his head. "It's like it happened in slow motion," he says. " 'All right, Rah-Rah, don't do it. Don't . . . you're going to do it . . . you're going to do it . . . SHIT! You did it.' " Bell says he was also angered because Phil Jackson said to him, "You fuckin' deserve it," when he protested about a noncall on Bryant.

Bell admits to a history that includes more than a few scuffles on and off the court. During his sophomore year at Boston University a coach sent him to a sports psychologist to discuss anger management. Bell attended a couple of sessions but nothing much came of it. "I didn't dig it," he says. "I never thought I had an anger problem. I just thought I was trying to find out who I was, trying to figure out how I fit in. In retrospect, yeah, maybe I could've talked to somebody. It might've helped me out a little bit."

Like, say, when it was time for Bell to take his league-mandated urine test a month earlier. He just couldn't produce under pressure and became so incensed that he almost tossed away his cup and walked out, which would result in an automatic suspension. "Raja, you can't get mad at a urine test," Dave Griffin told him. Bell stuck around and finally came through in the clutch. On numerous occasions during the season, Bell would go into a minitantrum, walking off the court and talking to himself, after missing three straight jumpers in practice. The assistant throwing him the ball, usually Gentry or Weber, would calmly wait for Bell to settle himself, and the warm-up would begin anew.

Bell's temper caused him and D'Antoni—mutual admirers—to get into it after the San Antonio Spurs drubbed the Suns 117–93 in Phoenix on March 9. It was a miserable night all around. Nash was out with a badly sprained right ankle. Barbosa had shown up for the game with a painful groin injury from one of his testicles having gotten twisted in its sack—"That's some Third World shit right there," said Iavaroni—and didn't play either. Marion and Tim Thomas were both recovering from the flu. The Spurs dominated for forty-eight minutes, and Bell, like almost everyone else, played poorly. Bell had snapped at Diaw during the game. "Pass the damn ball!" he said, an unfair criticism since Diaw had played unselfishly. Later, Bell angered D'Antoni when, in the coach's mind, he had pretended not to hear a play call that he had actually heard. So D'Antoni had snapped at him during a time-out.

After the game, D'Antoni decided to extend an olive branch to Bell. "All right, I shouldn't have done that with Raja," he says. "Raja, I apologize. We cool?" Bell didn't say anything or even look up. So D'Antoni repeated it. "Raja, we cool?" Finally, Bell sullenly nodded. That was not the Yalta moment D'Antoni had been looking for, and he lectured the team for ten minutes, after which Bell still looked angry. Coach and player then conferred behind closed doors, but the matter didn't get cleared up until two nights later when, before a game against Minnesota, Bell apologized to the team for snapping at Diaw.

"Raja will go off from time to time," says D'Antoni, "but if I had twelve guys like him, I'd feel pretty good."

Bell comes by his temper naturally. Presented with the Kobe

challenge, Bell's father, Roger, an athletic administrator at the University of Miami, would've possibly done something worse than a horse collar. Roger Bell has twice been kicked out of fifty-and-over basketball tournaments for overaggressiveness, one time breaking an opponent's nose. Raja, his mother, and his sister, Tombi, who was an outstanding college player, were there to enjoy the spectacle.

"I mean, damn, fifty-and-over, you'd think you'd be able to chill by that time," says Bell. "But I understand it because my dad and I have the same temperament. We lose it, then, by the time we get back in the car, it's 'Oops, we shouldn't have done that.' Some people who don't know me think I'm a complete asshole. I understand that. I know I'm not. I'm not like that at home at all. But, when I get on that court and people try to take something from me or get over on me, I *will* fight."

Though they are different types of players, Bell's career parallels that of Eddie House. They have both battled, convinced they have the talent to make it but looking for a coach to confirm it. They have to find a way to stay on the court, a way to get an identity. With House, it's shooting. With Bell, it's pit-bull defense and midrange competence.

Bell is convinced, or he is trying to convince himself, that his team will be just fine without him in Game 6. "Either Kobe's going to be passive and it won't matter," he says, "or he'll try to take over and dominate L.B. and mess everything else up."

When D'Antoni gathers the team together, he doesn't begin with the let's-get-fired-up-and-win-it-for-Raja speech. He wants to make it seem like any other game (though clearly it is not) so he goes over matchups and the importance of being as active on defense as they were in Game 5. Almost off-handedly, he says, "We'll get word about Raja soon. Whatever happens, I don't have any doubt we'll handle it. As the games go on, the Lakers are getting a little tighter. Trust me on that. It's going to be a great atmosphere. This is fun. This is what it's about."

After practice, Bell, obviously, is the big story. The press contingent is large, and everyone wants Raja. Julie Fie is nervous about letting him speak, but, in keeping with the Suns' policy, she makes Bell available after practice, an open target. He answers a few harmless questions, and then Fie, hovering around the outside of the group, hears the words "no respect for him," "pompous," and "arrogant." She swoops in and puts her hand gently on Bell's back, just to let him know she's there. But Bell is rolling, and Fie, with more than two decades in the business, recognizes a lost cause when she sees it.

"I think a lot of people let him get away with things and he feels like he's supposed to get away with them and I don't agree with that," Bell says of Bryant. "If you're going to keep hitting me in my face and then talking like you're not doing it on purpose . . . there's a reason both of my cheeks are bruised right now and I can barely open my jaw. Every time you stick your butt out [he means when Bryant posts him up by the foul line] and try to hit me in my genitals [he really says "genitals"], you're doing it on purpose. That's something you don't do inadvertently and it was enough."

Last night, after the game, Bryant had jokingly said maybe he and Bell should take their battle into the Octagon, the venue for Ultimate Fighting. Bell sniffs when someone brings that up. "We don't need an Octagon. There's plenty of space and opportunity right out on the court, man. When I get hit in the face multiple times, you've stepped across a line with me. It's not basketball anymore."

Bell also revealed the exchange he had had with Jackson during the game. "I thought that was kind of bush league from such a good coach," says Bell.

Out in Los Angeles, Jackson confirms that he and Bell did have words, though he obviously has a different take on it. "I told him, 'You're leaning in there all the time, so you deserve it,' " says Jackson. The coach says he did not use the F-word. And Jackson also poohpoohs the notion that the series is physical. "Fifteen years ago guys were thrown up into the seats, and it was really rough," says the coach.

"I think they're much more on edge than is necessary in this series. My guys are pussycats, and Phoenix has a bunch of pussycats, too."

Word has spread about Bell's comments, and Bryant is ready, returning to the I-am-king-and-I'm-not-sure-who-he-is theme. "Does he know me?" says Bryant. "Do I know this guy? I don't know this guy. I might've said one word to this guy. I don't know this kid. I think he overreacts to stuff. We go out there, we play and when we play during the season, we play each other. That's it. I don't know this kid. I don't need to know this kid. I don't want to. We go out there, we play the game and we leave it at that. Maybe he wasn't hugged enough as a kid. I look at him a little bit, he gets a little insecure or something."

If you're scoring at home, that's four "kids" and three "guys."

Kobe also says that Bell has "a glass jaw," and denies deliberately attacking Bell's genitals. "Whoa, I'm nowhere near doing something like that. We're out there playing basketball. He's a good defender. He's a good basketball player. Just go out there and play the game. There's no need to whine about it."

NBA Commissioner David Stern also weighs in on the Bell flagrant. He calls it "unmanly."

The one-hour flight to Los Angeles is quiet. It was decided among the players—in effect, by Bell, Nash, and Brian Grant, who are more or less the travel counselors, their wives being more or less the wives-in-chief—that significant others should not come along on the trip. It will be short and all business, and, superstitiously, no one had to bring up the fact that the Suns lost both games in L.A. when families were in tow. Jason March, the assistant video coordinator (whom Nash calls "Raef LaFrentz" because he bears a strong resemblance to that NBA player), was along on the Game 3 and 4 trip, too, and he took a lot of heat for being a jinx. So he's back in Phoenix.

At dinner, D'Antoni is asked what particular referees he doesn't want to see. He names one. "We just seem to have a personality con-flict," he says. "It's partly my fault, too. But we just don't get along." Not thirty seconds later, that ref walks by, having chosen to dine in the same restaurant. That means he will be working tomorrow night. He and the coach share polite nods. Between clenched lips, D'Antoni says: "Do I have the worst karma in the world, or what?"

CHAPTER TEN

[The Second Season]

Los Angeles, May 4 . . . .
LAKERS LEAD SERIES 3–2

"Make sure you mention Shawn. We couldn't have done it without him."

Raja Bell, who to everyone's immense relief has been suspended for only tonight's game, has decided to attend the morning shootaround. The only restriction on him in Los Angeles is that he must be out of the Staples Center two hours before tip-off.

"If you think that's the best thing to do, go for it," says Iavaroni, gently questioning whether in fact it is the best thing.

"Nobody told me not to," says Bell. "I'm not going to talk to the media, though. I did my talking yesterday."

Indeed, Bell's and Bryant's comments about each other dominate the morning sports pages in Los Angeles, as they do back in Phoenix. But the way the situation was handled by Julie Fie and John Black was absolutely correct. Some NBA teams would've kept Bell and Bryant from commenting, a ridiculous alternative. The players are grown men in the public eye, and they should get the chance to express their feelings. And what is the dire consequence if those feelings come out as antagonistic? It's not like the basketball-watching public isn't aware of the enmity the players hold toward each other.

One can only imagine what would've happened had this situation involved the clueless Portland Trail Blazers, who weeks earlier had announced a new media policy in which interviews with executives and players might be tape-recorded by the team, with a transcript or audio file of the interview posted on the Blazers' website. Also, reporters will be asked in some cases to provide a written list of questions before being granted an interview. The Blazers collect a bunch of reprobate players, blame the media when the inevitable negative stories come out, then construct policies that assure continued negative public relations. Today, that is what passes for media relations in some professional cities.

Besides, somewhere in the NBA offices in New York City, a few executives were silently conceding that a war of words is a good thing. One of the NBA's biggest problems with the consumer is the perception that the game is passionless, that teammates and opponents are bonded by a feeling of joint entitlement, and that those memorable and venomous team-against-team rivalries, such as the Lakers–Celtics and Pistons–Bulls, have gone the way of the two-handed set shot.

Bell has read Bryant's comments about him, and, even if he hadn't, everyone is quick to relay them to him. "See, to Kobe," says Bell, "this is like a movie. It isn't real life. To me, this is real. But one thing I learned is that they're going to spin everything and make Kobe look good." Bell doesn't identify who "they" might be, and his statement is a vast exaggeration anyway. The Kobe haters, and there are legions of them, will continue to hate him, and the Kobe lovers, or loyal Laker fans, will continue to love him. The new development is that Raja Bell—*I don't know this kid. I don't need to know this kid*—is now more than a blip on the NBA radar screen. He has an identity, which he has been looking for throughout his career at the fringes of NBA legitimacy.

At practice, Barbosa works with the first team, but D'Antoni does call on Bell later. "Raja," says the coach during a defensive drill, "get in here and be Kobe." Says D'Antoni: "I couldn't resist that."

• • •

Always interestingly dressed, Amare' Stoudemire—aka "Stat," "IsReal," and "ATM"—provided a season-long diversion that, for the Suns' brass, was often exasperating.

Late-season acquisition Tim Thomas was sometimes a tower of force, and sometimes an invisible man.

Boris Diaw (3), who started out the season as a giant question mark, finished it as the Suns' second most reliable ball handler behind Nash.

It's hard to imagine the Suns without a Colangelo *(Arizona coach Lute Olson is in the middle)* involved, but Bryan, left, went to Toronto, and godfather Jerry, right, feels increasingly distanced from owner Robert Sarver.

Diaw, the Frenchman, was known as a finesse player, but he could battle inside too, as he does here in the Western finals against Dirk Nowitzki and the Dallas Mavericks.

The author *(center)* pretends to understand the x's and o's discussed by *(from left)* Marc Iavaroni, Alvin Gentry, and Dan and Mike D'Antoni.

Dan D'Antoni, brother of the head coach, became the personal mentor of quicksilver guard Leandro Barbosa.

Eddie House, releasing his picture-perfect jumper against the Spurs' Tony Parker, never met a shot he didn't like . . . and kept the Suns loose with his banter.

A bit of strategic advice offered by the author must've tickled the fancy of head coach Mike D'Antoni.

Nash's flying forays to the basket, sometimes when he is seemingly off-balance, often stymied bigger and more athletic opponents such as the Lakers' Lamar Odom and Kobe Bryant (8).

Trying to look casual, the author lays on hands with Steve Nash prior to a preseason intrasquad scrimmage.

"Do I know this guy? I don't know this guy. I might've said one word to this guy. I don't know this kid."

The hand-to-hand combat between Raja Bell and Kobe Bryant defined the Suns' first-round series against the Lakers.

Marion frequently rises above the crowd, but feels undervalued in the Suns' hierarchy.

Suns owner Robert Sarver, holding his familiar foam finger, is an enthusiastic booster who doesn't back off from sideline confrontations. "He sure is getting his $400 million worth," one coach said.

When Shawn Marion smiles, the Suns smile with him.

The pregame wings meeting is a mixture of chalk talk, handled by Weber, and motivational talk, handled by Gentry. It seems like role reversal, for Weber is the relentless positive thinker and Gentry the old NBA hand who has courted carpal tunnel syndrome by drawing every conceivable X and O during his eighteen years in the league. But Weber has spent hours breaking down game film (even though the Lakers are Iavaroni's team), and Gentry knows that a game like this, played in the cauldron of pressure, might come down to intangibles.

The relationship between these two coaches is one of the linchpins of team harmony. While the D'Antonis battle like, well, brothers, neither wanting the other to get the last word, Gentry and Weber find a topic of contention, hit it quickly, then move on to the next thing. They rag each other constantly, enjoy every minute of it, and their interplay frequently defuses tension. Plus, it is highly entertaining. When Robert Sarver sent them off to talk to season ticket-holders before the season began, Iavaroni said, "Well, there goes Sammy and Dean."

After an agonizing 109–102 loss in Detroit on April 2—the Suns had blown a seventeen-point lead—the locker room had a certain unreadable atmosphere. Phoenix wasn't expected to beat the Pistons, then the league's best team, on their home floor, particularly since the Suns were at the end of an exhausting five-games-in-seven-days road trip. Still, it had been theirs to win, and, demonstrating that penchant for blowing big leads, they let it get away.

D'Antoni didn't want to say too much, but neither did he want to let the team forget it. "All right, guys, we probably ran out of a little gas. Look, they're good. I hope we have another shot at them. If we do, we'll make the best of it. You played well. Let's go home."

The assistants didn't want to express too much anger. But neither could they ignore how good it would've felt to have beaten the league's best team on the road. "That five-second call we got at the end of the game?" says Gentry. "That was bullshit. That was just rubbing it in. High school crap. You don't . . . Now, what the hell is this?" He holds his dress shirt in front of him. "Water leaked all over it."

Weber, dressing next to Gentry, starts laughing.

"Oh, I get it," says Gentry. "White Noise here determined which locker was all fucked up and he moved my stuff into it."

"I'm innocent," says Weber.

"What do you think about a guy who comes in early, scopes out the locker room and make sure he gets the good spot and says, 'Oh, I'll leave the leaky locker for the black guy,' " says Gentry. He turns to Eddie House. "You believe that, Eddie?"

"He did you wrong, Alvin," says House. "But, see, that's what Phil does."

Gentry and Weber reached the NBA by vastly different routes. Weber played at North Carolina State—"The kind of engineering school where they teach you how to wipe a cow's ass" as Gentry describes it about twice a week—having the misfortune to be redshirting when Jim Valvano's Wolfpack memorably won the 1983 NCAA title. Weber became an assistant at the University of Florida, but his real skill was developing players. When Danny Ainge was the Suns' head coach in the mid-'90s, he happened to watch Weber working out NBA prospects at UCLA's Pauley Pavilion. "A perfect workout was always in my mind until today," Ainge told him, "but you just gave one." He hired Weber for player development and Weber officially joined the staff as an assistant coach in 1999. He coached then as he coaches now—with a Tony Robbins power-of-positive-thinking energy that seems like nonsense until you see how consistent he is with it.

D'Antoni (and almost everybody else) gives Weber a hard time, endlessly flogging him about his reliance on his positive-thinking gurus and generally setting him up as the whipping boy. It's become a standing Suns' joke for D'Antoni to include Weber's "St. Agnes Drill" on the daily practice schedule, only to announce that time expired before it could be run. "Phil's drill is like that fifth guest on Carson that Johnny could never get to," says Gentry. Still, D'Antoni needs Weber's upbeat disposition and constancy, not to mention his skill at working with players individually. "Mike has to have positive people around him for what he's trying to do," says Laurel D'Antoni.

"Every single one of the four hundred books I've read, whether it be one idea or a couple of concepts, has added something to the way I look at life," says Weber. "Socrates said it best: 'The key to living is always to learn how to live.' That's what I am always trying to do, always trying to expand my knowledge base and figure out how I can be more helpful or what I can do. What I would really like to leave behind is the thought that I helped others."

It's hard to imagine a guy who thinks like that getting by in the cynical world of pro sports. But Weber is able to laugh when everyone slices and dices him about his beliefs, yet keep on believing them. Plus, Weber is single and some of his choices of female companionship impress even the players.

Gentry took a more conventional route to the NBA. After playing point guard at Appalachian State, he coached at the University of Colorado and the University of Kansas, then came into the NBA in 1988 as a San Antonio assistant via Larry Brown, under whom he had worked (and won an NCAA title) at Kansas. He got his first head-coaching opportunity as an interim with the Miami Heat and was then a head coach with both the Clippers and the Pistons. He got fired twice, but almost everybody gets fired in the NBA. (D'Antoni had been fired after one season as the Denver Nuggets head coach in 1999.) Gentry is, like D'Antoni, more of an offensive-oriented coach, but when D'Antoni hired him last season he wanted to tap into what he called "Alvin's big-picture skills." Perhaps because he's been a head coach and felt the sting of being fired, yet is confident in his abilities, Gentry just seems utterly *comfortable* doing what he's doing, as comfortable as any coach I've ever been around.

Thus, he's able to walk the line between telling it like it is and still managing to be a trusted confidante to the players. In the preseason story I wrote for *Sports Illustrated,* I had quoted Gentry as referring to Michael Olowokandi (a center who at the time was with the Minnesota Timberwolves) as "a pussy." It made some news stories and was the only item from the piece that could be construed as even mildly controversial. I included it for a number of reasons, the first being that it is classic Gentry, funny, perceptive, straight-from-the-gut, and second because the perception of Olowokandi as a soft and timid player is widespread. (After the quote appeared, someone from the league office called me and said, jokingly: "Publicly, we deplore the use of such language to describe one of our players; privately, we agree with the characterization.")

I found out later that Gentry did take grief for saying it, both within and without the organization. "Alvin," Bryan Colangelo would say when he left a coaches meeting, "try not to call anybody a pussy today." When the Suns went to Minnesota to face Olowokandi for the first time in December, Gentry stayed in the locker room before the game so he wouldn't have to confront Olowokandi or answer questions about the comment. (Olowokandi didn't play that night due to a minor injury, and, when Gentry came out for the game, a Minnesota fan behind him shouted: "Hey, Gentry, you were right; he *is* a pussy.") Gentry truly felt bad about having made the comment, and, though he never told me directly, he wished that I hadn't printed it. But he's a stand-up guy. He never said he didn't say it and never said he told me it was off-the-record.

Gentry manages to be both a student and a fan of the game. He's on top of every rumor—he tells you stuff a day or two before you read it on HoopsHype—and knows a story about everyone and everything. There is no meeting without a Gentry story. He tells the story of Doug Collins's college coach at Illinois State, Will Robinson, putting Collins in front of a mirror and saying, "Now, that's an ugly motherfucker." Then Robinson gets a basketball, hands it to Collins, and says, "Now you're a handsome motherfucker."

He tells the story of Kevin Loughery (under whom he coached

at Miami), who rose from the bench to protest a call with one referee, only to have the other two back the call. They were all African-American officials and Loughery looks at them and says, "What is this, the Temptations?" Gentry laughs. "It was probably racist," he says, "but damn, it was funny."

Gentry, who is black, is comfortable making jokes across color lines, but it bothers him that reporters invariably come to him looking for the black-man-with-a-hard-life story ("My father kicked our ass if we didn't do well in school and my mother cooked breakfast for my brothers, sisters, and I every day of our life when we were growing up") and angers him when he and other African-Americans are described as "articulate." "It's like a surprise we can talk," he says. "White people are never described as articulate."

He and Dan D'Antoni share a special bond because both are in mixed-race marriages, Gentry's wife, Suzanne, being white, and D'Antoni's wife, Vanessa, being black. "I got a movie for you, Danny," Gentry said one day. "It's called *Something New.* Black female CPA meets a white landscaper. Hell, it's your life story."

Stories get into Gentry's head and never leave. He tells another one from Miami, about a player named Ladell Eckles who stood up during a team meeting and wrote on the board: "No Your roll." Glen Rice said, "Sit down, dumb ass."

He tells the story of B. J. Armstrong coming to Charlotte and being greeted by Anthony Mason, a noted thug on the court. Gentry really rolls on this one.

"So, Anthony Mason tells B. J., 'Yo man, we all get together and pray after the game.'

"B.J. says, 'Well, that's cool, but it's not my style. I got my own beliefs and stuff.'

"But, see, this isn't good enough for Anthony. 'Nah, man, we do it after games. As a team.' And B.J. still says, 'Sorry, man.'

"So Anthony's getting more and more angry, and he says, 'So, you ain't going to pray with us?' And B.J. says, 'Sorry, but . . .'

"So now, Mason cuts him off. 'Well, fuck you, motherfucker, if you ain't going to pray with us.'"

D'Antoni laughs. "Now, there's the Christian spirit at work."

Gentry reaches beyond the NBA, too. One day the conversation turned to Al Gore, and, within two minutes, Gentry had gone to his computer and fetched from his extensive files the video clip of the speech in which Gore suggested that he invented the Internet. He recites endless dialogue from endless movies. Sometimes it seems like he has met everyone. We were talking about the space program one morning, and Gentry conjures up a story about meeting moon-walking astronaut Buzz Aldrin at a party at the Malibu home of Los Angeles Clippers' owner Donald Sterling.

"So it's a full moon, beautiful night," says Gentry, "and I'm trying to think of something to say to this famous guy, and finally I say, 'Buzz, damn, you ever look up and see the moon and think to yourself how people stare at it all the time and write poems about it, and you walked on it? You *walked* on it.'

"And Buzz looks at me and shrugs and says, 'No. Fuck no.'"

Gentry shakes his head. "Damn, you can even be cynical if you walked on the moon," he says. "Isn't that something?"

Cynical is exactly what Gentry and Weber are not. Neither is Iavaroni. He is a little more dour and can wrap himself up in celluloid gloom once in a while, particularly after watching three hours of bad defense. But all three of them come to work every day ready to be convinced that the world is a pretty good place. So does D'Antoni's brother and so does Todd Quinter when he's around.

"Whatever you ask of assistants," says D'Antoni, "the most important thing is that they're upbeat. Otherwise, it can be drudgery. Win or lose, around here, it's never drudgery."

The pregame checklist that Dan D'Antoni has given Barbosa includes this tip.

No silly fouls. Deny when possible. You have to start to become less aggressive. Work Kobie when he fights back.

"Kobe would be very upset, Dan," I tell him, "if he knew you spelled his first name wrong."

"Spelling was never my strong suit," says Dan, "but, frankly, I don't give a damn how Kobe spells his name."

If Barbosa is nervous about doing battle with Bryant, he doesn't show it. "I am thinking about your backyard," Barbosa says to Dan. The older D'Antoni had jokingly told Barbosa that he desperately needs the extra $60,000 that players and coaches earn for reaching the second round so he can make pool and landscaping improvements to his new home in Scottsdale. "That's the way to think, L.B.," says Dan. "Every time Kobe makes a move, just remember he's trying to reduce the size of my pool and take away a shrub."

D'Antoni's pregame speech is brief and to the point. He goes over the matchups, reminds them to corral Bryant in transition, warns against early fouls, and says, "Run 'em out of the gym."

On the way out of the locker room, a few players point to the number 19 jersey that Jay Gaspar has hung in an empty locker. "That's for Raja," says the equipment man.

As D'Antoni walks to his seat on the bench, he gets a hello from *Seinfeld* creator Larry David and comedian Ray Romano. They are seated just to the left of the Suns' bench. Jack Nicholson is in his customary seat to the right.

"Hey, you guys are great," D'Antoni says to them. "I like both of your shows." It reminds me of the time that I heard Kevin McHale, when he was a Boston Celtic, tell Kevin Costner in the locker room, "Hey, man, I saw *Dances with Wolves*. It was really great." Costner looked like he had just won an Oscar. Later, McHale told me, "Nah, I never saw it. It just seemed like the Hollywood thing to say." But this isn't Hollywood nonsense—D'Antoni really is a fan of Romano's *Everybody Loves Raymond* and David's *Curb Your Enthusiasm.*

"We like your team, too," says David. "The way you play."

"Yeah, good luck tonight," says Romano. "But only a little."

The Suns get off to a great start, grabbing a 20–10 lead. Barbosa's speed is giving the Lakers particular problems. On defense, Barbosa sticks gamely with Bryant, leaning in close, trying to move his feet instead of defending with his hands, the pregame tip that Dan D'Antoni emphasized. Early on, Bryant pump-fakes Barbosa and comes up high with his elbows, and Barbosa recoils, his lip split. The Suns coaches leap off the bench in protest, raising their arms and flapping their elbows, like chickens, trying to get the referees to make that call. It is impossible for a third party to determine whether or not Bryant is doing it on purpose since he is such a fluid and skillful player.

And then the Lakers get hot, going on a 27–10 run behind Bryant. But just when it seems that the Suns are back on their heels, they rally to retake the lead. When Barbosa goes out, Marion switches to Bryant and does an outstanding job. In a perfect world, Marion would guard Bryant. He matches up better size-wise, has the athleticism to stay in front of Kobe, and, being a superior leaper, has a chance to bother Bryant's jump shot. But the coaches still like Marion on Odom, a nod to the Iavaroni philosophy of letting Bryant have his but containing everyone else.

With twenty-seven seconds left before halftime, Bryant fouls Barbosa. The Brazilian Blur walks to the line, holding his jaw in severe pain, a chorus of boos raining down on him. But he drains both free throws, his fourteenth and fifteenth points of an exquisitely played first half, as Dan D'Antoni, the proud father, punches his right fist into his palm. When Bryant fails to get a call near halftime, he lifts his jersey up over his head in protest, the same gesture he made in Game 3. Quinter jumps off the bench and screams at the official to call a technical, and Iavaroni calms him down. "Let's not us get one," he says. The Suns take a shaky 60–57 lead into the dressing room.

The coaches meet outside briefly before going into the locker room. This is the time when D'Antoni says little and considers suggestions.

"Kobe's taking a lot of shots," says Iavaroni, glancing at the halftime box.

"Except for that stretch in the first quarter, we never went two possessions without scoring," says Gentry.

"Basically, we're getting what we want offensively," says Weber.

"Defensively, all I'd say is that we have to plug [get a defender stepping into the foul-line area to cover penetration to the basket] and have a softer trap," says Iavaroni. "It's become split city." (He means the Laker dribblers have been able to get between the Suns' double-team defenders.)

As Dr. Tom Carter sews together Barbosa's lip with three stitches, D'Antoni tells the team: "That's a helluva half. We weathered an injury to L.B. and a Kobe shot that banked in and might still be up there. Now, having said that, we can do a better job of rebounding. [The Suns have an egregiously low total of eight rebounds.] Keep tightening up our defense. Keep remembering their tendencies. Coaches?"

"When we can't trap," says Iavaroni, "we need more plug." D'Antoni grabs a marker and sketches a defensive alignment. Any assistant is free to make any comment during halftime, but it is almost always D'Antoni who draws. There isn't sufficient time for everyone to make a move to the greaseboard.

"And when we come down in transition, and they have to talk to each other and communicate, they get all screwed up," says Gentry. "So keep running."

"And keep doing a good job with your emotions," adds Iavaroni. "The pushing, the shoving, don't let that get to you. You haven't yet."

Barbosa is the last one out of the locker room. "It's okay, Leandro," says Carter. "The stitches will hold. Just don't bite down. I know it's difficult not to, but don't bite down."

133

The game continues to be tight. Bryant is fantastic, but the Suns don't get discouraged. Near the end of the third period, Nash drives by Vujacic, gets to the basket, draws a foul, and completes a three-point play to give the Suns an 88–85 lead. Vujacic, absurdly, has decided to pick up Nash near midcourt and crowd him when he has the ball, even though Nash gets by him almost every time.

"I need a blow," Nash tells D'Antoni in the huddle between periods. "I'm going back in the locker room. I'll come out with ten minutes to go." (Nash sometimes does that when there is not enough room to stretch near the bench.)

"I may send someone to get you before that," D'Antoni says, smiling.

Nash returns on schedule. The score stays tight. There is the feeling that this game will decide the series. The Lakers *need* to end it on this night; the Suns *need* to stay alive. With 1:45 left, Bryant has the ball in the deep left corner, near the Phoenix bench. The possession had been horrid and the shot clock is winding down. Marion is in Bryant's face. Kobe releases a line-drive jumper—"the raise-up" as Iavaroni calls it—and it goes in. It is just a ball-breaker of a shot, one that no other player on the planet would've made under pressure, and the Lakers lead 103–102.

Tim Thomas misses a jump shot, the Lakers score on a Bryant drive, and L.A.'s lead is 105–102. The season hangs in the balance. Nash misses a desperate three-point jumper, but Marion swoops in out of nowhere and grabs the offensive rebound. With the Suns needing a three-pointer, he has only one play—back out to a wide-open Tim Thomas, who is standing behind the arc. Marion makes the diagonal pass, Thomas takes his time, the same seemingly unhurried windup, the same deadpan concentration—*go ahead, wave in my face*—the same perfectly executed stroke . . . and the shot goes in. Tie game, 105–105.

The Lakers call time-out, with one more chance. Everyone from Larry David to the dimmest bulb of a Laker Girl knows it's going to Bryant. With Marion right up on him, Bryant gets it about twenty feet from the basket on the right side. Instead of driving toward the hoop and perhaps drawing a foul, Bryant settles for a fallaway that doesn't come close. Was it the best he could get with Marion on him? Or was it Bryant's excessive hubris at work, the I-can-make-anything mentality?

"Dumb-ass shot," concludes Dan D'Antoni.

The Staples Center is almost hushed. Over on the Suns' bench, the players and coaches struggle to keep their emotional equilibrium. Throughout the game, they had expected to win, but, as time ran down, it just didn't appear in the cards. The Stoudemire injury, the Kurt Thomas injury, the Bell suspension—it was all too much to overcome. But now they had life. Tim Thomas, the Rental, who had been sitting at home for most of the season, 2,500 miles from Phoenix, had perhaps saved the season.

And, suddenly, in the overtime period, Phoenix can do no wrong, the offense flowing as well as it had at any point during the season. Diaw jump shot. Diaw short hook. Marion layup. Diaw layup. Thomas jumper. Marion layup. Marion dunk. The Lakers are dying and forced to foul. Nash two free throws. Nash two more free throws. The Suns put up twenty-one points in the five minutes, which would translate to a fifty-point quarter.

With fifty-seven seconds left and the Suns ahead 118–111, I approach the bench.

"Is it okay?" I ask Dan D'Antoni and Todd Quinter.

"*No!*" they say in unison, remembering Game 4.

So I squeeze into a space next to Jerry Colangelo, who is standing behind the bench.

As the clock runs down, Nicholson sidles up to D'Antoni to congratulate him and praise him for the way his team plays. D'Antoni thanks him and says, "I can't believe the shots Kobe has made tonight." Bryant finishes with fifty points, having hit twenty of his thirty-five shots, many of them under severe duress.

"He's great," agrees Jack, "but he tries to do too much."

"Well, we could debate that," says D'Antoni.

The Lakers score thirteen points in the overtime but are overwhelmed by the Suns' onslaught. It was almost as if they were a dummy defensive team, ordered to stand around while the offense runs around and through them.

As the horn consecrates the 126–118 victory, Iavaroni, always thinking, warns the players: "Don't say anything to the fans. We'll be back here to play the Clippers in the second round."

The dressing room has the feel of a team moving on. Everybody warns everybody that there is still work to be done—a Game 7 at home—but, then, everybody starts celebrating again. It is almost impossible not to treat this like a series clincher. The list of heroes is long. Nash scored thirty-two points, made all thirteen of his free throws, and also had thirteen assists, squeezing his aching body into small crevices and getting off all manner of unorthodox shots, with Vujacic usually the victim. Nash says he felt like putting an arm around his opponent and saying, "Look, I don't mean to offer advice, but you can't guard me, so why do you play so close to me?"

Barbosa, stitched, had twenty-two points, and, though on the brink with five fouls, managed not to collect the sixth that would've disqualified him. That from a young player who had averaged only 9.7 minutes in twelve playoff games last season. Thomas had twenty-one points, and, well, all he did was save the season. Marion had twenty points, twelve rebounds (including the one that preceded the Thomas shot), and played brilliantly on defense against both Bryant and Odom; significantly, it was Marion, not Barbosa, who was assigned to check Bryant at the key junctures. Diaw had nineteen points and seven assists, two more than the combined total of the Lakers' point guards, the perpetually disgruntled Parker and the operatic Vujacic. Quiet James Jones had ten points and five key rebounds.

"All right, guys," says D'Antoni, clapping his hands, "the good news is, we won the game; the bad news is, Raja got in a fight in a bar, and he's out for Game 7." For a split second, a few players believe him, but D'Antoni's smile gives it away. Nash and Marion enter, having been detained for TV interviews. Nash signals for attention. "All right, we're only up four-to-two in this series," he says, referring to what he considers the gyp job in Game 4. "We only need one more." Everybody laughs.

"I gotta use that one in the interview, Steve," says Mike. "Okay?"

"Just give me a footnote," says Nash.

And then Tim Thomas comes in to wild applause. He holds up his hands, like a prize fighter who just earned a decision.

"Listen up," says Nash. "We have to get our energy back. Quick. Regroup. We're happy, but that took a lot of energy. Take some deep breaths. Relax. And let's come out and get 'em at home."

"Steve's right," says D'Antoni. "Saturday will be a five o'clock game. Get your rest. Make sure you take care of yourself. Get your emotions under control. And we are going to bust their ass on Saturday, all right?" Marion's "1-2-3 SUNS" is as loud as it has been all year.

Nash holds up his cell phone. "It's Raja, guys," he says. "He wanted to tell us, 'Good game.'" Another cheer goes up. Bell had watched the game from a Beverly Hills restaurant, accompanied by Kevin Tucker and two friends. Several fans had recognized him, but he managed not to get into a brawl.

The TNT postgame show is on and Pat Burke says, "Turn it up." Everyone wants to hear if Charles Barkley is going to find a way to blast the Suns. The volume comes up in time to hear Barkley say, ". . . you have to say this about the Suns. Steve Nash makes everybody better."

The din has quieted down by now and there is Marion sitting alone, a towel over his head, his feet in a bucket of ice, his downcast mood transparent.

"Great game, Shawn," I say.

He doesn't respond. Then, from under the towel, I hear: "We win, it's everybody but me; we lose, it's my fault. I don't understand that."

It doesn't seem to make sense, the cocaptain dispirited after the most important win of the season. But such is the Marion perspective. He played fifty minutes, most on the team. He went to war against both Bryant (outside) and Odom (inside); no other Sun could've done that, perhaps no other player in the *NBA* could've done it. He got the key rebound. He looked like he could touch the sky when he made two alley-oop dunks in overtime. But it is Tim Thomas who makes the big shot and Steve Nash who gets the props from Barkley and makes the locker room speech.

D'Antoni notices Marion's mood, too, and a few minutes later I hear the coach say to Jerry Brown, who covers the Suns for the *East Valley Tribune:* "Make sure you mention Shawn. We couldn't have done it without him."

An hour later, Bell walks onto the team plane, wearing an ear-to-ear smile.

"I am emotionally drained," he says. "Watching was much, much worse than playing. You can't even believe how I'm looking forward to Game 7."

It is 1:30 a.m. when the Suns' bus arrives back at US Airways Center, but a couple dozen fans are waiting with signs and cheers. The last time the Suns won three straight playoff games against the Lakers was 1993, when the first round was best-of-five. That team, led by Barkley, made it to the Finals.

One of the signs was for Tim Thomas: GLAD YOU'RE HERE, it reads.

TWENTY-SECOND TIME-OUT

March 2

The Rental Arrives; Boris and Amare' Go One-on-One

Tim Thomas is lacing up his sneakers in the Suns' locker room, beaming at his new environs, preparing for his first practice after signing a free-agent contract. D'Antoni, sucking on a Tootsie Pop, comes over to say hello.

"I just want to let you know," says the coach, "that I'm never going to get mad at you for shooting. I'm going to get mad at you for *not* shooting."

Could this be heaven? Chased out of Chicago and here's the coach of a championship contender telling him he has carte blanche to fire at will?

Just then Steve Nash walks in. Thomas springs up, all six-feet-ten-inches of him, rushes over to Nash, and lifts him a foot off the floor. "Hey, man, I am so glad to see you," he says.

Nash is surprised but hugs Thomas back. Then he looks over at Leandro Barbosa who is getting dressed.

"Hey, L.B.," says Nash, "when's the last time you fuckin' hugged me?"

Practice is light, as usual, and D'Antoni ends it by running the hilarious Pat Burke Hair Restoration Video produced by the Suns' marketing department. The bald-headed Burke, wearing a wig, plays the starring role and everyone is almost on the floor laughing by the time it's over. "I can't remember anything like this in Chicago or New York," says Thomas.

Everyone, including Thomas, lingers to watch Amare' Stoudemire go through one of his first strenuous workouts. Boris Diaw has been chosen to go one-on-one with him, and, in a way, this will be a test for Diaw, too. He came into camp as a guard or a forward—no one

139

was quite sure which—and also brought along a reputation for being soft. As late as December, there were still concerns about Diaw's competitiveness. But by that time there were no concerns about his talent. D'Antoni had started spotting him in at center (almost by default with Stoudemire out), and his ball-handling dexterity and court sense had become endemic to the Suns' attack. (It used to be that the coach would never have Nash and Marion out at the same time; now it's Nash and Diaw.) But now he's being asked to go to battle with a beast. Stoudemire's instructions from Aaron Nelson are: Go hard.

Everyone's attention is focused on Stoudemire at first. Nelson looks on with a critical eye, but Stoudemire appears fine. As the game goes on, something else happens: The bystanders begin to realize how incredibly gifted Diaw is as a one-on-one player. In games, he has for the most part resisted driving to his left, largely because he can usually get by his bigger and slower opponents by going right, but in this one-on-one duel he crosses over, backs Stoudemire down, and spins to his left for a couple of hoops. He even makes a baby left-handed hook.

After the highly entertaining twenty-minute showdown is over, most of the conversation is about Stoudemire, which is to be expected. Everyone is happy that, physically, he held up and that, while his conditioning must get better before he can return to action, it wasn't bad. Stoudemire himself looks pleased.

But it remains for Eddie House to give voice to what everyone is really thinking: "Boris brought the French pastry on Amare's ass."

Back in the locker room, Thomas smiles with pleasure. "Man," he says, "this is a lot different than teams I've been on. Mike is great, real loose. And that guy [he points to Nash] is somebody everybody wants to play with."

Later, I ask Nash what his history is with Thomas.

"I barely know him," says Nash. "I was surprised when he hugged me, too. It was great."

It could've been the most telling compliment Nash received all season.

CHAPTER ELEVEN

[The Second Season]

Phoenix, May 6 . . . .
SERIES TIED 3–3

> *"So, let me get this straight. The Clippers series is four-out-of-seven, right? Because this one we needed five."*

The last time the Lakers were in town, one of them left behind a page of their first-round scouting report at the Ritz Carlton. A friend of the Suns found it and passed it along. It isn't the first time the Suns had picked up a smidgen of Laker intelligence. Early in the season, they were preparing for a shootaround for that night's game at the Staples Center when audio of a Laker practice session filtered into their dressing room. The L.A. coaches were discussing how they were going to defend a certain Suns' play. So late in the game that night, D'Antoni changed the play and got Eddie House an easy basket.

The scouting report isn't that revealing and is not nearly as entertaining as the Orlando Magic scouting report on the Suns that was inadvertently left in a locker room last season. In describing the Phoenix offense, one of the Magic assistants had written: "Literally nothing is frowned upon."

It was one of D'Antoni's favorite moments of the season, and he referred back to it often, this idea that at least one team in the league saw the Suns' environment as rather the basketball counterpart of *Lord of the Flies,* chaos the rule of the day. "Remember, guys," he would say after the Suns ran an opponent out of the gym, "literally nothing is frowned upon."

Whoever wrote this page of the Laker report describes the Suns in predictable terms, which is to say potent on offense, impotent on defense. "We have a great chance to have success against the Suns if we use our heads as well as our hearts," reads the report. "Know what our objective is versus Phoenix and stay dedicated to exploiting their weaknesses and eliminating ours. Defense wins playoffs."

There are three parts that most amuse the coaches. One is from the offensive game plan: "Everyone must contribute offensively," it reads. "We can't win this series if Kobe shoots over 30 shots a game. Balance our attack." The second comes from the defensive game plan: "We must TAB (Tear Ass Back) on defense." And the final paragraph reminds the team: "The Suns set up this playoff to meet the Lakers. If they want to meet us in the first round, make sure we let them know how much we appreciate the lack of respect they have for us. Take them down!" The coaches get a laugh out of it, but it happens to be true—the Suns *did* angle for the Lakers—and they would've used that exact motivational ploy had the roles been reversed.

"Well, now we know what we gotta do," says D'Antoni. "We have to TAD—Tear Ass Down—before they can TAB."

Out in Los Angeles, that noted basketball scholar, Kwame Brown, has weighed in with his assessment of the Suns' offense. "They're not a fundamental team," Brown said. "They just go out and they just run a bunch of screen-and-rolls and have such good shooters." That is quite a telling comment. In Brown's world, "fundamental" equates not to movement and spontaneity but to isolation plays and set offense. It's not his fault, really. It's the basketball world in which he's grown up. It's all about one-on-one play. It's all about what I can do when I get the ball. The team that is able to get up a shot in seven seconds by passing the ball is by definition not fundamental. This belies the fact that basketball was once about freedom of movement and decisions made on the run, the sporting world's answer to jazz.

At the first official meeting in preseason, D'Antoni told his players: "We are in the entertainment business. Our fans came out last season because we were exciting to watch. The NBA wants an up-tempo game because they can sell it better. And when you start cutting up the pie, it's a lot bigger when the fans respond."

That is an extraordinary statement by a head coach in this day and age, "entertainment" being the last thing many of them would mention. For most coaches there is something frightening about turning a team loose. A coach must control his players lest the game descend into anarchy—that is the prevailing NBA thought. When D'Antoni last season announced his intention to get a shot within seven seconds, the immediate comparison was to the Denver Nuggets under Paul Westhead in the early '90s. Westhead's 1990–91 team led the league with 119.9 points per game. The problem was, the Nuggets surrendered a laughable 130.8 points per game, an NBA record for defensive futility. In one game (against the Phoenix Suns as a matter of fact) they gave up 107 points in *one half.* Westhead was eventually laughed out of the league, fired after a two-season record of 44-120. (He now coaches, ironically enough, the Phoenix Mercury of the WNBA where he is still operating a transition offense, albeit a little more sensibly.)

But D'Antoni saw no viable comparison between those Nuggets and his Suns. He would play defense—in Iavaroni he had one of the best defensive minds in the business—*and* push the ball. He had Nash, and that made all the difference. By definition, some of those quick shots would be three-pointers, the more the better, and some of them would be unwise shots. But D'Antoni lived with them. He couldn't on the one hand preach a seven-second offense, then castigate his players for making a few loopy decisions. There was, however, a governing principle to D'Antoni's offense: There are good shots, and there are *better* shots. It takes only one second to make an extra pass to a player who is more wide-open and better prepared to release his shot in rhythm.

And when the Suns finished with the best record in the league and virtually swept the postseason awards (D'Antoni was coach of the year, Bryan Colangelo executive of the year, and Nash the MVP), there were no more comparisons to Westhead's Denver Nuggets.

"Playing the Suns is like being a passenger in a car going seventy-five miles an hour," New Jersey Nets' coach Lawrence Frank said. "When you're driving, like they are, you feel comfortable. But when you're a passenger, you're uncomfortable. The trick is how to figure out to be a driver. But they don't let you do that."

Even when D'Antoni started working his magic again this season—without his leading scorer—there was resistance to that up-and-down style. Barkley, for example, loves the way Nash plays but, as always, declares the Suns ill equipped to win a championship. On the other hand, D'Antoni was treated like a savior in other quarters. At one point late in the season, a radio interviewer asked me, quite seriously: "You've been close to him all year now—is Mike D'Antoni a genius?"

I don't remember how I answered, but I hesitate to call anyone in the world of sports a genius. A hundred times I saw D'Antoni pick up a clipboard during a time-out, and, in ten seconds, draw up a play that is a slight variation of something the Suns ran three dozen times. Most of the time it resulted in an open shot. D'Antoni considers that spontaneous bit of sketching to be an important aspect of a head coach's job. "You can gain or lose confidence of the guys if you can't come up with a play," he says. "If you start struggling with it, they say, 'Hell, we're doing all this work and the general has left the battlefield.'"

But is that genius? Could a dozen other coaches do it as well? Perhaps. Coaching is at one level the art of repeating almost the same thing over and over so it doesn't *sound* like the same thing.

What I do know is that the closer you get to someone's work process, the more you resist calling it genius. That's because what you see at work are the sweat glands, not the brain cells. Had you been able to observe Hemingway pecking away in front of his old Royal, tossing away page after page until he got it right, you would probably conclude: "Damn, that guy rewrites a lot." D'Antoni and his coaches rewrite a lot.

Now, D'Antoni is particularly gifted in two areas. First, he has undying self-confidence, not so much in himself, but in what he believes about the game. You can tell him that this isn't going to work for these reasons, and that the Suns won't be able to accomplish this for these reasons, and he'll smile at you and say, in so many words, "You're full of shit. It *will* work."

He delights in cutting up every chestnut about the NBA. "I've heard you don't lose the game in the first five minutes," D'Antoni will say, "but if you get down six in the first five minutes, then you lose by five, didn't you lose the game in the first five minutes? I'm from West Virginia but I took a little math." Or: "Most coaches believe defenses are more vulnerable late in the shot clock, that you can get them out of position with a lot of passing. I don't know why defenses wouldn't be more vulnerable *before* they get set. That's why we play fast." Or: "People say that when you play fast you'll be a high-turnover team. I think you'll be a *low*-turnover team because you don't throw as many passes."

Or: "I'll hear people say, 'You blew a big lead because you play fast.' Well, hell, did they say that *before* we got an eighteen-point lead? Playing fast is how we got the lead." Or: "Coaches are always telling players, 'Hey, you can learn from this guy.' They told Leandro Barbosa he could learn by sitting behind Stephon Marbury. When I was playing, they told me I could learn by sitting behind Tiny Archibald. Well, guess what? I didn't learn shit, just like Leandro didn't learn shit. He doesn't play anything like Stephon, and I was about a hundred times slower than Tiny. So how was I going to learn anything?"

145

Secondly, he has the gift of distillation. For every minute of specific instruction D'Antoni gave his team—how to play this defense or what variation to run on that offensive set—he and his assistants had spent at least three hours deciding on those specifics. Maybe more. It is D'Antoni's belief that coaches must put in the time to devise the game plan, that they must know, to the best of their ability, everything an opponent is going to do. But the players don't have to know all of that, and, in fact, *can't* read and react if they have too much swirling around in their heads. Players become paralyzed, he believes, from watching too much video or getting too much pregame intel.

"What makes Mike so good is that he gets to the meat of what he wants very quickly, then trusts his players," says Gentry. "And it took me a bit of time to accept that. NBA Coaching 101 says: You gotta cover every single thing. And I found out from Mike that you don't."

At this point, with Game 7 tip-off a few hours away, the Suns have reclaimed the role of favorite. Two straight wins, confidence building, home crowd, Bell back, the Lakers on their heels, Bryant unsure of whether he should dominate or play the role of distributor. But basketball has always been a game in which one man can take over a game.

"Let me test this out on you," I say to Gentry. "You know you have the better team and now you have the momentum and all that. But the mere fact that they have a player like Kobe is reason enough to be worried. Without Kobe, you're thinking, 'We win easily.'"

"Absolutely true," says Gentry. "One game, one man can always beat you. I don't think he's going to do it. But he *could* do it."

As the endless afternoon wait continues—tip-off is 5:30, Phoenix time—Iavaroni, Weber, and Dan D'Antoni have gone downstairs to the locker room. Iavaroni always prefers to worry down there. Weber balances his nervousness with intense aerobic and weight work-

146

outs. Dan has been getting treatment for an aching Achilles tendon. On the upstairs office TV, the Kentucky Derby is about to come on, and Gentry turns up the sound. As the horses settle into the starting gate, D'Antoni suddenly turns and says, "All right, guys, I'll see you downstairs."

"Damn, Mike, the race is only two minutes long," I say. "Don't you want to see who wins?"

But he's already gone, lost in thought.

As Iavaroni prepares his board, a martial arts movie, holding the rapt attention of Eddie House, Brian Grant, and Kurt Thomas, plays at max volume on the large screen directly beside him. "Here I am doing Game 7 shit," says Iavaroni, "and all I got in my ear is Bruce Lee." One of the phrases Iavaroni writes is: *Pace. Space. Pass.* Dan had blurted out those three words yesterday when his brother asked for a way to summarize the game plan. "I like what the Old Ball Coach came up with," Iavaroni had said. "That's going on the board." Near him, the remainder of the week's schedule has been written, carrying the implication that Game 7 is a done deal.

MON, MAY 8TH SHOOTAROUND 9:45 AM.
MON NIGHT, GAME 1 VS. CLIPPERS

In the coaching office, D'Antoni nervously passes the time chatting with Jerry Colangelo and Mike Krzyzewski. As president of USA Basketball, Colangelo has named Krzyzewski head coach of the 2008 Olympic team, while D'Antoni, Portland Trail Blazers coach Nate McMillan, and Syracuse University coach Jim Boeheim will serve as assistants. They were potentially awkward appointments, a pro guy (Colangelo) putting a college guy (Krzyzewski) in charge of primarily pro players and in the process passing over his own coach (D'Antoni). But if D'Antoni feels slighted, he never says anything about it. With the possible exceptions of Phil Jackson and Larry Brown, Krzyzewski is better known among the general populace than any NBA coach, certainly better known than D'Antoni. Anyway, the pro-coach model had failed in the 2004 Games. Brown failed to connect with his younger charges, and the Americans limped to a bronze-medal finish.

Whether it's the influence of Colangelo or an instinctive basketball kinship with D'Antoni—Coach K's teams are known for pushing the tempo and being fundamentally sound, along with being solid citizens—Krzyzewski seems genuinely smitten with the Suns. If Phoenix wins Game 7, its next opponent will be the Los Angeles Clippers, whose roster includes three of Krzyzewski's ex-players—Elton Brand, Corey Maggette, and Daniel Ewing—but K sounds like he'll be rooting for Phoenix. "I just love watching Mike's guys play," he says. "They do it the right way here. With the right kind of guys."

Krzyzewski leaves before D'Antoni's pregame speech, but he wouldn't have picked up any motivational tips anyway. "All right, guys, real quick," says D'Antoni, his salutation the same as always. He goes over the matchups, reminds them to corral Bryant in transition and trap him in pick-and-rolls and make Odom turn baseline when he gets the ball down low. The Suns have been doing a particularly good job with that. "Offensively, do what we do," he says. "Push the ball, dive hard on pick-and-rolls. Keep spaced. Drive, kick, run the floor. All right, Noel, let's see what you got."

D'Antoni moves to the back of the locker room, folds his arms, and begins smiling. It is Gillespie's responsibility to put together this one-minute pastiche of offensive highlights, and the young video coordinator had another idea for this game. He ran it by D'Antoni, who was enthusiastic about it. Into the regular clips Gillespie has inserted a snippet of a commercial, running endlessly, in which a round-faced guy sings the Waylon Jennings song from the *Dukes of Hazzard:* "Just two good ol' boys/Never meanin' no harm . . ."

As splices go, it can't begin to match some of the stuff Phil Jackson has done over the years. During this series Jackson has been inserting snippets of the movie *Inside Man* into game film. But Gillespie's edit has its desired effect. Around the room, smiles form on the faces of the Suns. Raja Bell, whether he means Kobe no harm or not, begins mouthing the words. As a battle cry, it seems a little tepid, but it works. The series has been turned into a holy war, and the Suns' one certified jihadist has returned to the lineup. The Suns go charging out of the locker room.

The arena is full of signs. RAJA RULES. KOBE WHO? IT'S NOT RAJA'S FAULT THAT KOBE CAN'T LIMBO. THE GOOD, THE BAD AND THE UGLY, accompanied by photos of, respectively, Nash, Bryant, and Phil Jackson. Behind the Suns' bench, Bell is startled when he notices a few fans with cutouts of his face. Robert Sarver has purchased 12,000 extra clackers. It's bedlam.

Marion hits a jump shot, then tips in a miss. James Jones makes a jumper. Everyone is in tune. The Suns go up 16–6, the Lakers call time-out, and Nash waves his arms up and down, exhorting the crowd, which is something he rarely does. The Lakers look overmatched. Bryant, booed every time he handles the ball, is playing well, but his teammates have gone AWOL. Bell is steady and his replacement is spectacular—L.A. has no answer for L.B., who is frustrating them with his speed.

Midway through the second quarter, Barbosa attempts a three-pointer from the corner. Lamar Odom runs at him, and, without making a play at the ball, catches Barbosa in the face, the second straight game in which his face has gotten in the way of a Laker appendage. The Suns coaches leap off the bench, but no flagrant foul is called. Tim Thomas, however, does get whistled for a technical when he confronts Odom. Barbosa gets only his three personal foul shots and makes them all.

With 5:47 left in the half, Bryant, no doubt irritated that he is playing one-against-five, throws an elbow at Bell. The refs catch it and put Bell at the foul line. As a thunderous KO-BE SUCKS! chant fills the arena, Bryant cups his hand to his ear, urging the fans to give it to him louder. In considering the phenomenon that is Kobe Bryant, one must conclude that he is a Shakespearean fusion, part Henry V, part Falstaff, part hero, part knave.

The Suns lead by 60–45 at halftime. Comfortable but hardly decisive, given the capricious nature of the seven-second offense. The lead would be larger were both Nash and Marion not having subpar shooting games, and had the Suns not, typically, come up empty on six straight possessions near the end of the quarter. The coaches gather to fume about replays hastily put together by Gillespie and March.

"Lamar could've put L.B.'s eye out," says Gentry. It is an exaggeration, though a flagrant foul could've been called on the three-point shot.

They watch Bryant elbow Bell (it was called) and nail Diaw in the back (it wasn't).

"You think Kobe Bryant doesn't know exactly what the fuck he's doing on those kind of plays?" says Iavaroni.

"That's okay," says Gentry, "all we gotta do, I'm telling you, is kick their ass."

"Win the fucking game," says Iavaroni.

"They can't fucking guard us," says Gentry.

True to form, D'Antoni, though livid, says nothing to the team about the referees.

"I know some of our adrenaline went out of us," he begins. "You could see ourselves getting a little tired or not putting the hammer down on them, and guys, that's a mistake. That's a big mistake in a Game 7. Every inch of the game, every possession, you have to fight. You can't be, 'I'm up fifteen, I can force a shot now.' 'I'm up fifteen, I can take a defensive possession off.' You can't be that way. You gotta be disciplined enough to go frame by frame by frame. Now, within that, there will be mistakes. But you know what? That's fine. Go to the next frame.

"Just go out and bust their ass. We can win this defensively. Let's take care of business."

It's over by early in the fourth, the unofficial end coming when Bryant, covered tightly on a drive to the basket, deliberately slams his shot high off the backboard in an effort to get the rebound and put that back in. All he gets out of it is an offensive foul. At the other end, Tim Thomas dunks, the scoreboard reads 94–67, and Raja Bell lifts up his jersey and points to his number 19, a takeoff on what Bryant did after his victorious jumper in Game 4.

"Don't do anything now to get a technical or a flagrant," D'Antoni warns Bell during a time-out. With his flagrant foul penalty 1 (the one that drove D'Antoni crazy between Games 3 and 4) and the flagrant penalty 2 (for the assault on Bryant), Bell will be suspended for at least one game if he flagrant-izes again.

"It wasn't even in my mind," Bell says. "That was a one-time thing. I'm okay. That will never happen again."

The Suns win 121–90, becoming only the eighth team in NBA history to win a series after being down 3–1. The coaches exchange on-court congratulations, but the Laker players, with the exception of Jimmy Jackson, the former Sun, who had been waived, walk off without shaking hands, reportedly at the mandate of Bryant. The Detroit Pistons famously did the same thing after the Chicago Bulls swept them in the Eastern Conference finals in 1991. It was poor sportsmanship, but at least the Pistons, who had won the previous two championships, were *somebody*.

"So, let me get this straight," says D'Antoni, when he gets back in the locker room, "the Clippers series is four-out-of-seven, right? Because this one we needed five."

"Ah, hell, let it go," says Gentry. "No, on second thought, don't let it go."

An exuberant Robert Sarver bursts into the room like a stripper out of a cake. "Well," he says, "the price of doing business just went up." He is referring to the exquisite performances of Barbosa (who made seventeen of his twenty-one shots in Games 6 and 7) and Diaw (who had twenty-one points and the same number of assists, nine, as Nash, in Game 7). The Suns hope to sign both of them to contract extensions in the off-season.

"And consider this, guys," says Gentry, "those two guys who kicked the Lakers' ass are twenty-three years old." Nash describes it this way: "L.B. and Boris lost their virginity today."

D'Antoni's postgame speech is full of praise but carries a warning. "All right, guys, real quick. Unbelievable job. Down 1–3. Take tonight and savor it, but know we have the Clippers coming in on Monday. We know we can beat those guys so let's put our minds at the point that Monday is the most important game we'll play. One at a time. Keep it going. We kicked Laker ass. Now we're going to kick Clipper ass, all right?"

Before the Suns can huddle, Nash, in his role as camp counselor, the guy who lets his charges tell dirty stories but ultimately has to turn out the lights, raises his hand. "I know it's Saturday night and we should celebrate," he says. "But we need a lot of rest. Let's think about the next one."

After the huddle, someone cranks up Young Jeezy at full volume. Kevin Tucker turns it down, and says, "The media will be coming in. We don't want to be all ghetto." But Marion protests, and Tuck turns it back up. "Guess we deserve it," says the security man.

The great mystery of the game is why Bryant turned passive in the second half. He took only three shots, made none of them and scored one point. One theory is that, at halftime, Jackson had instructed Bryant to move the ball around since the one-man show hadn't accomplished anything; so Kobe took it to the opposite extreme and gave Jackson the see-what-happens-when-I-turn-it-over-to-these-clowns demonstration. Another theory is that weeks ago, after word had leaked out that Nash, not he, had been voted the league's MVP, Bryant decided to become a ball distributor rather than a ball hog, to out-Nash Nash as it were. A third possibility is that Bell had finally gotten into Bryant's head, that the grinding, never-ending mano a mano battle had finally extinguished Bryant's seemingly indomitable will.

Logic says the latter theory is the least reliable, but it's the one no doubt accepted by Raja's mother. Out in the hallway, decked out in a replica of her son's jersey, Denise Bell sees Bryant passing by en route to the postgame interview session.

"Kobe," she says, reprising Bryant's comments after Game 5, "do you need a hug?" Bryant glanced at her for a second but kept on moving.

In what seemed like a risky move, Jerry Colangelo had earlier that day scheduled a celebratory repast at Pizzeria Bianco, a few blocks from the arena.

"What if you had lost?" I ask Colangelo.

"I never considered that," he says.

I climb into D'Antoni's blue Porsche Carrera for the short ride. (He had bought it a month ago but for a week couldn't bring himself to drive it to work because he feared it looked pretentious.)

"Are you sure this is safe?" I ask his wife, Laurel, who will be following in the family car.

"He drove a Maserati in Italy safely," she says. "It's one of the reasons I fell in love with him."

The evening could hardly be more pleasant. Chris Bianco, whose restaurant has been rated the number one pizza eatery in the country by numerous sources, is a close friend, and he sends out plate after plate of food and bottle after bottle of wine. (Bianco is such a trusted soldier around the franchise that he sits in on Suns' draft meetings. Last season, Gentry, in his first draft session with the team, pointed to Bianco and asked Dave Griffin, "Who's that?" Griffin replied, "Oh, that's the pizza guy.") A large table has been set up outside and it's a beautiful night. McMillan, a veteran of ninety-eight postseason games as a player, and Boeheim, who won an NCAA championship in 2003, enjoy the positive vibe coming off a winning team that is moving on. Krzyzewski can't stop talking about how much fun it is to watch the Suns play.

"You do it like you're supposed to do it," he says to D'Antoni.

"Yeah, well, you've won a few big ones, too," says D'Antoni.

"But never a Game 7," says Krzyzewski.

After just forty-five minutes, though, D'Antoni rises and says his good-byes.

"It's still early," I say.

"Coaches will be in at seven tomorrow morning," he says. "The Clippers are coming to town. Or maybe you forgot."

CHAPTER TWELVE

[The Second Season]

Phoenix, May 7 . . . .
GAME 1 CLIPPERS TOMORROW

"I remember looking out the window of our house, watching Steve shooting free throws in the rain."

Today is Shawn Marion's twenty-eighth birthday. Julie Fie remembered it on her way into work—"Thank God," she says—and, in keeping with long-standing Suns' tradition, bought a cake. When I asked Marion whether he had spent last night thinking about the series that had passed or the series that loomed ahead, he said, "Neither. I thought about my birthday."

Today is also the day that Nash officially received his MVP trophy. In his prepractice briefing D'Antoni forgets to mention it, or never intends to mention it, but Brian Grant says, "Uh, Coach. Steve?" D'Antoni says: "Oh, congratulations to Steve. Man that's great. It really is. But you heard Steve say it [Nash had already completed his press conference]—we're a part of this. He couldn't have done it without you guys. And I know he couldn't have done it without me. [Everybody laughs.] No, I really mean it. Any individual award in a team sport is a team award. All of you guys should really, really be proud. Anything else?"

"Oh, yeah, Shawn Marion. Today's the day? Thirty? Twenty-eight? Congratulations, Shawn." Marion gets an enthusiastic round of applause from his teammates, some of whom are sensitive to his

155

feelings about being overshadowed by Nash. D'Antoni is relieved, in fact, that there was a reason to turn the spotlight on Marion on the day it should be on Nash. At that moment, Paul Coro is putting the finishing touches on a long story about Marion that will run in the next day's *Arizona Republic,* next to columnist Dan Bickley's more abbreviated piece about Nash and the MVP award.

Ninety minutes earlier, I had come upon Nash in an otherwise deserted locker room. He was standing in front of a mirror, brushing his teeth, preparing for his press conference to be carried live on NBA-TV. He wore jeans and a blue blazer, the latter his concession to the importance of the day. When the NBA dress code was announced, D'Antoni joked that "Steve will be in violation even when he's dressed up." On this day Nash looks like a middle school kid trying to spruce up (but not too much) for his first dance.

A pro sports team can have the best marketing and public relations people in the world, but if it doesn't have a player or players fans can respond to, it will have an unfavorable image or no image at all. End of story. And though a team may pick up a few bonus points because its coaches and reserves are nice guys, what really matters is that the best players—or, in most cases, *player*—connect to the masses. Nash is the Suns' connector. Mike D'Antoni is popular, Shawn Marion is popular, and, by and large, Amare' Stoudemire is popular. But the Suns' generally positive image is tied to the fact that people generally like Nash—the unorthodox but unselfish player, the citizen-of-the-world benefactor.

Nash is involved in so many charities it is pointless to list them. Suffice to say that he makes a lot of money but gives a lot of money away, too, in Phoenix, in Dallas, in his native Canada, and in Paraguay, his wife's homeland. He walks the walk. He puts his money where his mouth is. All those clichés. He is not the only Suns' player to visit kids in cancer hospitals, but he is the one who counts, and, moreover, the one who truly communicates with the patients. He doesn't pass through and give a few sad shakes of his head. He sits down with a young patient, asks what his or her treatment cycle is like, and then says, "Man, does that suck." Being able to communicate like that is part gift, but he has worked on it, too.

During the season I received an unsolicited e-mail from Mike Fernandez, who produces a radio show in Dallas with which Nash had a regular gig for five years. Fernandez wrote: "Any time the Mavericks were home he came into the studio (this wasn't part of his deal) to do the show . . . at 8:50 a.m.! He would do this even after a game the night before. How many athletes do you know will pick up a phone before 10 a.m.? He made everyone he came in contact with at the station feel good. Yes, he was getting paid. But he never took any money. The $10,000 a year we paid him went directly to the charity of his choice. When Steve left Dallas, it felt like a family member had passed away."

A couple of reporters who dealt with Nash in Dallas find him patronizing, feel that he talks down to the media. I don't get that. But a certain weariness comes through from time to time. In my view, Nash's ability to seduce the press would be less notable if he were a headline hunter, but, frankly, I don't think he enjoys his media responsibilities that much, certainly not the daily what-happened-today-that-didn't-happen-yesterday? aspect of it. He sees it as part of his job description, and Steve Nash is going to do his job.

"Got a speech prepared?" I ask him as he finishes brushing.

"I guess I'll just say thanks," he says.

"I think the people will be expecting a little more than that," I say.

"Well, I hate to disappoint them but . . ."

Nash proves to be charming, of course. He deflects credit to his coach and his teammates and, when someone asks him, predictably, what he thinks about when he considers the incalculable odds that an undersized kid from Canada would be a two-time MVP he says, "It's so ridiculous that I try to see the humor in it." My guess is, no MVP in any sport has ever given such an answer.

As a senior at St. Michael's University High in Victoria, British Columbia, in 1991, Nash made the outrageous decision that he wanted to play in the NBA. He had by then abandoned his first loves, soccer and hockey—his first spoken word was *goal*—because basketball had seized his soul. "I happened to have a group of friends that loved basketball more than the so-called Canadian sports," says Nash. "At the same time, the NBA was really, really big, with Magic, Michael, and Larry. So, for me, it was combustible. I totally fed into the game and totally fed into the hype machine. I don't know if it would've happened at any other time. Maybe I would've kept on playing soccer and hockey."

But, still, the NBA? There was sincere doubt that he was even the best basketball-playing *Nash*. His brother, Martin, younger by eighteen months, was a better natural athlete and a much more confident one. Both of them agree on that. They played together for one year in high school, Steve the workhorse point guard, Martin the cocky fireman who came off the bench. "I remember looking out the window of our house, watching Steve shooting free throws in the rain," says Martin, a pro soccer player in Canada. "I didn't do that. Look, I have no regrets. I played in three World Cup qualifiers. I had my chances. But with that little extra drive—that *Steve* drive—who knows?" Martin's superior athleticism remains a joke between them. When Nash was named Canada's outstanding athlete of 2005, Martin called him to offer congratulations and added, "But we both know the real truth, don't we?"

No one, least of all Steve, can explain where the *Steve drive* came from. His father, John, played soccer in his native England and also in South Africa (where Steve was born), but he was, and is, "a rather laid-back guy who never pushed me at all." Jean Nash supported her son in sports but was no stage mother. Though his basketball buds loved the game, none of them ever thought about taking it all the way. "How do you explain where drive comes from?" says Martin. "You can't."

It was one thing to have a dream, something else to realize it. Nash knew he would have to get himself to a Division 1-A program in the States but couldn't get anyone interested, including Syracuse and the University of Washington, the two schools he had targeted. Nash would more than hold his own in all-star tournaments against top high school competition, then hear nothing. "I don't want this to sound egotistical," says Nash, "but what I heard later was that scouts and coaches just didn't believe what they were seeing. It was too weird. A recruiter would see this average-sized white kid, and then he'd have to go back to campus and say, 'Hey, I saw this kid from Canada,' and before he finished everyone would say, 'Hey, we got a thousand kids like that.' "

Finally, Dick Davey, an assistant at Santa Clara (now the head coach), believed what he saw. Nash got his scholarship. "It felt good, and I owe so much to Santa Clara," says Nash. "But honestly? I wish it would've been Syracuse or Washington."

Nash worked and worked and worked and got better and better. In the summers he played for Team Canada, first for the junior national team and then for the national team. It was then that Del Harris, who was about to become head coach of the Los Angeles Lakers, became smitten with Nash's see-the-whole-floor game while working as an advisor to the Canadians. "I remember it like it was yesterday," says Harris. "I approached him and said, 'Steve, you may not know it, but you're an NBA player. You have a shot at having a good career. You remind me so much of a guy who nobody said could play named Mike Dunleavy.' " Nash remembers, too. "I had so many people who told me, 'Give me a break,' when I told them I wanted to be an NBA player. So when you hear someone from the NBA say it, it means a lot. When you're on the borderline of making it, when you don't have what everybody thinks you need to make it, it's important to have someone who believes in you. It's sometimes the *most* important thing."

What Harris saw in Nash was the kind of court sense that Dunleavy used to carve out a solid eleven-year career with four teams. (And now Dunleavy will be strategizing to stop Nash in the second round.) That's what the Suns saw when they made Nash the fifteenth pick of the '96 draft, primarily to back up Kevin Johnson. Suns' fans saw something else: A too-small Canadian from an obscure school. They booed the pick when it was announced at America West Arena.

During a rookie season of limited minutes, the Suns got Jason Kidd in a trade, and that seemed to spell doom for the Canadian Kid. "I figured I was the odd man out," says Nash. But by then Danny Ainge had taken over for Cotton Fitzsimmons as coach and, being a free-wheeling guard, Ainge liked small ball and he liked shooters. He frequently played a three-guard offense, Nash generally being the one to come off picks and shoot. "To this day," says Nash, "one of my biggest accomplishments was getting minutes my second year."

Eventually, though, the Suns' brass didn't see a tremendous upside to Nash and traded him to Dallas after the '97–'98 season. And over the next six years Nash grew into the perfect point guard for the Mavs, which is both praise and indictment. He and his team were offensive-minded, always entertaining, and, once Nash and Dirk Nowitzki got their pick-and-roll game down, a pretty good team. But Nash was almost as well known for being somewhat of a novelty act. He took his off-season see-the-world jaunts ("I wasn't staying in five-star hotels, but I didn't do the Europe-on-twenty-dollars-a-day thing either"). He was a fervent follower of English soccer and in particular Tottenham, the Premier League team in London that the Nashes have been following for generations. A reporter saw him reading *The Communist Manifesto* in the locker room and the tone of the subsequent can-you-believe-it? stories were along the lines of: Wow, a cat has been discovered writing lyrical poetry. "I just wanted to learn something about it," says Nash. "I was surprised when it became that big of a deal."

He took a lot of heat back in Texas—"the reddest of the red

states," as he puts it—for sporting a "No War: Shoot for Peace" T-shirt to a press conference at the 2002 All-Star Game in Atlanta. "But I got a lot of positive feedback, too, and I don't regret it at all," he says. "I'd do it again if the occasion arises. The idea was to get people talking, and that's what happened, even if I was the target."

He was the target again—for Phoenix—when Mark Cuban decided that Nash was expendable. And along came Mike D'Antoni.

This season, as Nash again orchestrated the D'Antoni seven-second offense with an aplomb that was exciting and effective—even without Stoudemire—the question that has spawned so much debate around the NBA last year surfaced again: Do Nash's abilities make the D'Antoni philosophy a success? Or is the D'Antoni style responsible for the dramatic elevation in Nash's game?

Hubie Brown, the respected commentator and former coach, belongs to the first camp, insisting that Phoenix's style only works because Nash is engineering it. After all, in the three years before Nash came to Phoenix, the Mavericks also had the league's top offense and Nash was running that show.

Sam Cassell, the Los Angeles Clippers point guard, against whom Nash will sometimes be matched in the Western semis, sees it otherwise: "The style they play, that's number one for Steve Nash being as good as he is," says Cassell. "The up-and-down style, when you're a point guard, and the coach allows you the luxury to control the ball, that, right there, accomplishes it all." Then, too, Nash wasn't even *mentioned* in the MVP voting before he got to Phoenix.

But the only accurate answer has to be a cop-out: Player makes coach and coach makes player. Nash and D'Antoni came together to their mutual benefit, a perfect marriage of form and function. Sometimes it happens that way. And it is spurious to argue, as some have, that Nash should not be an MVP just because the D'Antoni system happens to be a good fit for him. The Showtime Los Angeles Laker system was a good fit for Magic Johnson, the Chicago Bulls' triangle offense was a good fit for Michael Jordan.

Now, a better argument is that an MVP should be a better defensive player than Nash is. He is certainly not a bad defender, and from time to time is capable of being quite good. In regular season games against Washington's Gilbert Arenas, Golden State's Baron Davis, and Philadelphia's Allen Iverson, he did an outstanding job of keeping those players, all quicker than he, in front of him.

But Nash gets himself into defensive trouble when he runs around and overhelps, which is his tendency. (As a rookie assistant, Dan D'Antoni was reluctant at first to offer strategic advice, particularly to the Suns' All-Stars, but early in the season he did caution Nash about "staying put" more; Nash agreed but he is, by inclination, a wanderer.) Also, Nash is susceptible to fatigue, which is manifested most often on defense. And he can get overwhelmed physically by big guards who can back him down and/or shoot over him. Case in point: Detroit's Chauncey Billups.

An MVP should not be selected on the basis of a single criterion and certainly not on the basis of a single game. Nash won his first MVP during the 2004–05 season because of his consistent excellence—I thought it was an easy choice. But this year there was an abundance of legit candidates—the Cavaliers' LeBron James, the Lakers' Kobe Bryant, the Mavericks' Dirk Nowitzki, the Heat's Dwyane Wade, and the Clippers' Elton Brand, along with Nash and Billups. In a nationally televised game on April 2 at the Palace of Auburn Hills, Billups torched Nash with twenty-eight second-half points as the Pistons, then the consensus best team in the league, overcame a seventeen-point halftime deficit for a 109–102 victory. I couldn't get that game out of my head when it came time to vote for the MVP, and on my ballot I put Nash behind Billups and James. But in no way did I feel Nash stole the vote—he was a deserving winner.

Nash's defensive deficiencies are alluded to, but not dwelled on, by the Suns coaches. D'Antoni certainly doesn't like it when someone from the outside brings them up. It's the I-can-talk-about-my-family-but-don't-*you*-talk-about-my-family philosophy. Everyone agrees that Nash would be a better defensive player if (a) he didn't expend so much energy on offense, (b) he didn't have such a help mentality, and (c) the Suns were more of a defensive-oriented team.

One interesting question about Nash's game is the extent to which athleticism plays a part. Half the basketball world thinks he's an incredible athlete, the other half thinks he's the classic slow-footed, overachieving Caucasian. The answer isn't that simple. His athletic skill set is rich and varied. Pick a sport that involves hand-eye coordination, and he would've been good at it. He modestly believes, for example, that had he stuck with soccer he would've been a candidate for Canada's national team. During a typical practice, he might get in as much soccer work as other players get in basketball work. Whenever a ball rolls toward him, he toes it up his ankle, up his shin, up his thigh and, after gently toeing it around for a while, as if in a game of Hacky Sack, into his hands. "It feels as natural as catching it," says Nash. His how-to basketball video shows him dribbling a soccer ball ("dribbling" in the World Cup sense, with his feet) and kicking it into the basket, and it took only four takes for him to complete it. I asked Barbosa, who grew up playing soccer in the ultimate *futbol* country, Brazil, who was the better soccer player. "Oh, Steve, he is much better than me," says Barbosa. "Much better."

Nash is not that quick. On his own team, Marion, Stoudemire, Bell, and House are all quicker, never mind Barbosa, who's twice as quick. But Nash has great feet. He jumps rope like a middleweight boxer. "I'm more elusive than quick, and people confuse the two," says Nash. "I'm really good on the move, which involves coordination, timing and balance. Once I get going, I can do a lot of things. But I'm painfully bad at explosiveness." What Nash has done, then, has mastered ways to always be moving slightly. The Suns' offense is predicated on that principle, too, even in the half-court. Nash gives it up on the run and gets it back (via pass or dribble-handoff) on the run.

But the real keys to Nash's success are inborn (his court sense) or have nothing to do with basketball (determination and will). "Certain players are predisposed to creativity and decision making," Nash says, "and I guess I'm one of them. I do believe that, to an extent, point guards are born, not made. But you have to make yourself better. You have to take those natural gifts and expand them. You hear about so-called 'tweeners, right, guys who aren't quite point guards and aren't quite shooting guards. What do they usually become?" The answer is: Mediocre shooting guards.

The central dichotomy about the NBA's fastest offense, then, is that it is quarterbacked by someone who's not all that fast.

CHAPTER THIRTEEN

[The Second Season]

Phoenix, May 10 . . . .
SUNS LEAD SERIES 1–0

"I wish I had some genius thing to tell you, but the energy's not there. Why it's not there, I don't know."

D'Antoni had a theory that Game 1 would be easier for the Suns than Game 2. Everybody talked about the fatigue factor but he felt that Phoenix would still be running on its adrenaline from Game 7, and he was correct. The Suns' offense was in high gear in a 130–123 victory.

The frightening thing, though, was that the Clippers had played almost as well. Elton Brand (forty points) was unstoppable, and the primary reason the Suns won was a two-minute fourth-quarter spurt when, with Brand on the bench for rest, they extended a two-point lead to nine. Curtailing Brand's output is the top priority for the Suns, as Iavaroni says in the pregame bigs meeting.

"Game 2 is the real challenge, guys," D'Antoni said as he sent the team out.

He was so right. Marion misses four easy shots, then throws the ball away. Bell misses all five of his first-quarter shots. Eddie House, in the game early to possibly give the Suns a lift, falls asleep on defense, and Sam Cassell, creaky but crafty, grabs his own rebound, puts it back in, draws a foul and completes a three-point play. The coaches explode in anger—it's exactly the kind of play that will keep Eddie under House arrest—but it isn't any worse than a dozen others the regulars make in the first half. Walter McCarty, L.A.'s twelfth man, gets in the game in the first half, an embarrassing moment for the home team. The Clippers walk off with a 65–51 lead.

"Turn that shit off!" D'Antoni says, pointing to televised replays of the first half as he storms into the coaches' office. Then, realizing he sounded tyrannical, something he tries to avoid, he says, "Turn it down then."

"Guys, it's twenty-four to two on second-chance points," says Gentry. The coaches are unsure of where to begin, so horrible was the effort, but the Clippers' offensive rebounding is as good a place as any.

"We're not playing smart, either," says Iavaroni. "Technical mistakes. They're not great shooters, and they're going to drive to us, so why are we playing them outside the paint?"

"It's lack of hustle," says D'Antoni.

The only encouraging words come from Gentry. "Guys, we always say, to us, fourteen points is nothing."

D'Antoni relates that to the team, but it is all for naught. The Clippers win the third quarter, too, never failing to go more than two possessions without scoring. Marion almost air balls a left-handed layup from point-blank range. Diaw fumbles passes like a rookie playing in his first big game. It is hard to remember that James Jones, the somewhat invisible fifth starter, is on the court—he misses all four of his shots and has zero assists in nineteen unproductive minutes. Twice within a short span of time, Cuttino Mobley posts up Marion and launches moonballs over him, both of which go in. The average fan says: Nothing can be done about those shots. But the coaches are incensed that Marion is not more aggressive on Mobley, trying to deny him the ball, "golding" in Suns' vernacular. House never gets off the bench. Brand finishes with twenty-seven points and ten rebounds, and Cassell, jabbering away, outplays Nash with twenty-three points. Clippers win 122–97. Series tied.

"I wish I had some genius thing to tell you, but the energy's not there," D'Antoni tells the team. "Why it's not there, I don't know. All right, we're not having a good night on the offense end. That will happen. But that means you have to play harder on the defensive end. Goddamn.

"We make a mistake on the offensive end and go down to the other end and play *less* hard? We do a pretty good job on the initial trap, then we lose interest and don't get back? We're watching and hoping somebody else gets it. I mean it's the same theme all year, guys, the same stuff. Same stuff. Damn, you gotta dig a little deeper."

There is widespread dejection. D'Antoni can't figure out exactly what to say. He tries to explain his team's general torpor, not sure he believes it himself.

"Let's put it all in perspective real quick," D'Antoni tells the team. "One, we did not play well. And, as a coach, I have to feel what's going on in people's minds and my mind. We're two weeks with the Lakers. Elimination game, elimination game, elimination game. We have to say we were a little bit tired. Now, Friday we're going go bust their ass, and do it with all the energy we didn't feel tonight. Okay? It's an easy formula, guys."

Except it isn't an easy formula. The Clippers are bigger, stronger, and deeper than the Suns. And now they have home-court advantage.

May 11

As the coaches watch film, it becomes apparent how little animation came from the Suns' reserves on the bench in Game 2. Their spirit, or lack of it, seemed to reflect what happened on the court. Or did their lack of spirit in fact transmit to the regulars? That is a reach. But a dead bench is a theme that has echoed throughout the season.

The coaches thought it would be taken care of when Jimmy Jackson, aka the Chin—so named because his principal mode of communication was thrusting his chin out defiantly—was waived in early March. (The Lakers picked him up; one of the Suns' greatest fears was that Jackson would play well against them in the first round, but it didn't happen.) But even after Jackson left, on occasion a coach has asked Noel Gillespie to make sure he has isolated snippets of a Suns' bench in full repose for contrast with an opponent's bench that is full of life.

The coaches have yet to bring up the issue in a team meeting, but it smolders from time to time, particularly since the Suns had a gang of gung-ho cheerleaders riding the pine during last season's sixty-two-win ride. They included: Jake Voskuhl, a deeply religious backup center who talked about the team-that-prays-together-stays-together, that sort of thing; nice guy Bo Outlaw, who during an undistinguished career that began in 1993 has filled locker rooms with laughter and who rarely fails to get into conversations with courtside fans on the road; and Paul Shirley, who used his time on the bench wisely, ogling women and writing a blog that drew widespread attention in both Hollywood and the sports world. (Shirley turned up as an extra in *Glory Road,* the basketball flick to which D'Antoni took the team in Charlotte, and also cowrote a pilot, appropriately called "The Twelfth Man," that did not get picked up.) The reserves would joke about not playing much—whenever a loose ball would end up in one of their hands, they would quickly pass it down the bench and each of them would rub their hands over it, like it was a precious nugget of gold—but they were almost always in an upbeat mood.

The de facto captain of this year's bench is, clearly, House, Casa as he's known to his teammates. D'Antoni compared him to Outlaw. Casa is the circle dancer, who, earlier in the season, accidentally clipped backup center Jared Reiner in the knee during one particularly inspired bit of choreography, effectively putting Reiner on the shelf for a couple of weeks, which was, incidentally, where he was at the time and where he belonged permanently. (A player can't be released when he's injured, and Reiner milked his injury for as long as he could before finally being cut.) Toward the end of Jackson's tenure in Phoenix, the only time he had a smile on his face was when Casa went into his pregame dance. House is the one who gives each of the starters a special let's-go-get-'em before the game, a hug for Marion, a series of hand slaps with Nash, a split-second boxer's pose with Bell in which they face each other with fists raised. House picked up that particular move from one of his heroes, actor/comedian Martin Lawrence, who told him it is the universal sign for "respect."

House is also the one able to get to an insult with maximum expedience. He looked at James Jones's size-eighteen sneakers one day and said, "How do you play basketball with them big-ass skis on your feet?" When Diaw entered the locker room wearing a pair of retro short shorts (as Diaw pointed out, they are not retro in Europe), House said, "Damn, Boris, you gotta pull your shoes up." And when Bell showed up in a strangely patterned brown jacket, tight-fitting and zippered just below his waist, House took one look at him and said, "Damn, Rah-Rah, you look like motherfuckin' luggage."

House is still in an upbeat mood much of the time—at this point he says he wants to remain a Sun for next season. But he gets into funks, depending on how well his jump shot is or is not falling and how much D'Antoni is or is not playing him. He feels the pressure even if he doesn't show it. "Make a motherfuckin' shot, E. House," he'll say aloud when he comes to the bench after missing a few in a row. Like a hundred other players just holding on to regular NBA employment, he is sensitive to every slight and eager to correct what he considers to be inaccurate assessments of his play. What House must overcome is his reputation for being a poor ball handler and weak defender, both of them pretty much deserved. As the Suns were heading for the court to play the Philadelphia 76ers and Allen Iverson on January 5 at home, House stuck his head into the coaches' office.

"Hey, Mike," he said to D'Antoni. "Before the game, you say to Steve, 'Stay in front of Iverson.' But you tell me, 'Eddie, don't foul him.'"

"Oh, hell, Eddie, I can't remember what I said," says D'Antoni.

"It didn't mean anything. You'll do a good job on him, just like Steve will."

But for someone hanging on, House is not the most dependable of players. He is frequently the last one on the team bus, and, on a couple of occasions during the season, he strolled in just after the ninety-minutes-before-tip-off rule, blithely giving a friendly hello to the coaches as he passed the office. "Eddie, damn, at least come in the other door [the one the leads to the training room, far from the coaches office] if you're going to be late like everybody else does," Gentry told him. "Thanks for the tip, Alvin," answered Casa.

Once past House, the bench chorus is subdued. Barbosa is reliably upbeat, but, increasingly, he's on the floor. Brian Grant is Mr. Steady, a generally optimistic guy who hopes (against hope) that his aching knees will allow him a few minutes of action. He is widely respected, one of the only guys on the team who can offer words of encouragement to Marion and get him calmed down on the bench. But after twelve years in the league and a couple thousand anti-inflammatories to ease the pain in his knees, Grant isn't the jumping-around type. Nor is Kurt Thomas, who still harbors an outside chance of seeing playoff action after coming back from a broken foot. Nikoloz Tskitishvili, Skita, is a generally placid fellow, too; his biggest contribution of the year was anthropological—before a game against Portland on March 12, the team chose to perform a Russian-style circle dance. James Jones and Tim Thomas, usually one of whom is on the bench, are both low-key. No, when the coaches complain about a quiet bench, they are generally talking about Pat Burke.

In the eyes of the Suns' coaches, Burke has underachieved, not necessarily due to lack of effort but perhaps by trying too hard and pressing in game situations. There was a time during the season when it seemed as if he could be a major asset, particularly in the eyes of Dan D'Antoni. Dan would report to Mike from time to time that Burke had lost a little confidence, and the brothers would have a little sparring match about it.

"Well, hell, maybe I can run the whole offense through Pat," Mike would say. "Maybe that would get his confidence back."

"You wanna be coach of the year again, go ahead and do that," Dan would say.

At a game in Madison Square Garden against the Knicks on January 2, Burke stepped to the line with 1:24 left in overtime and Phoenix trailing 118–116. Over on the bench, Dan said: "This could make Pat or break him as an NBA player. He makes these two, he's a player. Because, I tell you, these are crap-ass shots." And Burke made them both. (Although the Suns lost that game in double overtime 140–133.) Burke may have finally fallen off the radar, in fact, when Dan got down on him midway through the season; before that, Burke had considered himself, along with Barbosa, one of "Dan's boys."

The coaches wanted Burke to evolve into an all-purpose backup big man, but it hasn't happened, and he finished the season with forty-six DNP-CDS—Did Not Play, Coach's Decision. But Burke hadn't caught many breaks during the season, either. A masseuse hit a nerve deep in his shoulder during a routine massage and his right arm ached for weeks. When he did get into a game, he was a whistle waiting to happen, a victim of that referee tendency to call a reserve for an infraction that he wouldn't dream of calling on a star. "You don't get minutes," Iavaroni says, "you don't get whistles."

And Burke does have his supporters around the arena. On most mornings when Dan D'Antoni arrives, he's immediately collared by a woman who works in security.

"Why doesn't your brother use Pat Burke more?" she demands.

Dan always plays along, nodding his head as if he totally understands where she's coming from. "I don't know why Mike does a lot of the things he does, Barbara," Dan will tell her.

Burke is a truly delightful man, a skilled mimic who took a couple of theater courses during his four years at Auburn. Before games he can sometimes be heard goofing on his bench-sitting buddy, Skita, in a thick Eastern European accent. "My Georgian friend here,"

Burke will say, pointing to Tskitishvili, "he give me the F.U. look. So, for that reason, I will assume right now Georgian comfort position." And he would fold his arms and pull his legs into his chest. His performance in the "Pat Burke's Hair Restoration Formula" video was flawless and hilarious. He and his wife, Peyton, have two-year-old sons, Graceson and Sadler. One day before Christmas, Burke came to practice and reported that one of the twins had picked up the Baby Jesus from the nativity set, and, wielding him like a weapon, held him above one of the Wise Men, yelling, "You want a piece of me! You want a piece of me!"

But Burke is not happy with his nonexistent role. After he made a three-pointer during garbage time in the final stages of Game 7 against the Lakers, he looked infuriated when the crowd gave him a resounding ovation. The way Burke saw it, the response was tantamount to fans applauding the handicapped high school kid when he finally scores a basket in his last game. D'Antoni didn't notice Burke's sour reaction when it happened but a few people told him about it the next day. He decided against saying anything to Burke. "Either I won't like what he says and I'll feel bad," says D'Antoni, "or he already feels bad and I'll make him feel worse by bringing it up. I suspect it's the latter anyway."

When anyone gets too down on Burke, though, another coach is liable to speak up in his behalf. As Gentry put it one day: "You don't really want a lot of guys on your team who think they're not supposed to be good enough to be playing."

The lack of bench spirit is just part of a larger problem, though—Laker hangover. The enervating seven-game series is just now starting to take its toll on players and coaches. "I tell you, I've never been so tired," says D'Antoni as he wearily picks up his bags and gets off the team plane when it lands in Los Angeles. "But I better not tell the team that. Look, all we gotta do is win one here."

"And it would be nice," says Iavaroni, "if it was Game 3."

CHAPTER FOURTEEN

[The Second Season]

Los Angeles, May 12 . . . .
SERIES TIED 1–1

"Now, everybody knows our character, right? We win one, we kinda take the next one off. We can't do that this time, guys."

In the category of mismanaged franchises, the Los Angeles Clippers should take a backseat to no one. No sooner would the beleaguered general manager (Laker legend Elgin Baylor) and one in a long succession of head coaches (there have been thirteen in the last twenty years, including Alvin Gentry) put together a unit that appears to be on the way up than owner Donald Sterling would refuse to spend the requisite money to keep the core together. Quick cut to Sterling laughing all the way to the bank: He bought the franchise for $12.5 million in 1981 (when it was the San Diego Clippers), and it's worth an estimated twenty times that now.

Making money has never been a problem for Sterling, ne' Donald Tokowitz, who is one of the largest real-estate tycoons in southern California and a recognized benefactor. He is best known for being, however, a trifle odd, still another example of F. Scott Fitzgerald's unassailable truth that "the very rich are different from you and me." Sterling rarely agrees to interviews, and, Gatsby-like, conveys an air of mystery and sometimes confusion. Before Game 1 in Phoenix Sterling insisted that someone was sitting in his courtside seats at US

173

Airways Center. It turned out to be Penny Sarver, wife of the Suns' owner. Sterling had missed by a section or two.

Though he is elusive to the press, people in Sterling's company find him to be a close talker and serial toucher. At restaurants, he generally insists on ordering for everyone at the table and feels no compunction about reaching over and snatching food from a fellow diner's plate.

In the summer of 2003, the details of a deposition Sterling (who is married) gave in a lawsuit he filed against a woman he admitted having sex with over a three-year period became public. They were, to say the least, fascinating. An excerpt: "When a woman excites you, sometimes that part of your body controls your mind. I knew from the day she came in she was a total freak and a piece of trash. How did I know? The girl immediately told me she lived with Mike Tyson."

It appears that this Clippers team is, at last, the one that Sterling is committed to keep together, witness his signing of Brand to a big deal through 2009. (The owner even seems to know the first and last names of most of his players.) Brand is no Kobe Bryant. But he has better teammates and, clearly, this challenge is a far more formidable one than the Lakers presented. And it took seven games to beat them.

The Clippers' 119–105 victory in Phoenix a month earlier represented one of the Suns' lowest moments of the season. It was somewhat of a showdown game at the time since the Suns were trying to hold on to the second seed in the West and the Clippers still had an outside chance of getting it. D'Antoni was incensed at the effort expended in the first half—"They're shooting fifty-eight fucking percent, and they got three guys who can't shoot"—and downright discouraged after the game. "It's not like you get ten chances in your career to win it all. We got one chance—this one—at making a real good run, and, with the playoffs coming, we go out there and play like we don't give a shit." Ironically, the Lakers came to town two nights later, and the Suns' 107–96 victory did a lot to reright the ship.

The Clippers' coach, Mike Dunleavy, got by as an NBA player

for ten years on smarts, determination, and, like Nash, an ability to hit shots when seemingly blanketed by the defense. (In contrast to D'Antoni, who never takes a practice shot, Dunleavy loves to challenge his players to shooting games and delights in reporting how he beat this player with a twenty-foot left-handed hook shot or that player with a twenty-five-foot over-the-head set shot.) In a pinstriped suit, Dunleavy bears a slight resemblance to Ed Sullivan, the old TV host, and when he appears on a clip, one of the Suns coaches is more than likely to remark, "Really beeg shoe tonight," Sullivan's catch phrase. But they respect what Dunleavy has done with the team.

The atmosphere at Staples Center for a Clippers game is completely different than it is for a Lakers game. There are fewer media types and fewer celebs, though about the same number of wannabe celebs. (Dr. Phil, for example.) There are no mystifying pregame words from Phil Jackson to be deconstructed. There is no sense of championship history, no collective air of hauteur, no Kobe, no magic, no Magic. "It's amazing," says D'Antoni. "Same building. Better team. Deeper into the playoffs. But there just isn't the buzz there is for a Laker game."

The Clippers have a different home locker room from the Lakers, but the visitors' is the same. It's hot and cramped, an afterthought by design. Weber remembers that Scott Skiles, when he was the head man in Phoenix, would take a chair and a desk and set up temporary shop in the shower room so he would have room to prepare before games in locker rooms such as L.A.'s. "Pat [Riley] would do better than that," says Iavaroni. "He would find space somewhere and put up yellow tape all around, like a crime scene, to give himself privacy."

When the bigs congregate, Iavaroni is clearly miffed by the atmosphere. Bell and House talk loudly and obliviously in the background, and Marion, who will be guarding Cassell, does not attend. The wings cram themselves into the small training room, where Weber goes over the game plan as Aaron Nelson and Mike Elliott tape ankles and Marion runs a small muscle stimulator over his body, its hum as pervasive as a vacuum cleaner.

It is reminiscent of the atrocious visitors' locker room at the Palace of Auburn Hills, home of the Detroit Pistons. Before a late-season game, Weber, desperate for a venue for the wings meeting, decided to send his charges back to the toilet area.

"Somebody is back there taking a shit," said Eddie House, "so you may want to rethink that." Weber did.

Digestion issues, to put it delicately, are never far from the surface. Forty minutes before a game, House will more than likely be chomping on a hot dog, and James Jones will be dipping into greasy chicken fingers. Nash, who loads up on fruit, even for his postgame meal, will look at House, smile and shake his head. Boris Diaw, who favors a nice *magret de canard* when he can get his hands on one, doesn't get it at all. To a French player, diet is crucial. On most European teams, players eat their meals together, lots of pasta and fish, all carefully planned by the team trainer. "Hot dogs in the locker room," he says, "is something I would not do."

Athletic trainers such as Aaron Nelson talk about nutrition, but in the American system they figure that players will get it eventually. In general, the older players do eat wiser, but Nelson knows he has to take care of both sides. So in the Suns' training room at home there are presorted containers of multiple vitamins, power bars, and other healthy snacks, as well as a few boxes of Krispy Kreme donuts.

"The human body really needs four hours to adequately digest food," says Nelson. "Players have to get to know their own bodies, they have to know whether it's really hurting them or not, and I guess these guys feel it isn't. Where you notice it is with all the farting and burping." Indeed, the locker room and team bus often smell like a sixth-grade gym class.

James Jones is an intelligent and friendly young man, the product of a stable home life. He is immensely proud of his father, who runs a nonprofit foundation in California. But there are other concerns about Jones (whom everyone calls Junior, a family nickname) besides the pregame noshing. He doesn't work out in the weight room, believing that shooters can get too muscular, but his lack of strength is a problem. The Suns want him to do two things—catch and pass or catch and shoot—but too often he catches and dribbles, a skill at which he is not adept. Every time D'Antoni tells him he's doing well, his play slacks off. And while he is a quiet and generally polite young man, he also has the knack of speaking up when he should remain silent. After a few losses during the season, Junior interrupted D'Antoni's postgame speech to offer up a few words of motivation. "We gotta get after it harder . . ." he began one night, and D'Antoni cut him off. "James," said the coach, "I got this, okay?" The coaches can never be sure what they are going to get out of him from one game to the next, partly because they consider him, as Iavaroni puts it, "a poor preparation guy." Which is borne out when Nash screams, "SEVENTEEN! LET'S GO!" and Junior is still putting on his sneakers.

WELCOME TO CLIPPER NATION reads the message on the scoreboard. If there is less of that ineffable something known as buzz in Staples Center, there is more team noise and more team colors. Laker fans are too hip to wear purple and gold, but thousands of Clipper acolytes have put on their blue and red in recognition of a team that has already gone where no Clipper team has gone before.

The game is played with intensity, though not precision. It is tied at halftime, 48–48. The first three Marion shots of the second half are a hastily released layup that clangs off the glass, an air-balled three-pointer from the corner, and a swat-back by the Clips' giant center Chris Kaman. Not promising. But then the Matrix shows up. He darts around and through the Clippers, and the Suns take a 74–63 lead early in the fourth quarter. Guarding the smaller Cassell, against whom he is doing a terrific job, has had a salubrious effect on Marion. From his position on the bench, Dunleavy is so intent on stopping Marion that he almost jumps in front of him when the Matrix zooms by en route to a layup. Frank Johnson, who coached the Suns before D'Antoni, once leaped out at Manu Ginobili during a game against the San Antonio Spurs and drew a warning phone call from the league office the next day.

But, then, things turn all Rad for the Clippers. With Cassell out of the game, Marion has been switched on to Vladimir Radmanovic, a six-foot-nine-inch outside sniper, and he quickly hits three three-pointers and a layup. D'Antoni is so angry with Marion that he almost runs out and tackles him. Radmanovic's shots were, to be sure, released with uncanny quickness. But Marion was late getting to him and the game plan was clear on this matter: Stay attached to Radmanovic like gum to a bedpost. The Clippers take a 79–76 lead.

During a time-out, Bell lobbies with D'Antoni that he should check Radmanovic, but the coach wants to keep him on Mobley. Bell feels that while Marion's quickness and length are ideal in some situations, he, Bell, is the superior "clamp" defender who just doggedly stays on his man come hell or high pick-and-rolls. Soon after, Bell and Marion get cross-switched in transition, and Bell says to Marion, "I'll stay on Radmanovic." As much as defensive technique, Bell's wanting to play Radmanovic is a product of his mind-set. He is an outstanding one-on-one defender (he got two first-team votes for all-defense, a monumental achievement for a Sun) but not a great help defender because, as Iavaroni sees it, "He's so competitive that all he wants to do is stop his own guy. A guy makes a basket on him, and all Raja wants to do is fuck the guy up."

During a game in Washington in late December, for example, the coaches considered Bell to be the obvious choice to defend Gilbert Arenas, the Wizards' high-scoring guard. But they put Nash on Arenas most of the time because they feared Bell's I'll-get-you-back mentality wasn't right for Arenas. Arenas would blow by him, and Bell would get up on him even closer on the next play. But by the end of the season, Bell had been able to curtail that mentality and play more fundamental lock-down D; ergo, his terrific job on Bryant in the previous series.

Whether or not Raja's playing Radmo is a factor, or whether the law of averages kicks in, the bomber does cool off. But the Clippers still lead 86–85 with 2:35 to play when Bell fouls out. If the Suns' situation is not dire, it is certainly desperate and reminiscent of Game 3 of the Laker series in this very building. But Nash and Thomas make four consecutive free throws, Marion scores on a driving finger roll off a pass from Nash, and the lead is a secure-looking 92–86 with forty-nine seconds left. Bell is so psyched that he charges off the bench to congratulate his mates, and the ice pack which he has on his swollen ankle bursts apart, sending water all over the floor. The Suns players peer up into the stands, pretending that someone threw something to deflect attention away from Bell.

D'Antoni, meanwhile, sidles over to Bennett Salvatore, the referee who worked the ill-fated Game 4 of the Laker series. "If Steve has the ball and it's a close game, we want a time-out," he says. "All of us are going to be screaming it, okay?" D'Antoni is smiling when he says it and Salvatore smiles back. But, really, it wasn't intended to be a joke, and Salvatore doesn't think it's all that funny.

At this point, I approach the bench and look hopefully at Quinter. It would seem like a safe time to try to get close to the bench to gain immediate locker room access. But Quinter, like a stern teacher, shakes his head no. I dutifully squeeze into the space next to Jerry Colangelo. Sure enough, Brand scores on a three-point play, and, after a Thomas miss, Ross makes two free throws to pull the Clippers to within 92–91 with 28.4 seconds left.

The Suns' theory in this situation is obvious: Keep the ball in Nash's hands for as long as possible with the hopes that he will get fouled and drain his all-but-automatic free throws. It didn't work in Game 4 of the Laker series, but it is still the soundest idea. But the Clips, with just enough time to get the ball back and get a good shot should the Suns miss, play tough and smart. The shot clock is almost expired when Nash lets fly with a running jumper, only his ninth shot of the game. It goes in. The bench erupts. And when Radmanovic misses a desperation three-pointer at the other end, the Suns have an important 94–91 win and a 2–1 series lead.

The locker room is ecstatic, reminiscent of the Game 6 overtime win over the Lakers. The subtext of the victory is almost as important as the victory itself. It was the Suns' first playoff triumph when they didn't score 100 points. They had only been outrebounded by one. They had played a gritty and determined game, the kind of game they are supposed to lose. They played with guts. They won ugly. Thomas had held Brand to twenty points and scored nineteen himself. Marion had been the Matrix, putting together a thirty-two-point, nineteen-rebound, four-steal game.

D'Antoni looks like a man who got a reprieve from the governor, but he tries to bring an admonishing tone to his postgame remarks.

"Hey guys, real quick. That's obviously a helluva job. Defensively, rebounding, all those things. Sometimes in the playoffs it doesn't come down to playing great. It comes down to playing hard. And you guys did that and made big shots."

Then his tone changes. He gets a sly smile on his face. "Now, everybody knows our character, right? We win one, we kinda take the next one off. We can't do that this time, guys. We can't come out on Sunday and, say, 'Well, we're going back home, we can take care of business there.' Get your bodies ready, get your minds ready, and come out Sunday and bust these guys up. We win Sunday, we know it's over . . . no, I don't want to say that. But we *need* this one."

For the next fifteen minutes, the sounds of a jungle bird (impossible to replicate on the written page) emanate from the shower room.

"What exactly is that?" I ask Nash.

"It's called immaturity," he says.

Barbosa started it, and I wonder if it's some kind of bird native to Brazil.

"No, it is just a sound I make," he says, "and see? Everybody want to follow me."

CHAPTER FIFTEEN

[The Second Season]

Los Angeles, May 14 . . . .
SUNS LEAD SERIES 2–1

"Tim's been hollered at so much during his career that it just rolls right off his back."

"VIKING LOVE!" Steve Nash shouts at the top of his lungs.

Raja Bell looks at him quizzically. "Viking love?" asks Bell.

Nash smiles and gives an I-don't-know-myself shrug. Every once in a while he just yells something, trying to pump up himself, his team, or both. Earlier in the year on a couple of occasions, Nash had picked up a Styrofoam roller and, in mock football fury, threw it across the room, shouting, "I'm fired up!"

But no one seems overly fired up this evening. It's twenty minutes before tip-off in what could be a series-deciding game, and the atmosphere in the locker room is strangely casual. The coaches are worried that the team believes the Game 3 victory has all but sewn up the series. "As up and down as we've been, it's unbelievable we would think that way," says Gentry. "But I've stopped trying to get into this team's head."

Bell seems particularly loose. As he dresses near Diaw's locker, he reaches up and grabs a loafer.

"You believe this?" Bell says, laughing hysterically. "Gum all over the bottom of it. Now, how can Boris not be feeling that shit?" Bell takes the shoe all over the locker room for examination.

"LET'S GO!" says Nash. Bell is still smiling about the shoe.

"Are they ready?" I ask D'Antoni.

"You tell me," he says.

A few minutes later Iavaroni comes out of the shower and takes a seat in front of Diaw's locker, the only available space in the dismal dressing quarters. He towels off and gets dressed, reaching for his loafers, one of which has gum on the bottom. It did defy logic that the meticulous Diaw, who dresses like a boulevardier, would allow a wad of gum to despoil his shoes.

Part of the up-and-down rhythm of a playoff series, particularly one like this in which the teams are evenly matched, can be explained by intensity and adjustments. One team loses and retreats, frantic, to the drawing board, looking for answers. *Let's tweak this and come out fighting!* But the most recent winner hesitates to make changes, even if they might be necessary. *Let's keep doing what we're doing!* And so the Suns made precious few alterations between Games 3 and 4. Why should they? "Our defensive philosophy is," Iavaroni had summarized before the game, "let's get better with our schemes." As for offense, the plan was fairly simple, too. D'Antoni had written the words "Do less on offense." He felt the Suns were running around frenetically instead of executing simple pick-and-rolls or what he calls "dribble-ats," in which the ball handler dribbles toward his teammate and either uses him as a screener or, more typically, hands off to him to keep the offense moving. In the D'Antoni system, it is imperative that the bigger players are adept at making the dribble-handoff. One of the reasons Diaw emerged as a valuable player was his ability to dribble at Nash, or, conversely, get dribbled at, and give the defense fits with a two-man game.

The Clippers, however, make two changes to their starting lineup, a fairly radical move this deep into the postseason. Dunleavy replaces center Chris Kaman and guard Quinton Ross with Radmanovic and Maggette, both of them forward-guard 'tweeners. Kaman is listed as having a sore shoulder, but it's likely he would've been replaced anyway. The new players are hardly strangers to the Suns—not after Radmanovic schooled Marion in Game 3—but they present troublesome matchups. The Suns are now reacting to the Clippers, not vice versa. Nash has to defend against Radmo, who is six inches taller, and Diaw has to check Maggette, who, while less skilled than the Frenchman, is stronger, faster, and more generally athletic.

There are bad signs early. The crowd is dead—do they see a certain inevitability creeping in after the Game 3 loss?—but only Bell seems energized. Diaw misses a wide-open layup. Nash shoots an air ball from fifteen feet. You could put Nash on the Suns' practice court and tell him to shoot one million shots from that distance and every one would at least draw iron. Indeed, he seems to be tiring as the series goes on; though Nash made the decisive basket in Game 3, he scored only twelve points.

An early lead is erased by a 12–0 Clippers run, and L.A. takes a 61–51 lead at halftime.

The locker room is subdued, as D'Antoni, quietly fuming, waits for Nash. The point guard always heads straight to the urinal, puts his arm across his forehead, leans against the wall, and waits for something to happen. On this night nothing happens for so long that Phil Weber checks on him to make sure he's all right. Finally, Nash emerges and takes a seat. His stomach muscles get constricted, which stops him from urinating easily—that's his theory anyway.

D'Antoni reminds them that "our M.O., not having that killer instinct, has come back to haunt us." But by and large he holds his temper, it being counterproductive to go off with half the game remaining. There is the danger, too, that the players feel all the heat is coming down on them when it should be spread around the coaching staff for errant strategies and schemes. Iavaroni tends always to look for strategic reasons that things didn't go well, that there must have been *something* overlooked in the game plan. D'Antoni, by contrast, generally feels that the Suns prepare extremely well; if the team screws up, it was most likely a screwup in execution. Still, he is sensitive enough not to always bring the hammer down on the players.

But the Suns aren't much better in the second half. Marion collects his third and fourth fouls within ten seconds early in the third quarter. Nash blows a layup. With about one minute left in the third quarter, Barbosa, whose biggest problem is trying to do too much, ignores a wide-open Bell in the corner and takes it hard to the basket, trying to get off a shot among three defenders. It misses. The Clippers lead 90–82 after three.

D'Antoni, or any of the coaches for that matter, can never decide how to approach Barbosa when he does something wrong because he is so sincere and tries so hard. After Iavaroni praised Barbosa for a good defensive play he had made in Game 3, the Brazilian grabbed Iavaroni around the temples with both hands and gently head-butted him. How can you get mad at a guy like that? So, since D'Antoni hesitates to get in Barbosa's face, he gets in the face of his brother, Barbosa's personal coach, a man who looks at each game, as Weber puts it, through "L.B.-colored glasses."

Their sparring is for the most part gentle and good-natured but sometimes has an edge to it, as brotherly battles do. Mike believes that the mistakes Barbosa makes are ones "you simply cannot make," fundamental miscues such as missing the open man. He's right about that. Dan believes that his brother overlooks Nash's mistakes and holds him accountable for almost nothing. He's right about that. Both brothers love the other guy's player, but they do feel territorial; Dan to the underdog Brazilian Blur who's trying to find his place in the league; Mike to the MVP and his personal sounding board, the quarterback he is most dependent upon to shepherd his seven-second revolution.

During a film session yesterday, Barbosa made a bad defensive play, and Mike cleared his throat and smiled at his brother.

"I'll tell you what," says Dan, "I'll get you a tape together of Steve on defense and we'll compare. And . . . look at that. See what my boy L.B. did on that play?"

"Well, hell, it's about time," says Mike.

"Look, if Steve runs off his man one more damn time," says

Dan, "I'm giving him a blindfold and a cigarette and handing you the gun."

As inconsistently as they're playing, the Suns never quite let the game get out of hand, mostly because of Bell who, left alone in L.A.'s eagerness to double Nash, is hot from outside. But when Phoenix draws to within 100–93 midway through the fourth period, Nash throws a horrible pass to the corner that leads to a turnover. Radmanovic promptly hits a three-pointer and Cassell hits a jumper and the Clips go back up by twelve.

During a time-out late in the game, D'Antoni tells Tim Thomas: "I'm going to get you out and put Boris back in." The Suns had made a comeback without Diaw, and it's always a tough decision for a coach as to whether he should put a regular back in during a rally that has taken place without him. But Thomas decides for him: "Leave me in, Mike," Thomas says. "I'm going to hit a big shot." D'Antoni accedes to the request.

Thomas has his chance with forty-five seconds left and the Suns trailing 108–105. Thomas ignores a wide-open Bell in the corner and launches a three that goes in . . . and out. At the other end, Cassell hits a game-clinching three-point jumper, punctuating his joy by running back upcourt and swinging cupped hands around his groin area, the Sammy sign that indicates, "I have big balls." He's done it before, and it's hard to believe that the NBA hasn't fined him for it. Still, it's pretty funny, unless you are the ones getting big-balled. The Clippers win 114–107 to tie the series.

D'Antoni makes the expected point—*we came to L.A. to get at least one and we got one*—but it sounds hollow, as does the "1-2-3 SUNS!" cheer. There are major concerns. The hesitant play of Diaw against the bigger team. The disappearance of James Jones, who has missed eleven of twelve shots in the last three games. With Thomas now starting, Junior represents the only other bench player besides Barbosa who is being counted on. The tepid play of Marion, who had been so strong in Game 3.

But the biggest would seem to be Nash, who had only eight points and seemed almost powerless to break down the Clippers' double-teams. Over the last three games, he has missed all eight of his three-point attempts, and, further, seemed to be laboring when he released them. D'Antoni, predictably, defended his point guard— "We're getting shots, and that's Steve's job, to get us shots"—but Nash's postgame response to a question about his physical well-being hardly engenders confidence in the Suns' camp. "Yeah, more or less, I'm doing fine," says Nash. "I'm just not playing real well at the moment."

The moment is getting more dire.

As the Suns leave the locker room, Donald Sterling, he of the fascinating deposition, and disposition, approaches D'Antoni and pinches his cheek. "We've got to get you out to Hollywood," he says. D'Antoni will be back at least once—and soon—for Game 6.

The flight back to Phoenix is quiet, the Saturday morning coaches' meeting somber. There is concern about balancing minutes among Diaw, Thomas, and Barbosa. Which two to have on the floor at the same time? "We need L.B. on the floor for offense," says Dan D'Antoni, "but we don't match up well defensively when he's in there."

There is concern about Nash, too. "He might be tired," says D'Antoni. "We may have worn him out this year." But why even talk about Nash? What are they going to do about it? D'Antoni's not going to play him fewer minutes—as it is, Marion and Bell are both on the floor more than Nash.

But what bothers the coaches, D'Antoni in particular, is that, while Nash's errors come from fatigue or even over-effort, Marion seems to be coasting from time to time. Nash makes mistakes of commission, but Marion makes mistakes of omission. The films show him failing to hustle back to cover Cassell, a player he could probably beat downcourt running backward, or he doesn't stay attached to his man, as was the case with the near-disastrous Radmanovic sequence in Game 3. But D'Antoni is fair-minded enough to wonder if he isn't too hard on Marion, if he deconstructs Shawn's mistakes under a harsher microscope than he deconstructs the mistakes of others. When, say, Tim Thomas doesn't hustle back, it's because that's who Tim Thomas is, a guy who doesn't hustle all the time. But when Marion doesn't hustle back, it's a violation of who he *should* be—a talent capable of dominating every game he's in.

There is always a conversation about which clips to show to the players and which should remain among the coaches. They are all sensitive about embarrassing a player in front of his peers. The only one D'Antoni doesn't worry about in that respect is Thomas. "Tim's been hollered at so much during his career," says the coach, "that it just rolls right off his back." They decide that they will indict everyone at practice that day, Marion included.

Marion comes into the practice gym looking absolutely miserable. He had gotten clocked in the left eye late in Game 4 and got four stitches—he holds an icebag over the swollen spot. The video session lasts longer than usual, twenty minutes, which by the standards of D'Antoni is the equivalent of showing *The Sorrow and the Pity.* Which is a good way to describe the Suns' play in Game 4.

Practice begins and Marion, with some reluctance, tosses his icebag to the side. He looks as if he's ready to take a standing eight-count. And, quite possibly, his team with him.

Then again, it has looked that way before.

FULL TIME-OUT

March 27

Say Adios to Amare'

At long last, Amare' Stoudemire returned to active duty on March 23 against the Portland Trail Blazers. He scored twenty points and collected nine rebounds in a 125–108 Phoenix victory. To Suns fans and the basketball world in general, it was an indication that Phoenix, now at full strength, could play with anyone. Stoudemire's teammates and coaches, however, saw a limping and limited Stoudemire who did what he did only because of his superior natural athleticism and the Trail Blazers' pathetic disinclination to defend him.

Two nights later, after Stoudemire scored six points and got five rebounds in a 107–96 victory over the Nuggets, the Suns' brass was *really* worried. Stoudemire hadn't been bad enough medically to sit him down, but he looked much worse than he had in his debut. He played only sixteen minutes, and, though D'Antoni presented it as the logical result of working Stoudemire back in slowly, allowing him to get his wind so he can be at full strength for the playoffs, in point of fact he didn't play Stoudemire because it could've cost him the game.

Still, on this night in lovely East Rutherford, New Jersey, hard by the Jersey Turnpike, the Stoudemire experiment will continue. No one on the inside is convinced it will work. Team doctors had long ago declared his surgically repaired left knee to be in game condition, but over the past few weeks, since about the beginning of March, Stoudemire had started to develop fluid backup in his right knee, or, in medical terms, a "Baker's cyst." He attributed it to "overcompensating," a predictable layman's theory, but doctors said the swelling in his right knee had nothing to do with his repaired left.

Since Stoudemire had started traveling with the team, he had been mostly a benign diversion. He wore mismatched outfits that defied classification, one night showing up in a green-checked shirt with matching pocket square, a tie that barely reached his navel, blue jeans, and boots. He looked as if he had dropped in from the set of *Green Acres 2006*. "The fashion police should absolutely arrest him," said Phil Weber.

In various cities, he did interviews in which he talked about how much he wanted to come back. Reporters like him—he is warm and friendly. Stoudemire would do some light workouts before the game, then return to the locker room, partake in some pregame banter, and take his shower with the assistant coaches, after the players had left for the floor. "Man, I look good when I shower up with you guys," he said one night, eyeing up a naked Gentry and Iavaroni, his own body a hard-chiseled six-feet-ten-inches, 245 pounds.

But there was almost always something going on behind the scenes with Stoudemire. He missed eight mandatory rehab sessions with Aaron Nelson, and sometimes he loafed through the workouts when he did come. He missed practices and sometimes never called in. Dave Griffin considered it a positive sign when he text-messaged an excuse. "It's hard to call it progress that he's trying to con me," says Griffin, "but at least he's putting forth effort on something." On March 15 Stoudemire didn't show up for a home game against the Clippers and never offered an excuse until his representative, Rodney Rice, chalked it up to "family issues."

A couple days after that game, the Suns decided that they had had enough. Jerry Colangelo summoned Stoudemire for a meeting attended by D'Antoni, Dave Griffin, Nelson, and Rice. When it was over, Stoudemire seemed refocused on getting back in the lineup, probably because it was made clear to him that fines would be rapidly forthcoming if he did not start taking his rehabilitation more seriously. "It was a good conversation," said Colangelo.

Clearly, the Godfather had spoken. Time to suck it up, Amare'.

The left knee had been ruled normal, and, as for the swelling in the right, well, Marion plays with pain, Nash plays with pain, a lot of guys play with pain, and, clearly, it's time for _you_ to play with pain.

So there was still hope on this Monday evening that Stoudemire could get back and start contributing on this tough road trip— tonight's game against the Nets would be followed by games in Milwaukee, Indiana, Toronto, and Detroit. There is a lot of doubt about whether Stoudemire can do it, but, then, the memories of what he did last year—the 29.9 points-per-game average in the playoffs, the way he almost disdainfully dispatched Dallas's and San Antonio's big men, the rim-ripping dunks—come back. As Stoudemire sat in street clothes watching the Suns play the Timberwolves in Minnesota the day after Christmas, he turned to Gentry on the bench and said, "You know, K.G. can't carry a team like I can." Gentry shook his head at Stoudemire's presumptuousness—declaring himself superior to Kevin Garnett, a former MVP and a perennial All-Star. "But then I started thinking, 'You know, he could be right,' " says Gentry. "That's how good this kid was last year."

At this moment, though, Stoudemire seems remarkably uninterested in the pregame bigs meeting taking place in the visitors' locker room at Continental Airlines Arena.

"Amare', you're starting on [Jason] Collins," says Iavaroni. "What's he known for?" Iavaroni likes to use the Socratic Method from time to time. It is not always successful.

"Rebounds. Blocks shots," says Stoudemire, who plucked a few words from the air. They could've just as easily been "eats buffalo wings, drives car."

"Well, not really a shot blocker," says Iavaroni. "He does rebound."

"He's dirty," offers Kurt Thomas, who is still out with a foot injury.

"All right, dirty," says Iavaroni. "Takes charges. Dirty screener. If you're not talking, one of our guys is going to get their heads knocked off. The main thing is, don't fall into their pace. Come out with the mentality that I'm going to run him until he breaks."

D'Antoni gives the same message before he sends the Suns onto the floor. "We gotta run the hell out of them," he says, "and their bigs don't run real well anyway." Clearly, against a team with a lumbering center, this is a chance for Stoudemire to show that he's back.

But from the beginning Stoudemire's only gear is glacial. The Suns foul continually, stopping the clock and wrecking their plans to run. Jason Kidd, who three years ago was the consensus best point guard in the league, shuts down Nash, the consensus best point guard in the league right now. And so the Suns' seven-second offense sputters, then clogs, when no one comes up to offer pressure release, and it's more like a twenty-three-second offense.

Between the first and second period, Stoudemire pedals a stationary bike next to the bench. When the action resumes, he misses an easy layup, barely getting off the ground. D'Antoni looks at Nelson. Nelson shakes his head. D'Antoni looks down the bench at Marion, who was getting a rest, and says, "Shawn, get Amare'."

"It looks like one of those nights," says Dan D'Antoni from the bench. He is dressed in brown suit and black T-shirt, "the Sopranos look in honor of being in New Jersey," he says.

"If Amare' doesn't start playing better," says Gentry, "it could be one of those *weeks.*"

"We don't beat Eastern teams by walking the basketball," D'Antoni says at halftime, which ends with New Jersey on top, 50–31. "And every time we foul or commit a turnover, the clock stops and they get to walk it up. The other thing is, we're passing up shots and we're not making the ones we have. We're, like, one for eighty thousand. Don't forget who we are and what we do."

But who they are and what they do, to this point in the season, has not included Stoudemire. The Suns are doing the reverse of what they normally do, which is live off of Nash's energy; tonight, they are dying off of Stoudemire's torpor. That includes Nash, who is getting blitzed by Kidd. Perhaps Kidd is tired of hearing about Nash, who, eight years earlier, had been traded away by Phoenix because the Suns felt so secure with Kidd running the show.

Is Stoudemire hurt? Is he out of shape? Is he not trying? Some combination of all of them? Nobody really knows for sure, except, perhaps, Stoudemire. About the most he says is that the right knee, not the surgically repaired left, feels stiff and is giving him "some pain." Well, does it feel stiff because he's not expending enough energy to loosen it? Does he have to play through some pain? Or, as is often the case with athletic injuries, is he truly in pain and no one outside of his body can tell him he's not?

"We're getting to a Catch-22 with Amare'," says Iavaroni, coming out of the locker room. "Does he have to play to get into shape? Or is playing making it worse?"

"Well, we gotta go one way or the other," says Gentry. "Either commit to him for twelve minutes or sit him down."

Midway through the third period, after missing all six of his shots, sitting him down becomes the only viable option. Stoudemire comes to the bench and pounds the back of his chair in anger, but he doesn't disagree that he had to come out of the game. On the court, Kidd banks in a three-pointer and the Nets lead 74–38. You had to look twice at the scoreboard to believe it's true. Even D'Antoni can't pretend there is a chance of coming back. At the beginning of the fourth period, Nash says to D'Antoni, with a sad smile, "I'm getting my ass kicked."

As the clock runs down on the worst loss of the season, the Suns continue to display their pleasant personality on the bench. Stoudemire tosses wristbands to some kids sitting behind him, and Marion responds to an autograph request during a time-out by leaning over and signing a ticket stub. The final is 110–72, the Suns' total nearly forty points below their league-leading average. Nash finishes with zero points for the first time in his career.

"I got a headache," says D'Antoni, putting his head between his hands.

His postgame remarks are brief and unmemorable. James Jones stands and says, "We didn't show toughness. San Antonio would've found a way to win." It rings hollow because Junior is hardly considered a bastion of toughness himself. But anything would've sounded hollow after that effort.

Ninety minutes later, on the team plane bound for Milwaukee, D'Antoni paces relentlessly, trying to decide what to do about his injured stud. He talks briefly with Stoudemire, trying to get a gauge on how he's feeling, then talks to Nelson and Nash. D'Antoni vacillates between being pissed off at Stoudemire or feeling genuine sympathy for him. He is injured . . . but he didn't work hard enough to get better. He had surgery . . . but that knee has been declared fine. "He has to get his pop back" is the expression everyone uses. But what does that mean? Is getting his "pop" back a matter of time? Or hard work? Or enduring pain?

D'Antoni has the team to think about, first and foremost. If Phoenix puts Stoudemire on the shelf, he will once again, in all probability, lose touch, kind of float through the locker room, which is what he has been doing for the better part of five months. That often happens with injured players even if they are the best of teammates, which Stoudemire is not. Further, if the Suns put him on the shelf, are they in effect declaring that they can't win the championship?

On the other hand, if Stoudemire plays, D'Antoni can see the team getting dragged down by him; if tonight is any indication, the Suns would be playing four against five until Stoudemire finds himself or his lost "pop." "Everybody was just watching everybody," Marion had said about Stoudemire's return. "The ball just stopped." In the Suns' system, being a "ball stopper" is the ultimate pejorative.

Finally, sometime after midnight, thirty minutes before the plane lands in Milwaukee, D'Antoni makes his decision: He will shut Stoudemire down. Everyone within the organization knows that it is almost certainly for the entire season, but, publicly, a Stoudemire return will be listed as a possibility.

What finally made the decision for D'Antoni, one that was unanimously supported by the players and the coaches, was factoring in the kind of player Stoudemire is. He is not someone who will help a team when he's not at his physical best. He doesn't give up his body setting picks, he doesn't pass well, and he is a weak defender. If he can't get up and down the court, he is semi-worthless in a half-court offense other than to put back offensive rebounds.

I ask D'Antoni if he is giving up on a championship this season in favor of making an all-out run next season with a healthy Stoudemire?

"Hell, no," he says. "We can still win it. And, with Amare' in there, was that a championship team you saw out there tonight?"

March 28

At the morning breakfast meeting, which will substitute for a shoot-around for tonight's game against the Bucks, D'Antoni tells the team what most of them suspected.

"We're shutting Amare' down, guys. So that means we have to turn it up one more notch. Playoffs are right around the bend. We got thirteen games, starting with tonight. We have to understand what we need to be better at. It's gotta be a concentrated effort of taking in what we say. Not everything we say is going to ring true all the time, but let's just try to get better as a team." That is D'Antoni's way of saying: It's time to rally 'round.

As Stoudemire leaves the meeting, Weber approaches him. As the rah-rah, let's-get-it-done guy, Weber will have a part in Stoudemire's on-court rehab, which, as the Suns see it, must continue apace. Plus, Stoudemire trusts him—Weber had made several trips to Stoudemire's off-season home in Florida last summer to supervise individual workouts.

"You wanna go over early tonight?" Weber asks Stoudemire. "Maybe get in a high-intensity workout?"

"P-Web," says Stoudemire, "are you crazy?"

Later, even the optimistic Weber concedes, "This isn't going to be easy."

CHAPTER SIXTEEN

[The Second Season]

Phoenix, May 16 . . . .
SERIES TIED 2–2

"If it goes to me, I'm going to make it."

Raja Bell arrives at morning shootaround to find a bunch of blue congratulatory balloons hanging in his cubicle. "B.G., I bet," says Bell. Brian Grant has indeed gotten the news that Cindi Bell is pregnant. The couple had been trying for quite a while and Raja is overjoyed. Eddie House had asked Bell a few days ago if he was planning on getting Cindi something for Mother's Day and Bell said, "A baby, I think." Now it's official. They already know it's a boy.

Tim Thomas offers his congratulations. "Same thing happened to me," says Thomas, who already has two young daughters. "My wife complains that every year I get in the playoffs, she gets pregnant."

Marion comes in, still looking like he had been in a bar brawl. Dave Griffin studies him during the short pro forma shootaround. "Shawn's going to be a monster tonight," says Griffin. "He has the I'm-a-bad-motherfucker factor going for him."

At this point in the series, the Suns have tried so many defensive tactics that they're not sure what is working and what isn't. If Elton Brand was not a good baseline driver before the series, he has sure figured out how to become one during the series, and he is now hurting the Suns no matter how they play him. The book on Cassell is to force him right, but he always manages to get left. Some players are like that.

Lenny Wilkens, a southpaw, could only go left, and he went in that direction into the Hall of Fame. As a rookie playing for the Kansas City–Omaha Kings, D'Antoni remembers an assistant coach delivering a pregame scouting report about Jerry West: "Okay, guys, West can only go right. But don't concern yourself with that because you can't stop him anyway. He's been going right for twenty years." Plus, the Clippers can throw so many different lineups out there that advance defensive planning has been rendered almost meaningless.

Aaron Nelson, the trainer—"call us *athletic* trainers," he's always careful to admonish, half-joking, half-serious—stops into the coaches office. The trainer is, in many ways, the second most important person behind the head coach in the daily affairs of the team. On many teams, including this one, he is responsible for making the travel arrangements, scheduling practices and shootarounds on the road, all the mundane details of moving around men and equipment. (Nelson is particularly fond of telling me, right before a trip, "There's no room on the main plane for you. Would you mind riding in baggage?") You know the trainer is important because, on the team bus, he invariably occupies the other front seat directly across from the head coach. No matter how crowded the bus gets, the head coach sits alone and the trainer sits alone, a canon that is inviolate unless their significant others are along—in that case they have to squeeze over and suck it up.

Nelson and the three men under him—strength and conditioning coach Erik Phillips, assistant trainer Mike Elliott, and equipment man Jay Gaspar—are often put in awkward positions. They are close to the players (you tend to build a relationship with a man when you slap and knead his body every day; plus, in the case of Elliott, he is a fixture in every poker game) yet they are considered management, at least Nelson is. Nobody knows more than Nelson does, for example, about how hard Stoudemire is really working to rehab his knee. But he has to figure out when to keep something between him and a player secret, and when D'Antoni or Griffin or some other member of the hierarchy should be informed. Nelson does it well and seems to have the trust of executives, coaches, and players. For the most part, D'Antoni leaves him alone to do his job, checking in only when he has to, usually with the comment, "You get anybody well this week, or are they all worse?"

Nelson is sometimes referred to as "N.G." for No Game, a nickname bestowed on him by Charles Barkley when, during a bachelor trip to Las Vegas years ago, Nelson came up empty. Every once in a while, usually when the team bus pulls into the parking lot after a road trip, a spirited chant of "N.G.,T.Y.T! N.G.,T.Y.T! will break out. "No Game, Touch Your Toes," the latter phrase a boys-will-be-boys reference to bending over.

"You give everybody a shot of adrenaline?" Jerry Colangelo asks Nelson.

"I just hit 'em in the heart," says Nelson.

"Anything going on?" D'Antoni asks breezily. He hopes the answer is uncomplicated.

"I think Steve will be ready," says Nelson. That is mostly why he stopped in.

"That's good to hear," says D'Antoni.

"He slept two-and-a-half hours this afternoon," says Nelson. "He needed it. He says it's nothing physical. He just hasn't been sleeping, and he says he's tired."

"I know what I feel like," says D'Antoni, "so I can imagine what he feels like."

The second-round playoff game between the Miami Heat and the New Jersey Nets streams along, soundless. The Nets' Vince Carter is heaving up more than his share of shots, most of which are errant. Dan D'Antoni watches for a while and delivers his verdict: "When it's nut-cutting time, Vince Carter supplies the nuts."

The Suns are painfully thin on celebrity fans. Sen. John McCain is a semi-regular, who, to his credit, rarely trolls for votes and seems to be there to enjoy the game. Once in a while Phil Mickelson occupies a courtside seat—his wife, Amy, was a Suns' dancer years ago—and on other occasions, Jimmy Walker, a well-heeled Arizona insurance man who handles investments and long-term planning for a slew of big names, will have someone from the glitterati sitting next to him. Often, though, they are there to root for the other team, as is the case on this evening when Billy Crystal sits down next to Walker.

But the big celebrity news of the evening is the arrival of Jack Nicholson, who, wearing his trademark dark shades, takes a seat behind the Clippers' bench. The Lakers' Alpha Dog Fan doesn't attend Clipper games in L.A., but, hey, a road trip is a road trip. He is accompanied by director James Brooks, who invited Nicholson to come along. Almost no one recognizes Brooks, but he was the one who helped Jack win Best Actor Oscars for *Terms of Endearment* and *As Good as It Gets,* and, Brooks's true hall-of-fame achievement, exec-producing *The Simpsons.*

Marion, true to Griffin's prediction, comes out smoking, hitting five of his first seven shots and finishing the first quarter with twelve points. Alas, his teammates don't add much, especially Nash, who, despite his nap, looks tired. The Clippers, per usual, dominate the boards, get several put-back baskets and take a 31–26 lead after one quarter. Nash finally comes alive in the second, hoisting up seven shots (he makes four) and pushes Phoenix to a 58–52 lead at halftime. Using a combination of Marion and Bell, the Suns appear to have gotten Cassell under control—he has made only one of six shots, and Dunleavy even turns the offense over to the youngster, Shaun Livingston, for long stretches.

There is a great sense of unease in the locker room, however. Six points, given the Suns' penchant for blowing leads, is no cushion at all. The coaches hope that Nash is back on track, and they're pleased with Marion, who has sixteen points and eight rebounds. They're shooting 50 percent and everybody except for James Jones seems to be in a groove. But, at root, it's not about the offense—the Suns are almost always able to score at home. The worrisome things are the things they can't do much about no matter how well they're play-ing—the size differential, the rebounds, the physical play inside. D'Antoni's remarks are brief, the real strategy handled by a series of individual meetings. Gentry talks to Nash, Iavaroni to Tim Thomas, and Dan to Barbosa (of course).

It appears to be working. In the first six minutes of the third quarter, the Suns outscore the Clippers 20–7. Some fans give it to Nicholson, and he just lifts up his shades and smiles; he rather likes the Suns' full-throttle offense, as he told D'Antoni during the Laker series. But, suddenly, as quickly as it came, it starts to go. Nash misses a layup; Tim Thomas loses the ball. Nash misses a three-point jumper, and Thomas, trying to get it back right away, misses almost the same shot. Then he misses a dunk. The Clippers keep whittling away, whit-tling away, and, by the end of the third, they're within six at 84–78. Marion was, again, great; everyone else was mediocre.

The Suns cling to their single-digit advantage through most of the fourth and lead 96–91 when, with 3:07 left, Nash drives to the basket, converts a layup, and draws a foul on Cassell. But Joe DeRosa, a veteran ref, waves off the play and says the foul was committed be-fore the shot, a call that wouldn't have been made in a high school jayvee game. Nash appeals to DeRosa and finally throws up his hands in exasperation.

Nash is not a major-league whiner or complainer, but he is con-vinced that he gets fewer calls than any of the league's stars and cer-tainly doesn't get them commensurate with being a two-time MVP. "The officials referee people, not plays," he says, "except for me." Nash is not alone in that respect, of course—to date, there is no record of an NBA player saying, "You know, they officiate me pretty fair." But the numbers do tell a tale. Nash finished the season as the league's thirty-third leading scorer with 18.8 points per game, averaging only 3.5 free throws per game. No one above him shot fewer free throws on a per-game basis, though Marion (who finished seventeenth at

21.8) was close, with 3.7 attempts per game. Philadelphia's Allen Iverson averaged 11.5 attempts. The league's other top five scorers—Kobe Bryant, Cleveland's LeBron James, Washington's Gilbert Arenas, Miami's Dwyane Wade, and Boston's Paul Pierce—were also in double figures in attempts.

Now, one could subject this to endless statistical deconstruction. The Suns as a team don't get to the line often because (a) they shoot quickly and (b) they shoot often from the perimeter rather than taking it to the basket, where contact most often takes place. Last season Phoenix was a middle-of-the-pack eighteenth in free throw attempts as a team, but that is misleading because Stoudemire (with 795 attempts) led the league. But, in Nash's case, logic says he should get more free throws because he has the ball so often and he *is* a driver who gets into the lane.

At any rate, instead of a probable three-point play and an eight-point lead, the Suns get the ball on the side, and, Nash, visibly shaken by the call, misses a wide-open jumper. And over the next couple of minutes, Nash can't seem to get his bearings, slipping, losing the ball, failing to find open teammates. This is a dream come true for an obnoxious fan who sits behind the press table and gives endless grief to Paul Coro of the *Arizona Republic*. The fan is convinced that Nash is overrated and that Coro, along with most every other reporter in America, protects Nash. He used to sit right behind D'Antoni, but the coach arranged to have his seat moved because he couldn't stand listening to him.

The game stays tight, and, finally, with the Suns leading 101–98, Cassell darts behind a hard pick set by Brand on Barbosa and drains a three-pointer from the corner to tie the score. Nash makes a brilliant long-distance pass to Marion but, as he is fouled by Brand, he can't convert the layup. With thirty-nine seconds left, Marion has a chance to win it from the line, from where he had converted 91 percent of his free throws in the first two rounds and 81 percent during the season. But after being the Suns' rock through three periods, Marion has faltered badly in the fourth, missing seven of his eight shots. Visibly nervous and shaken by the collision, he misses both of these. The Suns still have a chance to get a final shot, but Tim Thomas, instead of calling time-out, unleashes a wild pass downcourt, mistakenly thinking there was no time to set up a play. The game goes into overtime.

Once D'Antoni elects not to club Thomas over the head with his clipboard, his biggest decision is whether to start Barbosa or Diaw in the overtime period. Diaw was so routinely brilliant at times during the Laker series that it's easy to forget he is a young player in a new position, literally and figuratively. For the last two seasons he was a backup point guard in Atlanta, defending against players like five-foot-five-inch Earl Boykins of Denver, and his year ended with the Hawks' eighty-second game. Now he's an inside player going against an All-Star power forward, Elton Brand, and a scary-looking seven-foot center, Chris Kaman, in the second round of a pressure-packed postseason. (It will be a small miracle if Kaman, a stringy-haired, pasty-complexioned seven-footer, is not one day cast in some B slasher movie in which he plays the crazed school janitor who hangs out near the girls' locker room.) Diaw isn't soft by any means. He and his close friend, Tony Parker, the Spurs' point guard, developed their basketball chops by playing against men as fifteen-year-olds in France. But Game 5, at last, seems to have overwhelmed Diaw. It happens.

"Gimme two reasons you can help us in overtime," Iavaroni says to Diaw. Diaw doesn't respond.

"Okay, one reason," says Iavaroni. Still, Diaw is speechless.

"Okay, you gave me my answer," says Iavaroni.

"What do you mean?" asks Diaw.

"Your body language," says Iavaroni. "It tells me you don't want to play."

Iavaroni said it all gently. He didn't mean to put the player on the spot. But he had to find out if Diaw was ready to play. He wasn't. So D'Antoni goes with Barbosa.

Nash's problems continue in overtime, and, when Nash has problems, so generally do the Suns. With 3.6 seconds left, Cassell makes two free throws to give the Clippers a 111–108 lead. The Suns call time-out. The arena is all but silent. Phoenix had gotten by L.A.'s better-known team, but a defeat in Game 5 at home would all but guarantee extinction. Was the Suns' supply of miracles finally gone?

As D'Antoni huddles with his assistants out on the floor, Bell says, "If it goes to me, I'm going to make it." At about that time, D'Antoni decides that Bell should be the first option. As late as February, the Suns were mildly concerned about the number of times that Bell tended to shoot from just inside the three-point line—Weber called him "Mr. Long-Two"—but were loath to bring it to his attention. There is no play more distasteful than a shooter looking down to check his feet, then stepping *back* over the three-point line to release.

But at this point in the season Bell's three-point stroke is as reliable as anyone's, including that of a tired Nash. Anyway, the point guard will no doubt be smothered with defensive attention. D'Antoni comes into the huddle and sketches the play. Bell is to start on the baseline, come forward as if he were setting a pick for Marion, then veer toward the corner, catch the pass, and get his shot. Diaw, who had gone back in minutes earlier when Thomas fouled out, is given the assignment of throwing the ball in. Next to Nash, he is the team's best decision-maker. House, Bell's opponent in postpractice shooting games, peppers him with optimism as the huddle breaks. "You're going to make it," House says. "I know you're going to make it."

Dunleavy inserts little-used Daniel Ewing into the game to defend against Bell. No one is sure why. As the play begins, Ewing bodies Bell the wrong way, and Bell is able to head toward the corner. Diaw finds him with ease. Teams in that situation always have the option to give a quick foul to obviate the three-point shot. Some do; some don't. Dunleavy chooses not to foul. Bell gets a good look, shoots, and the ball goes in. Tie game. The fan who had brought the sign that read BELL TOLLS FOR THREE had been prescient. It is Bell's twenty-second three-pointer of the series, already surpassing by one Derek Fisher's record for a six-game series.

The shot seems to break the will of the Clippers. Phoenix dominates the second overtime, the decisive points coming from Marion (on a seven-foot bank shot off a pass from Nash) and two Barbosa free throws. The final is 125–118.

Fans flood the court like it's a championship victory. Robert Sarver runs from his seat to hug Nash. "Do you realize," says Phil Weber as he watches the scene, "that the two guys who saved our season weren't even with us last year?" He means Bell and Thomas, whose Game 6 jumper kept the Laker series alive. The Clippers file off the court, almost in a daze. "The most disappointing loss I've ever been involved in," says Brand, who finished with thirty-three points. Cassell says that, "We should've put him [Bell] in the fifth row with the popcorn man."

There is utter jubilation in the Suns' locker room. The game had started at 7:30, Phoenix time, and now it's 11:30. "A game like this just might kill Dad," D'Antoni says to his brother. "Ninety-four-year-old men are not supposed to be up this late." Lewis D'Antoni watches every game back in Mullens, West Virginia, which is on Eastern standard.

"I'm glad we won," says Gentry, "but I'm about to pay for my babysitter's college education."

Bell, for his part, is headed home to call his parents (Roger Bell always gives him the critique), then watch the TiVo replay of *CSI: Miami* with his happily pregnant wife. Marion, who finished with thirty-six points and twenty rebounds, a monster game even if he did miss those two free throws, heads out the door wearing a wide smile. "Shawn Marion gets very tired," Marion once said, "but the Matrix never gets tired." The Matrix showed up tonight. Marion still has the stitched-eye look going and he is limping slightly. He got taken down hard by Brand on the breakaway that preceded his two missed free throws and, later, in overtime, he had tweaked his ankle again. "I'm okay," he says.

A very long and eventful evening had belonged to the father-to-be and, as Griffin promised, the one with the bad-motherfucker look.

As for Barbosa, who had a terrific game with fifteen points and five assists, he walks out happily with his mother, who just arrived from Brazil. The last few weeks have been agony for Barbosa. Widespread violence had rocked his native city of São Paulo, the attacks on police stations and public buildings reportedly carried out by a criminal gang known in Brazil as the First Capital Command. Barbosa had hired security guards for his many relatives (brothers, sisters, nieces, nephews) but he was most worried about his mother, who is a kidnap target because of his fame. Ivete Barbosa has also been battling non-Hodgkin's lymphoma, after having lost her husband and Leandro's father, Vincente, to stomach cancer several years ago.

Barbosa is ecstatic that Ivete is safe and he also believes that she has turned the corner on her cancer treatment. He is closer to her than any person in the world. It was to his mother that Barbosa said, many years ago in Brazil, "Mama, I have a dream. I am going to play basketball in the NBA." That night, Ivete sleeps in her son's arms.

CHAPTER SEVENTEEN

[The Second Season]

Phoenix, May 17 . . . .
SUNS LEAD SERIES 3–2

"We've been through a lot of saying, 'Shawn this' and 'Shawn that.' But you know what? We've come a helluva long way. There's a helluva lot of ways you could screw it up by looking elsewhere for another player."

For months now, D'Antoni has been bothered by a giant photograph of Charles Barkley and Michael Jordan from the 1993 Finals that hangs in the fourth-floor hallway leading to the coaches office. He realizes that Barkley was important to the franchise, but that was over a decade ago, and there are other players the Phoenix Suns might want to highlight, guys with names like Nash and Marion. Anyway, Barkley has just been killing the Suns on TNT. "Every day I come in here," says D'Antoni, "and the first thing I see is Charles. I'm getting tired of it."

D'Antoni had mentioned it once offhandedly to Robert Sarver, and the next thing he knew the owner was out in the hallway trying, unsuccessfully, to yank it down. D'Antoni decides this is the day of departure for Messieurs Barkley and Jordan, and, a few minutes later, Noel Gillespie and Jason March are wrestling the photo off the wall.

"Where should we put it?" asks Gillespie.

"Put it in the Barkley Room," says Debbie Villa, the coaches' secretary. Around the corner is a large conference room that is also filled with photos of Sir Charles. "We'll work on that next year," says D'Antoni.

About an hour before practice, Marion calls and says he has "personal problems" that will prevent him from getting there. D'Antoni doesn't press him, though he does wonder what could've happened between one of the greatest victories in franchise history, one in which the Matrix played a big part, and 10 a.m. the following morning. But as D'Antoni sees it, the absence is excusable, even at this stage of the season, maybe *especially* at this stage of the season when pressure is at the highest. Practice will be light, and, besides, during Marion's seven seasons with the franchise, he has been reliable and diligent. After that horrible game against the Nets on March 27, part of the atrocious play was blamed on what Gentry called "New York–itis the night before." But Marion had been in his room, chowing down on room service, at 11 p.m. "The one guy I never worry about," says Kevin Tucker, who is responsible for monitoring players' off-court activities and trying to keep them out of trouble, "is Shawn Marion."

With the college draft six weeks away and the auditioning of prospects taking place, this is the time of year when trade rumors start to proliferate, and Marion's name has surfaced, not for the first time in his career. All that has to happen is for a player to be speculated about once—which in Marion's case happened in the *Chicago Tribune*—and it will be endlessly repeated. *Shawn Marion has been mentioned in trade talks.*

His All-Star status notwithstanding, it is not surprising that Marion's name is bandied about. Within the organization, his weaknesses are recognized—ballhandling in the open floor, a dearth of creative instincts as a passer, the absence of a back-to-the-basket post-up game—not to mention a sometimes lackadaisical attitude. The Suns also believe Marion is too quick to point out the faults of others and won't accept blame himself. This was Marion after a 113–106 loss to the Cleveland Cavaliers in late January, a game which Bell missed due to a strained right calf and Marion had to play LeBron James most of the night. "I didn't get no breathers," said Marion after James scored forty-four points. "I didn't get no help either . . . I was trying to guard him as much as I can. I had him pretty much. When you're hitting pick-and-rolls all day, there ain't nothing I can do about it because the big man is setting the screens and then I'm trying to go over or under, and I wasn't getting any help and that's what happens."

LeBron James can get forty-four on anybody in the world. Nobody even indicated that Marion was at fault, and, indeed, Marion's analysis is not flawed. He didn't get enough help. But why throw everybody else under the bus? During the season, the *Arizona Republic*'s Dan Bickley (who bet D'Antoni a dinner that his team wouldn't win fifty games; they won fifty-four), did a column on the coach. Here are Nash's comments: "Mike has a great demeanor, a great personality. He's bright. He's creative. He's competitive. He holds us accountable. He's fair and he makes it fun for us. He deserves all the praise he's getting and more." And here are Marion's: "One of the biggest things is, he realizes that we [the players] make the coaches. When we're winning, he's winning." Marion's knee-jerk defense of himself is, of course, built upon the foundation that he believes he will be held at fault for almost everything that happens.

On the other hand, Marion's strengths—the athleticism, the crowd-pleasing brilliance, and, most of all, the versatility—are eminently tradable. From time to time David Dupree of *USA Today* calculates a "divergent skills" index, in which he adds up dunks, three-pointers made, blocks, and steals and subtracts fouls; this season Marion blew away the competition, LeBron included.

Trades are a touchy subject, and a franchise, obviously, desires to keep speculation out of the media; just as obviously, trades are always a juicy subject, even outlandish trades that will never be made. Relationships have been irreparably harmed when a player learns he is on the block. The Suns are by no means "shopping" Marion, the term referring to a team actively making calls to get rid of a player, and the subject of a Marion trade rarely comes up in conversation. But it does surface from time to time, and is more liable to now without Bryan Colangelo around.

Trade speculation is a no-win situation for the franchise. Tell the player he's not being mentioned in trade rumors, and you could be exposed down the road as a liar. Tell the player he *is* being shopped, and, understandably, he gets pissed off and maybe stops giving his all. Earlier in the season Spurs' coach Gregg Popovich told Brent Barry that he was going to be traded, but the deal fell through and Barry remained. (Barry, one of the most down-to-earth guys in the league, played hard and well the rest of the year.) Marion was miffed that he had to come to D'Antoni to ask if there was any credibility to the trade rumors. D'Antoni told him no. But what if the Minnesota Timberwolves want to deal Kevin Garnett for Marion? The Suns would sure as hell take that call.

Rare, in fact, is the player who is a true untouchable. Nash is one at the moment, unless, as D'Antoni says, "The Spurs suddenly decide they want to give us Tim Duncan and Manu Ginobili." Stoudemire might be an untouchable, but that is partly because he just signed his new deal and the Suns have to give him a chance to make good on it. Anyway, trading him after knee surgery might not work. LeBron James is an untouchable, and the Lakers, having dealt away Shaquille O'Neal two summers ago, are not going to trade Bryant. The Heat wouldn't part with Dwyane Wade, and the Spurs wouldn't let Duncan go. But it's a safe bet that, no matter what their public denials, the Philadelphia 76ers talk about trading Allen Iverson, the Minnesota Timberwolves talk about trading Garnett, and the Boston Celtics talk about trading Paul Pierce. It's just part of the eternal challenge to improve. Carmelo Anthony is a brilliant young scorer who is expected to sign a contract extension with Denver, but it's a good bet that somewhere down the road 'Melo will be traded. Even great players get dealt. It's the nature of the biz.

But there is an unsettling aspect about the idea of unloading Marion, even if the return prize were someone as good as, say, Garnett. Just as some of Marion's weaknesses are sometimes undetectable to all but the most trained eye, so are some of his strengths. Back in early December, the Suns were engaged in a tight game at home with the Denver Nuggets. Marcus Camby had been killing them all night (he finished with thirty-three points and twenty rebounds), but, during a crucial possession late in the game, Marion, playing active help defense, brilliantly denied a pass to Camby (who is four inches taller) and the Nuggets were forced to accept Andre Miller's bad shot. Suns win 102–97. After the game, all the coaches could talk about was Marion's subtle defensive work, and there probably wasn't a fan in the building who picked up on it.

Plus, Marion was a big part of the Suns' renaissance last season, the fifth point in a star that would include Nash the point guard, Stoudemire the finisher, D'Antoni the architect, and Colangelo the brains behind the scenes. Marion is the Swiss Army knife, the all-everything. Trading Marion would nibble away at the essence of the Suns. What is amazing about Marion is the sudden and startling *release* of his athleticism, his kinetic energy. In practice one day, Marion was reclining against a wall, waiting to take his turn in a drill, when he suddenly sprang onto the court and tipped away a shot that Tim Thomas had released from the corner, his hand a good foot above the rim. Marion estimates his vertical leap at thirty-eight inches but says it was several inches higher years ago when he could almost reach the top of the backboard.

When you have that kind of natural ability, assumptions of greatness follow, and, as infuriated as the coaches get with Marion from time to time, they concede that it comes partly from their elevated expectations of him.

"I want him to be everything, do everything," says D'Antoni. "I want him to be stronger. I want him to get dunks, run the floor, guard his guy."

"We don't want him to just guard his guy," says Dan, "we want him to keep his guy from scoring. We don't always ask that of our other players."

"We've been through a lot of saying, 'Shawn this' and 'Shawn that,'" says D'Antoni. "But you know what? We've come a helluva long way. There's a helluva lot of ways you could screw it up by looking elsewhere for another player."

"I'll tell you what we take for granted," says Gentry. "Some of the rebounds he gets for us."

"And we did dodge a bullet with the personnel changes we had this year," says Iavaroni. "Whoever we want to give the credit to—and Shawn has to be part of that—you couldn't have expected to do any better than we did."

"We're two wins away from doing exactly what we did last year," says D'Antoni, meaning that they are two wins from a conference final.

On the practice court, Nash is trying to pump up Diaw. The young Frenchman has by no means played horribly, but Game 5 had been his worst of the postseason—he had only eight points and three rebounds and was on the court for only thirty-one minutes of a fifty-eight-minute game. He is tiring of the endless physical battles with Brand and Kaman, and, moreover, is afraid that he is letting down his team.

"Why the long face?" Nash says. "You know, every time you frown instead of smile it takes a month off your career. Hey, if anyone should be frowning it's me." Diaw forces a smile.

Actually, Nash *is* doing a lot of frowning behind the scenes. How many times over the last weeks has he heard the questions *What's the matter? Are you injured?* He truly doesn't know how to answer because he's not sure what's wrong. He just feels tired and sore, sometimes more tired than sore, sometimes more sore than tired. He speaks of "cumulative fatigue" that built up during a long and enervating regular season, and tomorrow night he will be playing his twelfth playoff game in twenty-three days. He knows there's something wrong physically, but he can't put his finger on it. Or, more to the point, he would need ten fingers to put his finger on it. Sometimes his congenitally damaged back hurts, sometimes it's his legs, sometimes it's his hamstrings, sometimes it's his ankles. "I'm going to feel better one of these days," Nash says. But he does allow that what he calls a general feeling of exhaustion is hurting the mechanics on his midrange and long-distance shots. Should the series go seven games, he would have three days to rest before Game 7.

Plus, Nash is fretting about his own team and its tendency to let down after a victory. "If we can come out and have a real maturity, and be extremely focused and professional, it would be a great opportunity for us," Nash says, talking about Game 6. Notice Nash's choice of words—*maturity, focused, professional*. All the things the Suns were not in Games 2 and 4, and, going back to the Laker series, Games 2 and 3.

May 18
LOS ANGELES

Noel Gillespie has unearthed a clip of Sarver exhorting the home crowd by pumping his arms like a madman. He looks like a signalman on an aircraft carrier revved up on amphetamines. Gillespie had put it on for the coaches that morning, and after it had run a few times, accompanied by the background music to "I Believe I Can Fly," everyone was convulsed in laughter. "That man," says Iavaroni, "is getting his four hundred million worth."

One of the things the Suns are hoping for from the Clippers is the emergence of a certain coming-apart-at-the-seams factor, which is what the Lakers experienced when adversity hit them in Games 5, 6, and 7. Suns' players and coaches had heard Mobley yelling at

Cassell's shot selection during the game and reliable reports had them screaming at each other in the locker room after the Game 5 disaster in Phoenix. I rarely express my opinion to the coaches about anything—why would they possibly want to hear it?—but I had ventured the theory before the game that Dunleavy will tether Corey Maggette to the bench, so inconsistent had his play been.

At the end of the first half, the Clippers lead 62–50 and Maggette has ten points off the bench. Further, the Clippers are cohesive and upbeat. They appear to be the kind of team that thrives under a kind of chaotic discontent, which isn't surprising since their leader is Cassell, a guy who hollers at you, then hugs you. Nothing the Suns try works very well. Brand is still manhandling them inside with fifteen points and four rebounds. Quinton Ross is suddenly shooting like the second coming of Steve Kerr (he has made eight of his ten shots). Kaman, the big center, is again turning Diaw (four points) into a nullity. James Jones keeps trying to make plays when all anyone wants him to do is catch and shoot or catch and pass. Tim Thomas has zero points and is playing like he's caddying for Brand, handing him the clubs that Brand will use to beat him over the head. The twelve-point deficit would've been even larger had Barbosa not scored eleven points in ninety-five seconds, which extrapolates to something like an eighty-three-point quarter.

The final is 118–106. Marion finishes with the quietest thirty-four points imaginable—Brand had thirty but was much more of a factor in the game. Thomas sleepwalked his way to a whole three points. That is what you get from Thomas—a season-saving show one week, a face-on-the-milk-carton game the next.

Diaw managed fourteen points but looks discouraged. Nash and Bell combined for thirty points but missed seventeen of their twenty-five shots. Bell's three-point accuracy came to an end—he missed five of his six shots beyond the arc. Without Marion and Barbosa (twenty-five points), the Suns would've lost by thirty.

"All right guys, real quick," D'Antoni says after the game. "We

213

didn't have that extra pop tonight. The way we have to play—and we'll talk about it on Saturday—we gotta run, we gotta hit quick, we gotta spread the floor, and we gotta go. We can double on pick-and-rolls, we can shut their ass down as we did toward the end of the game [he is reaching for a positive here], but we didn't get it done on the offensive end.

"We worked all year to get homecourt advantage, and that's what we have until the conference finals. That's pretty damn good. Let's get your minds straight and get it done."

Maggette, by the way, finishes with twenty-five points; any future theories I will keep to myself.

The players drift slowly out of the locker room and down the tunnel. Whatever happens in Game 7, this will be the last flight out of L.A. for the season—there have been four round trips since the Laker series. D'Antoni sees a morose Diaw. Earlier in the season Raja Bell, who knows something about mood swings, joked about how irritating it is that Diaw never seems to be down. Well, Diaw seems down now, and D'Antoni motions him to the front of the bus for a conversation.

"Boris, keep your head up, man," says D'Antoni. "You're not the only one struggling. You've been doing fine. We're gonna get 'em in Game 7. We're gonna take care of business at home."

"These games," says Diaw, "have not been fun for me."

Growing up in France, Diaw tried all kinds of sports, including fencing, judo, and rugby, before finally deciding on basketball. "I want to grow to be six-feet-eight and play point guard," Diaw told his mother.

"You cannot be six-eight and be a point guard," she told him. "At that height you must be a center."

"What about Magic Johnson?" Boris told his mother.

Diaw reached his desired height, but, now that he has made it as an NBA player, he finds himself battling beasts like Kaman under the boards. It's not how he envisions the game. He is a smart player and understands, at some level, that his success has come largely because D'Antoni has put him in a position where he can out-quick most of his opponents. But in a protracted series, where tempo inevitably slows down, that advantage in quickness is being mitigated. And he just hates physical play.

During a 136–121 win over Charlotte on February 25 in Phoenix, things turned chippy in the fourth quarter and Diaw took an elbow from the Bobcats' combative point guard, Brevin Knight. As elbows go, it wasn't anything extraordinary, but Diaw looked over at the bench in shock and said, "He elbowed me." Everyone just kind of shrugged, but Diaw couldn't believe it. "He elbowed me. Why would he elbow me? He had no reason to elbow me. Why would he do that?"

Boris, sometimes there's just no good answer. An elbow is an elbow is an elbow.

D'Antoni tries to find an answer for Diaw now. "Boris," he says, "every series is different. It's not always going to be like this. And one thing you gotta understand is how much you figure in our plans. We want you here. You're our guy."

With another Game 7 on the horizon, D'Antoni will likely need *all* his guys.

CHAPTER EIGHTEEN

[The Second Season]

Phoenix, May 21 . . . .
SERIES TIED 3–3

"That's officially the end of the Barkley Room."

At practice, the talk is not of the Los Angeles Clippers, but of pro wrestling, the arena being host to a sold-out WWE event that night. Boris Diaw mentions that he might attend. "Maybe I will learn something I can use against the big guys," says Diaw. Tim Thomas walks down the stairs and strikes a Hulk Hogan pose, having spotted some of the wrestlers in the hallway. Brian Grant arrives and announces that he just introduced himself to the Undertaker. He said it in the same awed tone of voice that one might've said, "I just met the ambassador to China." But no one is more excited than Eddie House, a major pro wrestling fan who plans to be in attendance that evening.

"I'm telling you, they really hit each other with the hard part of the chair," House is insisting to anyone who will listen.

"And I'm telling you, this shit ain't real," says Gentry. "I know these guys. I've seen it up close. They came to L.A. and I met Bret 'Hitman' Hart. He's tough, but how in the hell are you gonna get hit with the damn hard part of the chair and not get a broken skull? They hit each other with the cushion."

"I'm not saying *all* the shit is real," insists House, "but I've seen these guys get hit with the damn hard part of the chair. Maybe they miss accidentally or something."

"No," says Gentry. "It's like when they hit each other in the face and stomp on the ground, so it sounds like they're hitting each other in the head." He gets up and demonstrates.

"I know that ain't real," says House. "But where does the blood come from when they get hit with the chair? Tell me that."

"What are you, Eddie, with this WWE stuff," says Nash, "honorary white trash?"

Nash has already been through a one-hour workout with his physiotherapist, Rick Celebrini, who had arrived last night from Vancouver. Celebrini, who once played pro soccer in Canada with Nash's brother, Martin, was supposed to be on a weekend trip with his wife but, when Nash called, off he went to Phoenix. It was just the two of them at the far end of the practice gym, Nash shirtless and sweating, just like in one of their summer workouts in a deserted gym. Nobody likes to say much to Nash when he's working with Celebrini, and Nash doesn't like to say much either. When Celebrini breaks down what they work on, talking about things like "body mechanics" and "core movements," Nash knows it sounds like mumbo jumbo, and he is uncomfortable, and perhaps a little superstitious, about sharing it with the general public.

"Are you the shot doctor, too?" I ask Celebrini.

"It's all connected," says Celebrini.

About all Nash will say about it is: "My [shooting] mechanics can't survive some of the physical stuff I'm going through." Plus, just having Celebrini around is mentally restorative—Nash believes that he didn't become a real player until he started working with Celebrini six years ago.

Over the last week, D'Antoni has fielded more what's-the-matter-with-Steve? questions than he did all of last season when, to be honest, there was almost never anything wrong with Steve. The questions anger D'Antoni—if he started losing confidence in Nash,

217

his offensive engineer, he might as well pack up and head back to Italy—but they are legitimate questions. Down deep, even D'Antoni realizes that, as do the assistants. They can't obsess about Nash's subpar play and, really, there isn't much they can do about it, but they know it's a reality. "If you would've told me after the Laker series that Steve could be playing the way he's playing, and we'd be here, in a seventh game," says Gentry, "nobody would've believed it." The prevailing theory—at least, the *hopeful* theory—is that Celebrini's visit, combined with the three-day rest and the homecourt advantage, will be just the palliative the MVP needs.

After practice, Nash is submerged in his daily training room ice bath when I wander past, my eyes on a Krispy Kreme. "Way to work, Jack," he says. Just to make me feel guilty, Nash makes that comment every once in a while after I've finished up a grueling practice session that involved sitting on my butt and scribbling in a tablet.

Later, with Nash not around, I find Celebrini. We're just about to start discussing what he found about Nash's mechanics—"His right hip was dropping so his shot naturally is . . ."—when Nash materializes.

"Let's go," he says to Celibrini, flashing me a gotcha grin.

May 22

The atmosphere in the upstairs coaches office is tense. They began playoff preparation on Thursday, April 20, one day after the regular season ended, three days before they played the Lakers in Game 1. The coaches have not had a day off, not one single day when they haven't sat around a room, tossing around ideas, their theories bouncing around like molecules under heat. They have spent far less time with their wives (or, in Weber's case, girlfriends) and children than they have with each other.

There are ten men on a basketball court at one time and only one ball. And, in the case of their own offense, they don't call many different plays. What else could they possibly have to talk about?

At this stage, the coaches are all like mad scientists, drawing up plays on scraps of paper and showing them to D'Antoni or dashing over to the blackboard to see what they look like in chalk. They're not looking to change the offense, but, rather, for one little wrinkle, one little *something,* that could make the difference between winning and losing a Game 7. Gentry even retreats into his cubicle and digs out an old playbook from his days as an assistant with the New Orleans Hornets.

"If we use a Hornet play," says D'Antoni, "we can be damn sure nobody's ever seen it."

Understandably, tensions are high; emotions are ragged.

"I don't like that matchup," Dan D'Antoni says after the coaches watch Nash score against the much taller Radmanovic.

"Well, we scored on him every time," says his brother. "Any particular reason you don't like it?"

"I just don't like it."

"So you'd prefer we score another way?" asks Mike.

"Can't I just not like it?" says Dan.

"Well, shit, Danny, you can just not like it," says Mike, "but specifics would be nice."

"Brothers," says Iavaroni, shaking his head.

Dan also insists that the Suns' main advantage is that they play harder than the Clippers. Gentry and Dan are frequently on the same page, but not this time.

"Elton Brand will play like a bitch from start to finish," says Gentry. "And no one in the league will play harder than Corey Maggette."

"But sometimes he doesn't play smart," says Dan. "I don't think you can play hard and play dumb."

"My point is, on the nights when Corey is going good, he'll

219

have twenty points and fifteen rebounds," says Gentry. "So you better hope things don't go good for him."

"I'm just saying that we can play—we don't always do it but we *can* play—at between fifty-five miles an hour and seventy miles an hour," says Dan. "They have a governor that stops them at fifty-five."

"I strongly, strongly disagree," says Gentry. "I think they play hard as shit. They play every bit as hard as we do. If we're depending on us playing harder to beat them we're depending on the wrong thing. I think if we win, we win for one reason: We make shots."

"How about Game 3 when we won but only shot thirty-eight percent?" says Weber.

"That was an aberration," says Gentry, "and you guys know it."

"Well, just to borrow the old cliché," says Iavaroni, "we can throw out all the statistics for one day. And I'm Mister Numbers."

"How long until tip-off?" asks Mike.

Still seven hours to go.

Marion comes into the locker room two hours before the game, looking calm, wearing what Weber calls a "schmedium" T-shirt, i.e., tight-fitting, somewhere between a "small" and a "medium." He is finishing up a good-luck call from Joe Johnson, the former Sun who was traded to Atlanta and whose season has now been over for a month. Dave Griffin looks worried when he hears "T-shirt" because this is a TV game and the Hammurabis behind the NBA dress code will be watching. That's pretty much how the league office monitors violations: A camera shows a player entering the locker room in gold chains, cap on sideways, and a long retro jersey, and someone in the league office, watching the telecast, writes him up for not complying with the "business casual" edict. It's a little Big Brother. But Marion should be okay because the T-shirt has a collar. A few weeks ago, Nash had been caught wearing a sweatshirt to a game, though Griffin, by sketching out an extremely liberal definition of "sweater," was able to convince the league it really wasn't a sweatshirt.

However the NBA chooses to describe its dress code, which was put into effect before this season, it is about one thing: Making a concession to the red states, where the NBA does not play well. The league can argue that it is color-blind, because it theoretically targets Steve Nash the same way it targets, say, Allen Iverson. But believe this: It is more about Iverson than Nash. (What the red states should see is Nash's T-shirt that says GOOD BUSH above a sketch of a woman's lower abdomen and BAD BUSH above a photo of George W.) If the code is not inherently racist, it is certainly *racial*.

Personally, I wish Iverson didn't dress like a sixth grader when he shows up in public, mainly because, to some portion of the public, his choice of wardrobe perforce defines him as a thug. You can talk about his talent and his guts and his intensity and all of that, but it doesn't make a scintilla of difference to that portion of the public that defines him by his cornrows, his tats, and his sideways cap. But to levy fines against a grown man for what he wears just seems wrong. Had the code been in effect in the 1970s, a whole generation of leisure-suit-wearing players and coaches would've spent half their waking hours writing checks to the league office.

Actually, it's interesting how few player protests there have been during the season. Both the fines and the subsequent team appeals were made quietly. One wonders if the red states noticed how well players reacted to rules that most of them detested.

Out at courtside, L.A. superfan Penny Marshall, who by now has seen way too much of the Suns, having attended almost every game in both the Laker and Clipper series, is tapping Robert Sarver on the shoulder. (Behind her a fan holds a sign that says KOBE STILL SUCKS.)

"Are you the owner?" she asks.

"Yes I am," says Sarver.

"I don't like the Gorilla," she says, talking about the Suns' well-known mascot. "I don't like some of the things he does."

"I'm sorry about that," says Sarver. "He's been around for a long time."

"Some of the things he does aren't right. I think you should get rid of him."

Sarver considers that for a second, then says: "We'll get rid of you before we get rid of the Gorilla."

Sarver reports that Penny, who is friends with Gentry from his stint coaching the Clippers, calls him an asshole. If it's true, again, it's not the first time.

On the blackboard in the locker room, Weber has written the phrases *mental toughness, we have been here before, stay focused,* and *be ready to ride the wave.*

"What does that last one mean?" I ask Gentry.

"Nobody knows exactly, least of all Phil," he says. "But we coaches have to say stuff like that once in a while. It's expected of us."

It's Game 7 night in San Antonio, too, and the players are watching the Dallas Mavericks surprise the Spurs in the other Western Conference semifinal.

"Damn, Dallas is playing hard," says Kurt Thomas.

"In about one hour," says Raja Bell, "the motherfucking Phoenix Suns are going to be playing harder."

D'Antoni's speech is calm and routine. He goes over the match-ups and reminds them again and again: *They have no answer for our speed. They have no answer if we keep running and moving.* "All right, go ahead, Noel."

Gillespie puts on the video, and, with Lionel Richie's "All Night Long" playing in the background, the players watch a smorgasbord of fast breaks, dunks, nifty passes, and three-point shots. Marion is mouthing the words. Bell is grinning and nodding his head in rhythm.

Tim Thomas looks so relaxed he might be going to the beach instead of a Game 7. Of course, he always looks like that.

"I could be wrong," D'Antoni says, "but I think we're ready."

Dunleavy deeply respects Nash, but he couldn't help having some gentle fun with all the talk about Nash's fatigue. When someone asked him about Sam Cassell, Dunleavy, obviously referencing Nash, said, "Sam is really worn out. Very tired. Old legs. I don't know if he can make a shot."

Whether it is the Celebrini visit, the three days' rest, or simply the blood rush of the moment—Nash has a 3-0 record in Game 7s—Nash looks like he is playing on a different pair of legs than he had over the past two weeks. He makes his first three-point shot, grabs a rebound, assists Marion on a three-pointer, assists Diaw on a layup, hits his own drive, and makes a steal in staking the Suns to a promising though hardly comfortable 32–28 lead. An even better sign for the Suns is what happens when Nash goes out for a four-minute rest in the second period—behind Bell and Barbosa, they extend the lead to nine points, and, when Nash comes back, he and Marion play well as the Suns protect the margin.

The 65–57 halftime lead somehow seems safe despite the Suns' well-established predilection for letting opponents back in the game. If not safe, then *safer* than other such leads in the immediate past. Perhaps it's because Nash (fourteen first-half points), his body mechanics having been fixed, has rediscovered his long-distance shooting touch (three of four three-pointers). Perhaps it's because Marion (ten points, including two three-pointers) seems so comfortable. Perhaps it's because the indefatigable Elton Brand (twenty points, five rebounds) seems to be the only Clipper doing damage, much as Bryant seemed to be playing as a one-man team in the first half of Game 7 of the Laker series. "Elton's played every damn minute at top speed," says Gentry, "so maybe he'll wear down." Perhaps it's because Bell sent Livingston into the seats to break up a layup, setting the tone that this is the Suns' house and this is the Suns' game, and managed not to get called for a flagrant.

Dan D'Antoni makes one plea to the assistants: Stop yelling en masse at L.B. "You're getting him all excited and confused," says Dan. Everyone agrees that they had shouted too loudly and forced Barbosa into taking a hurried shot with the 24-second clock winding down.

Late in the third period, Barbosa's brief, turbo-charged career is capsulated in one play. With the clock running down and the best option clearly being his one-on-one isolation drive against Livingston, he inexplicably gives up the ball to James Jones, the one Sun guaranteed not to be able to make a play. The bench goes apoplectic, so Barbosa runs over, gets the ball back from Jones, and takes it hard to the basket, all at warp speed. In two different spots in the pregame tip sheet he gives Barbosa, Dan D'Antoni had used the words "be aggressive." Barbosa's driving layup gives Phoenix a 94–79 lead after three periods.

The Clippers, relatively unshakeable throughout the series, finally fold, much as they did in the second overtime of Game 5. Marion scores twelve points in the fourth quarter to finish with thirty, and, with 1:52 left, D'Antoni takes him out to a huge ovation. Nash is still scurrying around when the buzzer sounds, wrapping up a deeply satisfying twenty-nine-point, eleven-assist game. The final is 127–107.

And, so, for Nash, it is on to Dallas, the team that let him ride off into free agency, something that has unquestionably helped his career but still hurts him inside.

Bell, who played with Nash for one season (2002–03) in Dallas before leaving to sign a free-agent contract with Utah, encounters Jerry Colangelo in the deliriously happy locker room.

"Thanks for bringing me here," Bell tells him.

"It's been our pleasure," says Colangelo.

D'Antoni's words are typically brief. Again, there is no time for celebration, Game 1 of the Western Conference final being two nights hence.

"All right, we're going to Dallas," he says. "What you guys did was unbelievable. We run into Dirk Nowitzki, but I don't know if he can be too much better than Elton Brand. Wednesday comes quick. So get with Aaron, take care of your bodies. Let's go. Let's keep it rolling." Then he goes into the coaches office and grabs a handful of the ubiquitous popcorn. "I'm so happy I can't see straight," he says. He turns up the TNT recap of the game. Charles Barkley is on the tube, now saying that, *Okay, yes, I admit it, the Suns have been surprising, but the Dallas series will absolutely be the end of the road for them.*

"That's officially the end of the Barkley Room," D'Antoni says. He thinks for a second and conjures up a Suns' player from the early days. "We're renaming it the Neal Walk Room."

Back in the training room, Nash and Bell are sitting in their respective tubs of restorative ice, Bell sipping a beer, Nash downing an energy drink. They, too, are watching the broadcast. Bell shakes his head and says to Nash, "Is Barkley retarded or what?"

At that moment, Robert Sarver leads a delegation of minority owners in a congratulatory processional through the locker room and right into the training room, stopping to shake, wetly, with the be-tubbed Nash and Bell. Sarver has been the owner of the Phoenix Suns for exactly twenty-three months, and he will be going to his second straight Western Conference final. Donald Sterling has owned the Clippers for twenty-five years and has never gone once. This Robert Sarver is one lucky man.

TIME-OUT

March 31
TORONTO

Reuniting with a Departed Family Member

The Suns followed up disastrous losses in New Jersey and Milwaukee with a win over the Indiana Pacers. They arrive in Toronto at four a.m. after a marathon session at airport customs.

"I think I'll call Bryan," says D'Antoni. "See if he's up."

"He probably is, worrying about the game," says Gentry.

Six hours later, Bryan Colangelo, now the general manager of the Raptors and the protagonist in one of the most sudden general manager exits in sports history, picks up D'Antoni and shows him his new digs in Toronto. D'Antoni and Colangelo had a close relationship when they were together in Phoenix. In all likelihood, D'Antoni would never have made it to his present position had Colangelo not brought him in as an assistant in June 2002. Actually, Colangelo's wife, Italian-born Barbara Bottini, was largely responsible. Long before D'Antoni and Colangelo knew each other, Bottini and Laurel D'Antoni had worked together for the Milan basketball team that participated in the first McDonald's Open in Milwaukee in 1987. (When pressed, and sometimes when not pressed, D'Antoni will remind you that he had a triple-double in that game against the Bucks, although the Italians lost.) Bottini was always telling her husband, "You should keep your eye on this guy. Really sharp, really-popular over in Italy as a player, then a coach." They finally met in Italy in the summer of 2001, when D'Antoni was still coaching Benetton Treviso, and, within a year, D'Antoni was an assistant with the Suns. And Colangelo, with the blessing of his father, was the one who elevated D'Antoni to the head position after Frank Johnson was fired in December 2003.

Colangelo seems energized by the challenge of being general manager of one of the least successful franchises in the league. But he is sad about how suddenly and bitterly it ended in Phoenix. He had been executive of the year for the 2004–05 season and he and Dave Griffin had arguably done a better job this year, bringing in players like Boris Diaw, Eddie House, and Kurt Thomas. True, the front office hadn't been able to convince Sarver to keep Joe Johnson, but Phoenix had traded away Quentin Richardson (for Thomas) and, in truth, the Suns simply didn't miss Richardson and felt the trade was a good one even after Thomas got hurt.

At Air Canada Centre that evening, Colangelo makes his appointed pregame rounds, shaking hands with the Suns' players and sitting down for a few minutes with the coaches. Jerry Colangelo is along on the trip, too, though he is due back in Phoenix the following morning to make a breakfast speech at seven a.m. He has come to be with his son.

The big change since the younger Colangelo's departure, the coaches tell him, is restaurant choices. Colangelo is a bit of a gourmand and oenophile; the tastes of D'Antoni, now the team's GM and head coach (during the season he is concentrating almost totally on the latter and letting David Griffin do the former) and the one who whips out the credit card, run to pasta, burgers, and Diet Coke. "Yesterday in Indianapolis," Gentry tells Colangelo, "we went to Steak 'n Shake. Kind of place you wouldn't be caught dead in, B."

Bryan Colangelo is wearing, as is his custom, a suit and custom dress shirt with a high collar. (No tie.) Dick Van Arsdale, a former Suns player and now a team executive, calls it the "Flying Nun look." Colangelo seems reserved, but, then, he always is. Jerry is from the old school, a product of the era when you courted the press, told them stories so they would sell your product. Bryan used to joke that "the only way to keep a secret about the Suns was to keep it secret from Jerry." The son, who has a degree in business management and applied economics from Cornell and worked in commercial real estate in New York City before his father asked him to come back and take a job with the Suns, is from the new school. He's more official, more button-down. But in recent years Bryan had relaxed a little bit, the cumulative effect, possibly, of hanging around the casual D'Antoni.

Having a reporter around goes against Bryan's essential nature, his "comfort level" to use Phil Weber's phrase. But he fought those instincts and went out of his way to make me feel at home. And I felt bad when it went wrong between him and Sarver.

A schism was perhaps inevitable. Since 1968, the year that a twenty-eight-year-old Chicago Bulls executive and former University of Illinois point guard named Jerry Colangelo was asked by a group of owners to oversee the basketball operations of a new franchise in Phoenix, the Suns had been essentially a family organization. Or, more properly, a Jerry organization. Colangelo, a lower-middle-class kid from Chicago—his father worked in a mill and painted houses—shepherded the team through its early years, stepping in as coach on two occasions when he had to fire the incumbent. He turned down an opportunity to be the top sports exec at Madison Square Garden, running the NBA Knicks and the NHL Rangers, because "my instincts told me to stay in Phoenix." Also his wallet. In October 1987, with the franchise at an all-time low because of a drug scandal, Colangelo and a team of investors paid $44.5 million to buy the Suns. He owned only 1 percent of the team but he was the chief exec. Eventually, he upped his stake to 38 percent. And in April 2004, he sold to Sarver and his group for $401 million, the highest price ever paid for an NBA franchise.

Through most of that time, 1968 to 2004, Jerry made the big calls. If Jerry didn't like you, you were gone. Bye-bye, Dennis Johnson. If you had personal problems that made the newspapers, you were gone. Adios, Jason Kidd. In 1987, Jerry brought back a gravelly voiced college coach named Cotton Fitzsimmons, whom he had first hired in 1970, to run player personnel, then made him head coach a year later. A plaque outside of Griffin's personnel office on the fourth floor of the arena still carries the name of Fitzsimmons, who died from lung cancer in July 2004. Probably not a week goes by when Cotton's name is not conjured up somewhere in the building. During film sessions, Iavaroni is liable to offer up Fitzsimmons's immortal quote about a poor albeit energetic effort put forth by a reserve. "You're playing hard," Cotton would say in his raspy voice, "but you're killing us." Cotton's widow, JoAnn, still has two prime seats behind the Suns' bench.

It was a close-knit, "small" organization. Many former Suns— Dick Van Arsdale, Alvan Adams, Connie Hawkins, Mark West, Eddie Johnson, John Shumate, Dan Majerle, Tom Chambers—took jobs with the franchise after their playing careers had ended. Cedric Ceballos is the arena emcee, becoming the first former player to debase himself in this manner. Al McCoy has been the Suns' broadcaster since 1972. Ruthie Dryjanski came with Colangelo from Chicago in 1968 and is still his assistant.

Jerry brought in his son in 1990 to assist Fitzsimmons in personnel and six years later he made him the GM.

So along comes Sarver, an outsider, a banker who lives in San Diego. Sarver didn't know, or particularly care, about the "Original Sun" (Van Arsdale) or the Hawk (Hawkins) or the infamous "heads" call on a 1969 NBA coin flip that turned up "tails," and enabled Milwaukee to draft Lew Alcindor (who became Kareem Abdul-Jabbar, the leading scorer in NBA history) and Phoenix to end up with Neal Walk. Sarver had his own style. One of first questions he asked the Colangelos and D'Antoni was whether the Suns should pursue Kobe Bryant, a free agent at the time. Sarver was all about flash and dash. He danced with cheerleaders, cavorted with the Gorilla, started the wave, dunked from a trampoline, launched himself along the floor like a human bowling ball during a time-out diversion, waved a foam finger in the air, insulted the San Antonio Spurs. He fired, then "reassigned" a security guard who stopped him one night from going into a restricted area because he didn't recognize the new owner. He e-mails D'Antoni quotes such as this one from Mario Andretti: "If things are running smooth, you're not moving fast enough."

Stylistically, Sarver is, let's say, one hundred and thirty degrees removed from Jerry. And one hundred and eighty degrees removed from Bryan.

Before Sarver bought the team, he told Jerry that he would not be taking that active a role in running the team. It is beyond naive, however, that Colangelo counted on that. When you pay your $401 million, it's your circus and you're wearing the top hat. Going from the anonymity of banking to the large-font type on the daily newspaper clearly agrees with him.

One of the words Sarver never heard in the banking business was "renegotiation." Banking is a heavily regulated industry, and, by and large, his top executives stayed without getting extensions or new deals. Bankers are generally not pursued in the open market. Customers do not form lines in front of Sarver's banks and yell, "Yo, you gotta get Will Forrester here, man. He da man on mergers and acquisitions, dog." Talk radio does not jawbone about your accounting department.

But it is what happens in sports. And in early February, the Raptors, having fired Rob Babcock, came at Colangelo, whom they had first identified as a candidate in 2004. Bryan said he wasn't interested, though their financial package was lucrative, perhaps as much as $3 million per year, more than three times what Colangelo was making with the family organization that was becoming less like family. But Sarver, surprisingly, gave Colangelo permission to talk to the Raptors. The implication was: I hope they *do* talk.

As Colangelo's discussions with the Raptors grew increasingly serious, that would've been the time for Sarver to intercede and guarantee that Colangelo would get a new deal commensurate with his track record of drafting players and making free-agent deals that turned the Suns into a contender. Colangelo never asked Sarver to match the Toronto offer. He wanted a three-year package worth about $5.2 million, broken into $1.5, $1.7, and $2 million. Given the size of the Raptors' offer and his accomplishments, the request seemed beyond reasonable. But Sarver wouldn't say yes, agreeing only to the *possibility* of giving him a new contract at the end of the season. It was then that Colangelo decided that he was not wanted by Sarver, and he accepted the Raptors deal. He was officially introduced as the new general manager on February 27. The kid who had once been a Suns' ballboy; the kid who told his father that he shouldn't trade Dennis Johnson for Rick Robey; the kid who had learned the business through a kind of genetic osmosis, listening to Dad negotiate with agents during summer vacations or exchange information with talent scouts; the kid who had drafted Shawn Marion and Amare' Stoudemire and signed Steve Nash—that kid was leaving.

Sarver admits that the idea of renegotiation is hard for him. "In sports, you have a good year and all of a sudden everyone wants more money," says Sarver. "I understand it at some level because people in sports are getting fired all the time, whereas such insecurity is not present in other businesses. So the sports business breeds insecurity, and I'm not used to having people work for me who have that insecurity."

But one man's "insecurity" is another man's "ambition." A team came along, recognized Colangelo's talents, and wanted to give him a lot more money. That's how it happens in sports. And Sarver, a self-described man of action, took none. The only logical conclusion is that Sarver wanted Colangelo out, because he didn't like him, didn't like his work, or could put himself closer to the action without him. Colangelo didn't want to leave, his wife didn't want to leave, and their children, Mattia and Sofia, didn't want to leave. "Any thought or notion that I wanted to leave or that there was something concrete for me to stay is absolutely a misnomer," says Colangelo. But, the way he sees it, he had to go. Were he a player, Colangelo would've almost certainly said, "I was disrespected."

At root, the Colangelo-Sarver story is a story about fathers (as it so often is). Jack Sarver was a self-made man who built a mini–hotel empire and began a savings and loan in 1964 in Tucson. When Robert was sixteen, he got a call from his dad. "Put on a coat and tie and get down here. You're going to work." He started his son as a teller.

Jack Sarver valued education above all else, having not had the money to attend college himself. He sent Robert to the University of Arizona, but the son, as freshman often do, spent most of the first semester screwing around. He managed just a 2.1 cumulative grade-point average that put him on academic probation. "It crushed my dad," says Sarver, "just crushed him. He couldn't go to college, so he really wanted me to do well. And look at what I did with the opportunity." Sarver shakes his head. "I was on academic probation when he died."

Jack Sarver had a fatal heart attack when he was fifty-eight, leaving behind a self-made estate of $6 million. His widow, Irene, gave Robert $150,000 in 1984, when at the age of twenty-three he became the youngest person in the United States ever to start a successful bank (the National Bank of Tucson). Irene added an investment of $250,000, and that was all the capital Sarver needed to get started. Once he got started, he never stopped. Sarver owns four million square feet of commercial office space, 3,500 apartments, 700 hotel rooms, and a couple thousand acres of land, along with being CEO and chairman of Western Alliance Bancorporation. And the only thing he is really known for is owning the Phoenix Suns.

Irene Sarver attends games frequently, sitting next to the Sarvers—Robert; wife, Penny; and sons, Max, Jake, and Zach. "My mom is beyond proud of me," says Sarver. "If I robbed a bank, she would figure out why that was the right thing to do. But I think about my father a lot. I wish I would've been able to show him my success." He turns serious. "I've been luckier than I've ever deserved to be, in life and in business. I talk about this with Steve Kerr, who also lost a father too young, all the time. [Kerr, a former NBA player and now a TNT commentator, is part of Sarver's ownership group and a respected advisor; Kerr's father, Malcolm, president of the American University in Beirut, was assassinated in 1984.] 'There is someone up there looking after us, Steve. It's probably our fathers.' "

By contrast, Bryan Colangelo's father was always around. They were close. Bryan ached when he sat in the stands and heard Jerry criticized and got in more than a few fights protecting his father's name. And the son made the father proud, too. No academic probation for Bryan. He was a terrific student and a solid basketball player at Central High in Phoenix, then at Cornell. When he graduated from college, Jerry would've been overjoyed had Bryan come back to join him. But the son felt he needed some time away, some time to forge his own identity before coming back, which he did in 1990.

Bryan put in six years as the second-in-command in personnel before Jerry anointed him and said, "Congratulations, and the first thing you're going to do is trade Charles Barkley." Bryan did it. The joke around the franchise was that every time there was credit to be taken, Jerry would step forward, and every time there was blame, it fell on Bryan, standing in the background. That was okay with the son. He didn't need the attention.

But though the son was a button-down man, he was a bold GM. He hired and fired coaches and reshaped the team a couple of times, most notably when he traded Stephon Marbury and Penny Hardaway to New York, a move that cleared cap space to sign Nash, Quentin Richardson, and a few other pieces. He wore suits and custom shirts. But he had *cojones*.

Still, there was that shadow. Bryan always refers to his father as "Jerry" in public, but what he really needed was a new surname for himself. "A lot of people still think I'm here only because of Jerry," he said back in January before the Raptors' talk had started getting serious. Had Sarver treated Bryan differently, let him know he was wanted and upped his salary via the nasty but necessary business of renegotiation, Colangelo would've stayed in Phoenix. But deep down, he also knew that he needed to get out, to get *in* the sun instead of *being* the son.

Perhaps it will work out for Bryan in the long run. The Raptors, after all, have nowhere to go but up. The saddest person in all of this, though, might be Jerry Colangelo. He doesn't say much about it in public, but he wanted his son to stay and perpetuate what he had started. Jack Sarver would've probably wanted the same from Robert.

D'Antoni doesn't mention the let's-beat-Bryan angle before the game. The Sarver-Colangelo split monopolized headlines in Phoenix for a few weeks, but, in truth, the dispute had markedly little effect on the team. The players generally liked Bryan, but they are, after all, players, interested in the outside world only as it happens to intersect their own. "If it doesn't affect the flow of money on the first and fifteenth of each month," says Gentry, "everything's pretty much okay with them." One school of thought even holds that the players would've been disappointed in Colangelo if he *hadn't* taken the Raptors' offer: He's getting all this money—why wouldn't he go?

Anyway, any Colangelo-against-his-old-team talk is obscured by this being the Steve Nash Favorite Son/Sun game. "Whatever happens tonight," says Gentry, "I'm hanging with the Canuck after the game. The whole country is his 'hood."

"Yeah, like he wants you around," says Weber.

Nash finishes with twenty points and ten assists as the Suns win an entertaining, offensive-minded game 140–126. Gentry terms the Raptors "the Chevrolet version of what we are," which is accurate. Clearly, Colangelo has some work to do.

Accompanied by his father, the new Toronto GM comes into the Suns' locker room to congratulate the players and coaches. Bryan is flying back that night on a private plane with Jerry to see his wife and kids, who are still in Phoenix. He is friendly but clearly disappointed that the Raptors—*his* Raptors—did not perform better.

"They got a lot of diseases up here, B?" D'Antoni asks, his eye on Colangelo's heroically sized vitamin bag. Colangelo is a bit of a germaphobe, and D'Antoni always kids him about it.

"SARS, I think," says Gentry. "Isn't that big up here?"

"Right now it's losing I have to worry about," says Bryan. He shakes everyone's hand solemnly. "I hope you guys go all the way." He departs the locker room no longer the GM of a championship-caliber team he had assembled, but, rather, the boss of one trying to find some measure of respectability.

CHAPTER NINETEEN

[The Second Season]

Phoenix, May 23 . . . .
GAME 1 OF MAVERICKS SERIES TOMORROW

"We can play the underdogs to the outside world, but in here we know we're gonna bust their ass."

From the upstairs coaches office at US Airways Center, Alvin Gentry places a call to San Antonio coach Gregg Popovich, whose Spurs had been eliminated by the Mavericks twelve hours earlier. Gentry and Popovich were fellow assistants on Larry Brown's staff—it seems like Gentry has been on everyone's staff—and wants some feedback on what Popovich believes did and did not work against Dallas. Such calls are not unusual in the NBA; if a coach feels like he can use a prior relationship to gain intelligence, he will do it, and if the other coach feels comfortable dispensing such intelligence, he will do it. In this case, the Suns know they won't get all that much because the Mavericks coach, Avery Johnson, is also close to Popovich, having been his point guard when the Spurs won the championship in 1999.

Pop isn't in, but his secretary says that she'll get a message to him.

"I know what you mean," Gentry says to her. "It's sort of like playing the Iraqi national army team."

Gentry is exaggerating his negative feelings toward the Mavericks. But only slightly. There isn't much of a natural rivalry between Phoenix and Dallas, other than, based on empirical evidence, they seem to be vying for the title of Boob Job Capital of the U.S. But there is little love lost between the teams. Some of the animosity (if that's not too strong of a word) was hatched during last year's conference semifinals, which the Suns won in six games. Even though they were the higher-seeded team, the Suns felt that the Mavericks took them lightly; their star, Dirk Nowitzki, was among those who said that Dallas had the superior team even when it was over.

Moveover, they messed with Nash. Don't mess with Nash around Phoenix, certainly not when you're the team that told him you didn't want him. In that playoff series last season, the Mavs espoused the theory (other teams did, too) of allowing Nash to shoot but taking away his passing lanes, i.e., turn him into Kobe Bryant. It worked in Game 4 when Nash had forty-eight points but the Mavs won. But in Games 5 and 6, both of which Phoenix won to close out the series, Nash scored *and* distributed (thirty-four points and twelve assists in Game 5, thirty-nine and twelve in Game 6), absolutely torching his old team. Nash finished the six games with an average of 30.3 points.

Plus, Phoenix and Dallas are, to some degree, perceived as doppelgangers of each other—entertaining and talented, yet hard-wired to fall short of a championship because they lack some toughness gene. Each hates that reputation and wants to slough it off on the other. Both franchises have crawled their way to near the top of the NBA food chain, and now both are looking to beat the other to the *very* top.

But they want to do it in different ways. Phoenix accepts—nay, *embraces*—the idea that an entertaining and talented team can win a championship. D'Antoni hates it when Dallas's offense is spoken of in the same sentence as his offense. "If we don't score a hundred and ten points a game," he said in the preseason, "we're Dallas." The Mavericks, by contrast, grew tired of being called "soft" and have attempted

237

to remake themselves as a down-and-dirty team that hangs its hat on defense. They would scoff at the notion that Phoenix's defense is even in the same league as theirs.

To some extent, the teams can be defined by the demeanor of their head coaches—the smiling, loose and affable D'Antoni wants to have fun while he's beating you; the defiant, Napoleonic Johnson, who roams the sideline with his lower lip thrust out, wants to stomp you while he's beating you. Dallas's personality change can be traced to the hiring of Johnson, who replaced Don Nelson late last season. Nellie liked to run and play small, and his 2002–03 team, which started Nash and Bell in the backcourt, was a kind of precursor of D'Antoni's teams in Phoenix. (Except that he insisted on playing a stiff of a center, seven-foot-six-inch Shawn Bradley, who established a world record for covering up when someone dunked on his head.) Nellie has admitted that part of his heart went out of coaching when Nash left for Phoenix. Nellie is a former forward with the heart of a running point guard; Avery is a former point guard with the heart of an aggressive forward.

It so happens, too, that Johnson and D'Antoni finished 1-2, respectively, in balloting for coach of the year. D'Antoni professes not to be bothered by it—"Hell, I'm amazed I won it last year," he says—but he would like nothing more than to outcoach the Little General, Johnson's perfectly apt nickname. They respect what Johnson has done with the Mavs and it's difficult not to like him. Nash and Bell do—they were with the Mavs when Johnson was winding down his playing career in 2002–03. (Bell says that Johnson was the one who got him to attend chapel services on a regular basis, where, apparently, he picked up a lot, though not that turn-the-other-cheek thing.)

Johnson notwithstanding, there is something irritating about the Mavericks. Jason Terry, who plays both point and shooting guard, for example, runs onto the floor with his arms spread like an airplane because his nickname is "Jet," a fact that most fans outside of Dallas are unaware of. Plus, Jet believes God has a "destiny" in mind for the

Mavericks. Jet had no comment on what God thought of his punching the Spurs' Michael Finley in the groin in Game 5 of the Western Conference semifinals.

There is a certain collective smugness about the Mavericks, much of it stemming, obviously, from their deep-pocketed owner, Mark Cuban. The dot-com millionaire has turned American Airlines Center into his own version of the Twilight Zone—"a dimension of not only sight and sound, but of mind"—all geared toward ragging on the opposition and lifting up the Mavs.

Cuban would be the last person to admit that the Mavs have a rivalry with the Suns, not after he had spent the previous two weeks insulting San Antonio with the hopes of amping up the intrastate antagonism for the future. He sold the idea that Finley, a former Maverick (and former Suns player, too) and about as classy a guy as the NBA has to offer, was somehow at fault when Terry low-belted him. The scoreboard poked fun at Finley, and Cuban told the newspapers that "Dirk wants everybody to come out and boo Fin." Then Cuban repeatedly found ways to insult the Riverwalk, San Antonio's major tourist attraction. (Being a fervent patriot, he left the Alamo alone.)

Cuban unquestionably saved the franchise, which was among the worst in pro sports when he bought it six years ago. But in the process he has also coarsened the culture, turning the majority of his fans into bleating homers who don't respect opponents and who treat every official's call that goes against the Mavs like a crime against humanity. Cuban no doubt senses that his Mavs could not beat the Suns in a personality contest. So in his sights are the Spurs, bland as broth in their no-nonsense black and silver uniforms, not the Suns, all smiles and lightness in their purple and orange. Some of it has to do with Nash. Cuban somehow sold the idea during the San Antonio series that Finley had deserted Dallas—in point of fact, Dallas waived Finley, once the cornerstone of the franchise, to save money with the amnesty clause—but he would have trouble turning everyone against Nash. Nash is too popular. Nash wanted to stay in Dallas but Phoenix guaranteed $60 million over six years, and Cuban didn't think Nash was worth that much. He liked Nash personally and loved what he did for the franchise, but he believed that Nash wore down over the course of the season and was not the point guard to take his team to the Promised Land.

Nash understood that it was a business decision, but there is no denying the redemption he felt last season when he and the Suns stuck it to his old team in the postseason. Nash has never publicly blasted Cuban, but he does get in his shots from time to time. After a recent press conference unveiling the new Wheaties edition bearing Nash's face, he was asked if he would be sending a few boxes to Cuban. "Sure," said Nash, smiling. "Looking at his waistline, I'm not sure how healthy he eats." That had to sting Cuban a little even though Nash was kidding; the owner is a workout freak who conducts sweaty pregame interviews from a vertical climber.

Still, the Mavs are a strong team, and, to their credit, they kept their entirely legitimate complaints about the NBA's seeding system largely to themselves during the season. They finished with six more wins than the Suns yet were consigned to the fourth seed in the Western Conference because Phoenix and Denver, by dint of winning their respective divisions, were seeded second and third, respectively. That meant that the Mavs had to meet the top-ranked Spurs in the conference semifinals rather than the finals. (The system will change for the 2006–07 season, with the NBA going to a system that seeds the top four teams in the conference based on wins rather than divisional alignments.)

The Mavs are such a strong team, in fact, that there is a consensus among Suns coaches that they would've matched up better with San Antonio. There is much work to be done, particularly in devising a plan to stop their high-scoring power forward, Nowitzki, and not much time to do it. The good news is that they feel they know the Mavs fairly well, having split four games with them during the season.

Dan D'Antoni is alone in his opinion that the Mavs are not as good as their record. All year long that's what he's been saying, and, when Dan believes something, you're not getting him off it. "He'll fight you to the death," says his brother, "even if he's wrong. Sometimes he *prefers* it when he's wrong." But like all the assistants, Dan has learned to compromise, learned to stop arguing so the strategy sessions don't continue right up to tip-off. Watching Dan's adjustment from high school (he won more than five hundred games in thirty years as a head coach at Socastee High School in Myrtle Beach) to the NBA game has been a fascinating process, akin to watching any rookie trying to find his way. This one just happens to be fifty-nine, four years older than his younger brother/boss.

In one respect, it was easier for Dan than for any other high school coach making the leap from high school bench to pro bench— he was going to get a measure of initial default respect. *We like Mike, so let's give his brother a chance.* But as the season progressed, it was on the elder D'Antoni to find his own place within the team. He couldn't be Iavaroni, for Dan's trust in film and stats and his familiarity with the minutiae of the NBA game is not that strong. He couldn't be Gentry, for he does not have eighteen years of NBA coaching experience and an intuitive knack for handling pro players. He couldn't be Weber, for his ability to work one-on-one with players, at his age, is limited (as is his faith in the eternal worth of mankind). He couldn't be Quinter, the chief scout, for his intimate knowledge of personnel on other teams is limited.

And he couldn't be his brother. He never has been. From time to time Dan reprises a version of Tommy Smothers's Mom-always-liked-you-better routine, which gets Mike groaning except that he is forced to admit it's true: Mom *did* like him better. Dan was the outlaw, Mike the model son. Dan was the athlete, Mike the *student*-athlete. Dan was the fighter (during a brawl at a high school game, he threw a policeman over the scorer's table), Mike the diplomat. Dan has what Laurel D'Antoni calls "the thrill gene." Mike, by contrast, is a creature of habit. When they were in Italy, Laurel left Mike a fortieth birthday card at each of a half dozen of his daily stops—espresso bar, newsstand, lunch counter, etc.—and he picked up all of them. "My life is a roller coaster," says Dan, "and Mike's is a merry-go-round." I found that out myself on the road. If Mike and I went to a Starbucks together at 7:20 a.m. on one day—he would invariably order a latte and a blueberry muffin—then we would meet to go there at 7:20 a.m. the next day. We didn't even have to talk about it.

They never played on the same high school or college team, which both agree was fortunate because Dan had his identity as a player and Mike had his. They argued all the time but never mixed it up physically, and, independently, both give the same answer as to why: Dan: "I would've killed him." Mike: "Danny would've killed me." (For a decade in Myrtle Beach, Dan was a bar bouncer along with being a basketball coach.) So they were competitive but rarely were they competitors. On the playground, Dan would select his little brother and give the other captain the next three picks. "I'm not saying we never lost," says Dan, "but we didn't lose much. I was pretty damn good even if I was small [Dan made it to the final cut with the Baltimore Bullets in 1971] and, from the time he picked up a ball, Mike just knew how to play the game. He almost never made the wrong play."

Dan is not in the habit of puffing up his brother—they are more likely to be found battling over politics, theology, music, or which is the superior crossword-puzzle solver—but Dan extends D'Antoni the younger his ultimate coaching compliment. "If you stand on that sideline and all you have is X's and O's to guide you," says Dan, "you got nothing. Mike feels the flow of the game as well as anybody I've ever seen."

They had one class together at Marshall, when Mike, an incoming freshman, took the same summer biology course that Dan needed to graduate. From the front of the room, Mike, who had studied hard for the test, used elaborate sign language to communicate the answers to Dan, who had not. A couple of months later, Dan was Mike's assistant coach on the freshman team and later, for one year, an assistant on the varsity staff when Mike was the star.

Years ago, they talked about coaching together somewhere but always figured it would be in college. When Mike got enough leverage within the organization to add an assistant, he knew it would be his big brother. The fact that Mike, the younger, is more famous is a family joke rather than a conflict between them. Last year, one West Virginia newspaper listed Mike's winning coach of the year as the state's biggest sports story, while Dan's leaving Myrtle Beach and joining the Suns was sixth. "I had fifth all locked up," says Dan, "but then some sumbitch died." Mike claims he frequently receives mail from Marshall addressed to "Mike D'Antoni" and "Mike's brother," to which Dan replies, "Shit, I got into the Marshall hall of fame before he did."

In his own way, though, Dan, like Mike, was always a leader. For thirty years he ran his own program, was respected as a motivator, and was recognized as a character. During one regional final, he grew tired of the relentless advice he had gotten from one leather-lunged fan, so, during a third quarter time-out, he marched his team up into the stands, gathered them around the fan, and said, "Okay, you got your thirty seconds. Tell 'em what you want and shut the hell up." The guy just stammered.

With the Suns, Dan has gradually come to assume three roles. First, he is Barbosa's personal coach. He can no longer get out on the court and *show* Barbosa how to, say, gather himself and try to draw a foul when he drives to the basket, as Weber is able to do, but he can *tell* him. He can be there day after day, the constant voice in L.B.'s ear that the player needs to keep up his confidence.

Second, D'Antoni the elder has become the anti-NBA voice of the staff, the guy who always preaches "Do less, not more." Since he had never been around the NBA until this season, he takes even more delight than his brother in ridiculing some of what he sees as the over-strategizing of coaches. "At Socastee, I had one assistant," says Dan, "and when he asked me what he should do during games, I said, 'Sit there and chart what we do, so when the newspapers ask me I'll know.'" He swears that NBA coaches call so many set plays only so they will be able to have an answer when asked about it after the game. Dan claims to have had one guaranteed-to-work strategy late in a close game: "Call time-out so that the other coach will get his team together and screw something up."

Dan is convinced, too, that the other Suns' assistants shouldn't yell out the other team's play call when they know it. "I think it messes up our guys more than it helps them," he says. From my limited experience, I think he's wrong about that. I think most players want to know and search the opposition bench for clues. (Nash and Bell do all the time.) But Dan is consistent with his do–less–not–more philosophical position, and that mind-set undoubtedly helped the team from time to time, particularly when it elected to call off a certain defensive scheme.

But the Old Ball Coach exerts the most influence when he doesn't even realize it—in those private moments with his brother. At root, they approach basketball in the same way. "If I had a tape of my team in high school it would look like Phoenix," says Dan. "We played small ball, little guys, quick, high pick-and-rolls, fast-breaking, aggressive." But what he does for his brother is more philosophical than strategic. In those dark and lonely moments when the head coach wonders if he's doing it the right way, it was the assistant on the bottom rung who tells him that he is.

"Obviously I wouldn't have gone to South Carolina to get a high school coach if he wasn't my brother," says D'Antoni the younger. "Danny knows what I want and sometimes you have a crisis of confidence that you can't get it. You have a road you're trying to go down, but there are going to be some along the way, and, next thing you know, you're veering off or going the wrong way. Danny understands and gets me back where I want to get."

. . .

At practice, D'Antoni sidles up to Eddie House. "You ready to roll?" he says. "We're gonna need you this series."

"I been ready to roll," says House. "Bring it on."

As if to emphasize that, House politely interrupts D'Antoni when he starts the video session. "Uh, Coach, you got that paper from the other day?" House asks.

D'Antoni cracks up. Eddie had won about $400 in a shooting contest to be paid for out of fine money. "I'll get it to you later," promises D'Antoni.

The theory of using House in this series is based on three factors. First, Dallas does not have a strong, lock-down defensive guard except for little-used Darrell Armstrong. And if Armstrong is checking House, House will be asked to give up the ball immediately. Second, Phoenix feels it can beat the Mavericks by outscoring them rather than with hard-nosed defense, and hard-nosed defense is definitely not House's strength. And, third, as Gentry puts it, "There will be more possessions in this game, so each one is not quite so valuable." House, who is point-guard-sized (six-foot-one) but not point-guard savvy, is capable of committing turnovers.

Further, as with all shooters, House is in a Catch-22. (Or, as Weber observes, it is a Catch-and-Shoot-22 with House.) Casa needs shots to get going, but, if he can't get going, it's difficult for D'Antoni to leave him in. The best advice is something the coaches have told him repeatedly—"Let the ball find you"—but, as D'Antoni says, "The main thing I worry about with Eddie is that he's out there running around like a little Chihuahua looking for his shot."

When it's time for what passes as the D'Antoni pep talk, there is a palpable ease in the practice gym. The pressure will come later, of course. But the Clippers have been disposed of, and the Mavs seem, if not soft, then somehow *familiar*. Nowitzki is damned good but he's also solvable, certainly less of a puzzle than Brand and certainly less frightening than Kobe Bryant.

"You're gonna hear over the next couple of days how good they are, and how balanced they are, and how they beat San Antonio," begins D'Antoni. "All that's well and good, but I'm telling you right now that we are better than they are. We busted their ass twice and had them down seventeen another time. [The Suns blew that big third-quarter lead against the Mavs in the first game of the season at home and lost 111–108 in double overtime.] We can play the underdogs to the outside world, but in here we know we're gonna bust their ass."

CHAPTER TWENTY

[The Second Season]

Dallas, May 24 . . . .
GAME 1 TONIGHT

"If they don't think that little motherfucker is the MVP now, they can kiss my black ass."

Until I step off the team bus at American Airlines Center for the morning shootaround and see four dozen reporters and photographers, I have no sense of how, suddenly, everything must look and feel so different for the players. Now there are only four teams left, nothing else to refract attention from Suns-Mavs in the West and Heat-Pistons in the East.

Watching the interview tableau from the perspective of a semi-insider is a fascinating demonstration of the NBA caste system. The head coach and the star—D'Antoni and Nash—are whisked away for private network interviews or massive group sessions. Nash will answer a hundred questions about his "return" to Dallas and his friendship with Nowitzki, even though this is his dozenth return to Dallas and he and Dirk regularly see each other off the court. They plan to have dinner together between games.

Marion is also a popular target, and so is Bell, who is known as a *good talker*—there is nothing more valuable than a *good talker* to a journalist—and, further, an emerging postseason hero.

Then there are the "middle men," players like Boris Diaw, Eddie House, James Jones, and Tim Thomas. Actually, Diaw has emerged from that pack since he has been named the NBA's Most Improved Player and word has gotten around that, while he doesn't love analyzing the game during interviews, he can be a charming guy. The other middle men don't command as much attention as they should. Jones is a thoughtful player, and both Thomas and House are friendly sorts who are liable to say something cocky, just what a reporter needs. Nobody is sure about Barbosa's command of the language, so most reporters stay away from him. (Though he struggles with some nuances of the language, L.B. is smart and picks up almost everything.)

The guys who aren't playing much—Pat Burke, Skita, Kurt Thomas, Brian Grant, and the injured Dijon Thompson—congregate in a corner of the locker room, taking united solace in their outsider status. Occasionally, they are sought after for that local angle, that end-of-the-bench perspective, or that knowing-veteran comment (Grant is especially valuable for those), and, in truth, any one of them would be able to address the Suns' strengths and weaknesses if they were asked or were in the mood. (Skita could do it in five languages.) But it gets more difficult to be a reserve at this time of year—the lights are brighter but you're still stuck in a dark corner.

The Suns' assistant coaches retreat to a small room near the entrance to the locker room. Experienced reporters know enough to tap the minds of the assistants, who are often freer with their tongues than the head coaches and just as plugged in to the X's and O's. Certain head coaches, Pat Riley being the prominent example, don't allow their assistants to speak to the media, preferring that one message—the Riley Report—make it to the outside world, a paranoid viewpoint that earns him a lot of scorn among the media, and, in all likelihood, among the fraternity of assistant coaches. D'Antoni, of course, has no such edict, and Gentry and Iavaroni, in particular, get interviewed as much as any assistants in the league. Weber is recognized by veteran reporters as an enthusiastic dispenser of information, and Dan D'Antoni's rep is growing because of his relationship with Barbosa. On this day, though, they are being ignored while the head coach gets deluged.

"Are you worried about matchup problems?" I ask them with faux TV-interviewer enthusiasm, thrusting an imaginary microphone under Dan D'Antoni.

"Alvin's sock and tie combination is a big matchup concern," answers Dan.

One of the major lines of questioning, obviously, is the grim mathematical precedent that presses down upon the Suns. Since 1966, only seven NBA teams have even played in two consecutive seven-game series, and, of those, only one has emerged victorious in three seven-gamers. That was the Los Angeles Lakers, who in 1988 twice needed seven games in the conference playoffs, then went the max to defeat the Detroit Pistons in the Finals. It's been only four years since the NBA went to a best-of-seven format for the first round.

For a team already thin on reserve strength; with a point guard who, given the every-other-day schedule of games, will not be able to get in restorative work with his personal biomechanic; and without a center (Stoudemire) who killed the Mavs in last year's playoffs with 28.8 points and 12.5 rebounds, the task seems daunting indeed.

"All I can tell you," says D'Antoni, "is that we definitely plan to show up tonight."

The highlight at a casual shootaround occurs when Tim Thomas, standing almost on the baseline, rears back and heaves a ball, like an outfielder trying to nail a runner taking the extra base, at the far basket. It swishes. "I might have to try that tonight," he says, nodding, as if it were nothing.

Amare' Stoudemire has made himself more and more available to the media as the postseason has gone on. He probably gets interviewed about *not* playing as much as anyone besides Nash gets interviewed for playing. At shootaround that morning, Stoudemire had announced that he has a new nickname. "Call me ATM," he says after winning a shooting game, "because the cash always comes back to me." Stoudemire always gives himself his nicknames. "STAT" means "Stand Tall and Talented." That was his favorite until he decided he wanted to be called "Is-Real" because, you know, his game Is Real.

Now, an hour before tip-off, he is putting the finishing touches on his wardrobe. "Charles called my green coat 'relish' and my yellow coat 'mustard,'" says ATM, slipping into a jeans-colored coat that looks perfectly apropos for, say, a square dance in Compton. "So tonight I'm throwing blueberry at his ass." Like most players, Stoudemire professes negative feelings about Barkley as a basketball commentator, yet courts his attention.

D'Antoni had talked about playing the Mavs relatively straight-up, but that isn't exactly the plan. The Suns plan to trap Jason Terry on all pick-and-rolls; there is not unanimous agreement on that, but D'Antoni fears that Terry will get loose and start making three-pointers. They want to "raid and recover" on Nowitzki, i.e., send a second defender at him who would then retreat to his own man when Nowitzki's penetration has been stopped, and, as was the case with Kobe Bryant, "catch" his spin move. They talk about corralling the speedy Harris, then, in the half-court, playing off him and making him shoot perimeter jumpers. They have to be aware of Josh Howard driving hard left and Jerry Stackhouse driving hard right.

"Everything else, guys, is activity," says D'Antoni. "We do that, as usual, we will be successful. Let's go get 'em."

As the coaches retreat to their small office, and the players lace up before Nash hollers out "NINETEEN ON THE CLICKETY!", someone passes wind, heroically so.

"Someone has died," says Diaw, calmly moving away from the stench, "but does not yet know it." Even when he talks about bodily functions, he sounds positively French.

As the players exit, one of Iavaroni's blackboard messages is there for study: **HURRY UP OFFENSE EASIEST You get the best shots in first :07 seconds.**

Marion knows that. Six times in the first half he streaks downcourt and takes a pass for a wide-open layup. The Mavs aren't quite sure how to play Nash, either, finally electing to switch on his pick-and-rolls, which allows him to score twelve points in the second quarter or find Diaw posting up a smaller guard. At halftime Phoenix leads 62–58; the Suns would be up by a greater margin if not for the inspired play of Devin Harris, who looks every bit as quick as Barbosa, a daunting thought. The plan is to force Harris to drive left into what the Suns call "the muck," the congested area in the paint.

"Offensively, they haven't had an answer for a lot of things," says D'Antoni. "Our speed, what to do with us in the open floor. So do your dribble-ats, move the ball, it will open up, and we do not have to settle [for perimeter jumpers]. They haven't had an answer for our pick-and-rolls over the last two years, so I don't know how they'll be able to do it over a halftime."

"The more jump shoots they shoot," chimes in Nash, "the better chance we have to win."

But an old problem haunts the Suns in the second half—giving up offensive rebounds. Harris stays hot and the Mavs pound them inside and take a 114–105 lead with 3:43 left. By that time Bell has left the game with a strained left calf muscle that came on suddenly, one of those bizarre noncontact injuries. Even the coaches can't escape injury. As Barbosa battles for a ball near the sidelines, he bats a ball directly down into Iavaroni's face, like a volleyball spike. For Iavaroni, who once wore a mask on the court after suffering a horrific eye injury, it brings back bad memories.

Out on the court, it is time for Nash. Spurred on by the first mass booing he ever received in Dallas—the *Dallas Morning News* had declared that it was time to stop loving Nash and start booing him, a decision Cuban applauded—Nash hits two three-pointers and a circus layup in between to put the Suns ahead. But Harris makes a jump shot with four seconds left, his twenty-ninth and thirtieth points of the game, and Dallas leads 118–117 as Phoenix takes a time-out with just four seconds left.

"They're going to run a play called 'Charlotte,'" I say to my seatmate, Marc Stein, from ESPN.com. "Everyone thinks Nash is going backcourt to get it and go one-on-one from there, but they're going to pass it in to Diaw and Nash is going to go backdoor off him for a layup." It's actually a play that D'Antoni stole from Scott Skiles. When he sent the Suns out to run it in a December 31 game in Chicago, he said to Iavaroni, "You think Scott will recognize it?" Whether Skiles did or not, the play worked to perfection.

For once, I'm right. But if I know something, surely the Mavs know it, too, and, as Phoenix lines up, the Dallas players are all hollering, "Nash is going to get it! Don't let him go backdoor!" Tim Thomas inbounds to Diaw, but the warnings pay off—Nash isn't in position to get a return pass. So Nash yells, "Go, Boris!" Diaw begins backing Stackhouse in toward the baseline, and, when he gets there, pump-fakes and goes up for a jumper that nestles softly into the basket. Suns lead 119–118.

I watch the final seconds from the tunnel that leads to the dressing room. Bell is out there by now, balancing on crutches.

"I hope it's broken," a fan yells down at him. A section of the crowd can see Bell if it looks down.

Bell smiles and flashes him the finger.

The Mavs lose the ball, and Tim Thomas stands at the free-throw line for two foul shots that will ice the game. He makes the first, the "swish" audible even in the noisy arena because of the microphones placed around the basket.

"Ooh, I love that sound," Bell shouts to the fans, pointing to them with one of his crutches. "Can you all hear it?"

Thomas makes the second.

"Ooh, I hear it again," says Bell, pumping his crutch in the air. "Did you all hear it, too? Time to go home now. Drive safe, everyone."

The Suns come charging through the tunnel, Bell there to greet them, the 121–118 victory now history.

"If they don't think that little motherfucker is the MVP now," says Gentry, speaking of Nash, who finished with twenty-seven points and sixteen assists, "they can kiss my black ass."

"Guys, obviously, a helluva job," says D'Antoni in the animated locker room. "We're gonna get Raja well as soon as we can, but we gotta take up the slack. We came here to get two, guys, and we can get two. We're better than this team, and it'll be a disappointment if we don't get two. Let's get our rest, get with Aaron, and we're gonna bust their ass on Friday night, too."

Nash, in the role of camp counselor, steps in, ever the voice of reason. "Hey, guys, we got one more to get here," he says. "We can do it." The roar indicates they believe it.

As the coaches review a replay of the final satisfying seconds, they see Barbosa, during the time-out huddle that follows Diaw's basket, stroll up to the Frenchman and plant a kiss right on his cheek. Diaw looks surprised. Barbosa is beaming like a little kid. The coaches can't stop laughing.

"It took a while," says Dan D'Antoni finally, "but it's Brokeback Playoffs time."

CHAPTER TWENTY-ONE

[The Second Season]

Dallas, May 25 . . . .
SUNS LEAD SERIES 1–0

"Zone the little fucker."

The Suns had won by the thinnest of margins, getting a basket on a broken play, yet their world couldn't be brighter. Had they lost, had the Frenchman not been able to back in Stackhouse and release that croissant-sweet baseline jumper, they would be miserable, nagging at each other as they searched for answers.

"Dallas is going through that right now," says Iavaroni at the morning meeting in D'Antoni's suite, "*What's wrong with us? What do we have to do different? Can we turn it around?* All that and look how close that game was."

"We all know exactly what they're going through," says D'Antoni, "but better them than us."

The unexpected thirty-point performance by Devin Harris brings up a classic dilemma: Revamp the defensive game plan to contain him? Or treat it like the anomaly it might've been? The problem is exacerbated, of course, by the injury to Bell, who is definitely out for Games 2 and 3. And there is quiet concern that he could miss the rest of the series. Before Game 1, the percentage of time the Suns spent dealing with Harris as opposed to Dirk Nowitzki would've broken down to about 95 to 5, Dirk. But at the very least, general answers must be found in this morning meeting to curtail Harris's penetration. "We can let Dirk have thirty," says Alvin Gentry, "but we can't let Devin Harris have twelve layups." But how to stop it? Switch Nash onto Terry and let Barbosa play Harris?

"Who's the better guy one-on-one against Harris?" wonders Iavaroni. "I would think L.B. would be a little better."

"Why?" asks D'Antoni.

"Because at this point Steve isn't very good," answers Iavaroni.

Nash has done well for most of the season defending against quick point guards. But it's been a long season, and in Game 1 there were far too many of what Iavaroni calls "blow-bys."

"So, knowing we're going to trap Terry anyway, why don't we put Steve on Terry?" continues Iavaroni.

Gentry favors picking up Terry earlier and making him stop his dribble out front. Dan would rather keep Nash on him but tell him to play way back in the lane—"Zone the little fucker" is the way he puts it—and dare him to shoot outside. Then he wonders that if the Suns put Nash on Terry, would the Mavs respond by moving Terry to the point and taking Harris off the ball.

"I think they'll just keep having Harris handle it until he gets wild," says Todd Quinter.

"Well, is L.B. a better defender than Steve?" asks Dan. "I'm just throwing it out there."

Again, the question. No one offers an answer because it's not an easy one. Both Nash and Barbosa have what the coaches call "happy feet" on defense, the former because he is always going away from his man and looking to help, the latter because he jumps around so much trying to get in the proper position. To a certain extent, as Gentry suggests, the solution comes down to worrying about only one of the guards, Harris or Terry. "If Jason Terry gets out of the box with thirty or so," says Gentry, "I can guaran-damn-tee you that Devin Harris is not going to get to thirty. So they'll just flip-flop. We'll weather it."

The conversation goes on for more than thirty minutes before

Iavaroni says: "Okay, pack it in on Harris and trap Terry. Let's move on. We've had meetings that have lasted twenty minutes and this one has gone forty on the same situation."

"Good thing we won, huh?" says Dan.

As the coaches review the tape, Quinter shakes his head at the repeated glimpses of the Dallas owner in the stands, usually berating a referee or demonstrating some other form of irritation that his team is being vastly mistreated by the authorities. "Jeez, they show Cuban every play," complains Quinter.

"They're teaching hate here," says Weber. There's a general distaste for Cuban's aggressive, rub-it-in brand of advocacy.

"Remember November twenty-second, nineteen sixty-three?" says Iavaroni. "They got hate down here."

"Hey, speaking of Kennedy," says Gentry, "we should have a moment of silence for our boy, the senator from Texas."

"Yes, good old Lloyd Bentsen," says Iavaroni. Bentsen, Michael Dukakis's running mate in 1988, died yesterday.

" 'I knew Jack Kennedy, sir,' " says Gentry, going into Bentsen's famed retort to Dan Quayle at a debate, " 'and you are no Jack Kennedy.' "

"Alvin, is there any useless information you don't have rolling around in that head?" asks Dan D'Antoni.

"In other Kennedy news," says Iavaroni, "they're erecting an NBA conspiracy museum in New York City."

"It'd be nice if we won this thing before seven games," says D'Antoni. "Help take away the conspiracy theories."

The Game 1 win notwithstanding, it won't be easy. A major reason the Mavs are difficult to prepare for is that the Suns can't even be sure which of a variety of lineups they will use. Like the Clippers, Dallas is deep. The Mavs have two big men to choose from in Erich Dampier and DeSagana Diop. Three reserves, Jerry Stackhouse, Adrian Griffin, and Keith Van Horn, are potential starters; Stackhouse finished third in the voting for the NBA's top sixth man this season.

Marquis Daniels seems to be in Avery Johnson's doghouse, but he is an all-court player to be feared, too.

"If they're concerned about running with Shawn, based on what happened last night, they could start Stackhouse instead of Dampier, put Josh Howard on Shawn, and have Nowitzki on Boris," says Gentry. "That leaves them Jason Terry, Devin Harris, and Stackhouse to guard Steve, Raja, and Tim. To me, that's their best lineup."

"But you're forgetting the NBA rule," says Dan. "You can't start your best five guys."

"I think they'll start Dampier," says Mike, "because it's also a rule that if you pay a bad player seventy million you have to start him."

One of the things all coaching staffs do is try to compare players they are scouting with other players they have just seen. They find similarities to the Clippers' Corey Maggette, for example, in Stackhouse, an aggressive off-the-bench scorer who doesn't like to pass and who, if hot, can kill you. Stackhouse is also one of Gentry's all-time favorite players, having spent three seasons with him in Detroit.

"I tell you right now," says Gentry, "nobody's tougher than that boy right there. Remember when he got into it with Kirk Snyder, that young player from Utah last year? Here's what happened. Stackhouse tells the kid, 'I'm going to kick your ass,' but the kid doesn't think anything about it. Game's over, Stackhouse, who dresses all *GQ*, goes to the equipment manager and asks for a warm-up suit, puts that on, goes out into the tunnel, sees Snyder, kicks his ass with a couple of punches, goes back in the locker room, returns the warm-up and puts on a nice blue suit. All in a day's work."

For all the joy he felt after the game, Gentry confesses to having an unsettling dream just hours after the big win.

"I dreamed that Mike traded the entire coaching staff to the Nets for Jason Collins," he says. "So I kept going up to Dan and asking, 'How could your brother do that? Why would he get rid of us?' Can you believe that? Why would I dream that after one of the biggest wins of the season?"

"The reflexive insecurity of being a coach?" I suggest.

"No," says Mike. "That wasn't a dream. I made the offer and they wouldn't do it. They don't love Collins all that much, but they said they had to get a lot more than that."

Raja Bell didn't have any bad dreams, but his nightmare came anyway, as he explains at practice. In the early morning hours he needed to use the bathroom, so he reached for his crutches and took a few steps. "Hey, it feels pretty good," he said to himself, so, like a pilgrim at Lourdes, he threw down the crutches. And promptly collapsed on the floor.

"What are you doing!" screamed his wife, who helped him back into bed.

With the kind of injury Bell has—small tears in his calf muscle, or, officially, "microtrauma"—the first twenty-four to forty-eight hours are the worst. The injury isn't really dangerous, but it is time-dependent. Aaron Nelson is treating him with manual therapy and a mix of modality treatments (ice and electrical stimulation). The Suns insist on calling the injury "day-to-day" but, privately, they have ruled him out for tomorrow night. So, as he did before Game 6 of the Lakers series, which he missed due to suspension, Bell waxes philosophical about how the Suns can fare well without him.

"Obviously I want to play," says Bell, "but remember they were trying to hide Dirk on me. A lot of times I just found myself standing in the corner. Now, I had plans to change that in Game 2. I was going to start diving and making him move. But they can't do that with L.B. He'll slash them to death."

Conceding that the opponent more or less hid a weak defender on him is an astoundingly humble admission for an NBA shooting guard to make. Bell has a lot of pride and is ecstatic at both the progress he's made as an offensive player and the fact that D'Antoni, the league's most offensive-minded coach, has confidence in him. Further, he sometimes gets defensive when his overall athleticism is questioned. He used to be, as he says, "one of those guys who played up around the rim," and was even capable of winning a dunk contest. During a game against the Knicks in New York on January 2, Nash passed him up on a fast break and instead shoveled a pass to Marion. "Somebody tell Steve I can dunk," Bell hollered to the bench.

But circumstances have turned Bell into a defensive stopper and a capable but not spectacular offensive player. And he is honest enough to concede that, in the short run, Barbosa is the greater burden for a defense.

Eddie House is paging through *USA Today,* meanwhile, reading about the upcoming Antonio Tarver-Bernard Hopkins light heavy-weight match.

"I thought it was in Vegas," says House. "It's in Atlantic City."

Amare' Stoudemire looks up. "Where's Atlantic City?" he asks.

I'm not sure if he's kidding. He isn't. "South Jersey," I say. "I was born there." He nods, no doubt thinking that the fact it's my birth-place is the only reason I have that bit of arcane knowledge at my disposal.

Later, as Stoudemire watches practice, his gaze settles on Iava-roni, who is working with the big men. It's hard to figure out whether Stoudemire wants to be on the floor. Certainly he wants to be out there tomorrow night, tearing down the rim with twenty thousand people in the stands. But practice is another matter. Suddenly Stou-demire smiles, and, like a kid reciting a nursery rhyme, says: "Iavaroni. Andrew Toney. No baloney." He doesn't know where Atlantic City is, but he can spout off a line from a Philadelphia 76ers video about their 1983 championship team, of which Iavaroni (and Andrew Toney) were members.

"Coach Iavaroni's got a ring, right?" Stoudemire asks. He says "Iavaroni" quickly, like it's three syllables instead of four. *I've-rone-ee.*

"Yep," I say. "From nineteen eighty-three."

"Damn," he says. "I was one year old when that shit happened."

Stoudemire gives no outward sign that anything is different about his life. But tomorrow morning, in a courtroom back in Maricopa County, Arizona, Carrie Stoudemire is scheduled to stand before a Superior Court judge and officially accept a plea deal over her DUI crash into a freeway barrier in October of 2005. Amare' is staying with the team and will not be attending. It's a pro forma hearing—Carrie has already agreed to a three-year prison sentence (including credit for one hundred and sixty-two days already served) that helped her avoid a possible four-year sentence had she been found guilty at trial. But some in the Suns' camp think it's significant that her son is not returning to Arizona to be with her, a sign, perhaps, that he's breaking away from her. Stoudemire doesn't talk about his mother except in the most general of terms. *I love her. I'm still behind her.*

Though there is absolutely no chance that D'Antoni is going to play him in this series, the press is full of speculation about it. Stoudemire feeds it. He takes shots before and after practice, and, unless Iavaroni is monitoring the drill, never once do I see him feed the ball back to a teammate. That is what he should be doing. Shawn Marion's jumper is, at this moment in the season, infinitely more important to the Phoenix Suns than Stoudemire's jumper. But ATM just keeps putting them up, putting them up, never rebounding, never seeing himself as part of a whole, a spoke in the wheel. Small things often reveal big deficiencies.

Not a day goes by that the Suns coaches don't study the whole Stoudemire package—the two surgically repaired knees; the tendency to work on the fun part of rehab (out on the court) and skip over the private part of rehab (stretching and strength drills); the increasing distance he puts between himself and his teammates—and worry that he won't return as the same force he was next season when he averaged thirty-seven against the San Antonio Spurs, the eventual NBA champions, in five conference finals games.

But for a variety of reasons, I get a smile on my face whenever I see Stoudemire. As Gentry often says, "Amare' just cracks me up." Stoudemire is friendly and open (except on the subject of his mother, which is understandable), never failing to give me a cheery "Whassup, Jack?" He would probably be the player voted least likely to discuss books, yet he is one of the few who has questioned me about the project.

"How long's it take to write a book?" he asked one day.

"Well, *Moby-Dick* took a long time, but I have to write this one pretty fast," I answer.

"A book," he says. "Yeah, huh? Word for word. Straight up."

I'm not sure what he means but I nod.

One day Stoudemire came in wearing that Rolling Stones T-shirt bearing the image of a cartoon figure sticking out his tongue, the cover of *Sticky Fingers*.

"Now, STAT, tell me," says Gentry, "can you name one single Rolling Stones song?"

"Can't help you, Chief," said Stoudemire immediately.

On another day, he was wearing a T-shirt bearing the likeness of a 1930s *Time* cover on which Al Capone appeared.

"What's with you and Capone?" I ask him.

"Don't know anything about him," Stoudemire answers, "except that he was a bad guy."

I gave him the one-minute primer on Capone, Chicago, and Prohibition.

"Damn," he said. "There was a time drinking was illegal?"

CHAPTER TWENTY-TWO

[The Second Season]

MAY 26, Dallas . . . .
SUNS LEAD SERIES 1–0

"I got a house in Scottsdale I will give you if he didn't walk."

Like most teams, the Suns run two buses to visiting arenas on game days. (A third bus during the playoffs is for family and friends.) The first bus carries, in trainer Aaron Nelson's words, "the hungry"—the assistant coaches, trainers, and those players who either don't see much action and need extra work, those who are rehabbing an injury and need extra work, or those who just want extra work. Leandro Barbosa is the only one who always falls into the latter category. Typically, Brian Grant, Pat Burke, Nikoloz Tskitishvili, and, these days, Kurt Thomas, are on the "hungry" bus. The "nonhungry" bus follows an hour later, bearing the head coach, the regulars, the broadcasters, and other hangers-on such as myself.

Eddie House, who in Game 1 played eight minutes and made three of his five shots, a limited night's work but a nice one, strolls onto the "nonhungry" bus seven minutes late, ten minutes after Nash and Marion, the superstars, came on. One could argue that House would do himself a favor by taking the hungry bus, but, no, he takes the nonhungry and also shows up late. D'Antoni gives him a quick glance but doesn't say anything. House will find a slip of paper in his locker the following day informing him that he has been fined $250.

262

• • •

Over the last twenty-four hours, a clip of Avery Johnson using the phrase "transition defense" has dominated the evening sportscasts. In response to a question about what Dallas had to improve for Game 2—the Suns scored thirty-two fast-break points in Game 1—Johnson said it three times in a row, and, though only Faulkner could truly capture the coach's distinctive Louisiana patois in full verbal fast-break mode, it came out sounding something like TRANZISHON-DEEEFENCE-TRANZISHONDEEEFENCE-TRANZISHONDEEEFENCE. Naturally, it was added to Gillespie's video, and the coaches and players have already seen it a dozen times. TRANZISHONDEFENCE. You can hear it being said around the locker room before the game.

In the bigs meeting, Iavaroni says: "Whoever is near Nowitzki when the ball goes up, you got a free shot at him. Take it. It's legal. It's okay." That is old-school ball—that's how Iavaroni played the game when he was the forgotten fifth starter with All-Stars Julius Erving, Moses Malone, Maurice Cheeks, and—no baloney—Andrew Toney. "Who do you think they wanted to collect the fouls?" he always says.

I happen to be sitting next to Marion, and, when Iavaroni mentions giving Nowitzki the extracurricular shot, Marion turns to me, shakes his head, and giggles. That is not in Marion's arsenal. That is not what he does.

On the board Iavaroni has written two other interesting messages. The first says PACK-TIVE and F.U.S.D. DISCIPLINE. He constantly looks for new phrases. The first one instructs his defenders to "pack it in" and "stay active" while doing so. The second is a familiar Suns' expression that, believe it or not, is not an obscenity. "Fake Up but Stay Down" refers to a close-out technique in which the defender, coming out to contest a jump shot, fakes as if he's going for the shot but keeps his balance (stays down) to protect against the more dangerous drive.

The second message is more clear-cut. It reads:

94   *:07*   *4*
Feet   *off the shot clock*   *quarters*

D'Antoni sketches out the defensive matchups and reminds them, "Our game is offense. If we run, we'll have mismatches and cross-matches and, I'm telling you, Nowitzki and Van Horn can't guard anybody. Keep running. All right, Noel." The pregame video includes not only Avery Johnson's by now familiar phrase but also a slow-motion reply of Iavaroni getting hammered by Barbosa's spike. "I am sorry, Coach," says Barbosa, genuinely contrite. Everyone else is laughing. "Damn," says Tim Thomas, "Coach was looking straight up at that shit."

A few minutes later, Nash shouts, "NINETEEN ON THE CLICKETY!" but most of the team is watching a TNT pregame package on Diaw, who is being interviewed with his mother. "Let's go," says Nash, "we can watch Boris on TiVo."

The coaches listen to Barkley's follow-up to the Diaw feature. "Well," intones Sir Charles, "Boris Diaw is a pretty good player. But when Stoudemire comes back next year, Boris is going back to the bench. He'll be behind Shawn Marion at 3."

D'Antoni shakes his head. "I'm so glad we took down that photo of Charles," he says.

Dan D'Antoni, hobbling in his protective boot, and Raja Bell, hobbling with his crutches, walk onto the court together. "The crips are here," Dan says.

"Wear a tie!" a few fans shout at them, for both are going with the stylish T-shirt look that fits into the NBA's mandated business-casual.

Dan just smiles. Bell smiles, too, and adds, "Suck my dick, Homes." The quick, secret-assassin comeback has become somewhat of a specialty for Bell. During a game in Philadelphia on January 31, a

76ers fan seated behind the Suns' bench rode Bell on and off the whole night with a single line: "Hey, Bell, go back to Utah." Finally, in the fourth quarter, Bell turned around, noticed the fan's mottled complexion, and said, with a big smile, "ProActiv, my man. Clear that right up." Even the fan's seatmates laughed at him.

It takes D'Antoni less than thirty seconds to make a defensive change. Dallas forward Josh Howard, who was considered doubtful because of a sprained ankle he suffered early in Game 1—his loss was to be the compensating factor for Bell's injury—jetted by Diaw for a layup, and D'Antoni orders the Suns to trap him from now on. So, though the Suns wanted to play Dallas fairly straight up, they are (a) trapping Jason Terry on high pick-and-rolls, (b) trapping Howard when he gets the ball in scoring position, (c) faking at Nowitzki to discourage his penetration, then coming late when he does go, and (d) being aware that Nash might need help on Harris's drives. For the most part, they are treating tonight's fifth starter, Keith Van Horn, like he's the Invisible Man. Plus, whichever Sun happens to be nearest Van Horn when the Mavericks are on defense, is automatically given the ball and invited to embarrass him one-on-one. Exploiting Van Horn is a major factor as the Suns build a 52–47 halftime lead with Nash and Diaw again leading the way.

There is real excitement in the locker room. Steal this game, another one on the road, and, well, you can almost kiss the Mavs good-bye. In the locker room, the coaches all offer tidbits.

Iavaroni: "We're doing too many panic things when the ball is at the free-throw line." (He continues to suggest that the Suns play more straight up with fewer schemes.)

Gentry: "We can't leave Steve down there with Adrian Griffin." (Griffin is a stocky forward who can post up.)

Weber: "We've done a great job with their spins. Four times Nowitzki and Stackhouse spun and we were *right there*." (Weber is much more likely to offer something that the Suns did right rather than wrong.)

Dan D'Antoni: "We have to make it so at the end of the game it becomes about [he goes into the Avery Johnson voice] *transition defense, transition defense.* We have to play harder than they do."

D'Antoni never says much during this time (unless he's angry about something). He digests each coach's offering, considers his own strategic thoughts, and makes a quick decision about what to tell the team and what is too complicated to communicate at halftime. To an extent, the coaches make their suggestions as much to remind themselves of what might have to be said later during a crucial time-out.

"Great job," D'Antoni tells the team. "Only thing is, don't panic on defense, just like you don't on offense. Keep your principles. Fake at Dirk, then come late. We have to judge when we have to hit him.

"Now, we also have to recognize that when Steve has Adrian Dantley down—shit, not Adrian Dantley, I'm going back about twenty years—when he has Adrian Griffin down there, we have to be able to understand who he's going against. He wants you to come, so you don't. But when he goes to shoot, when he *doesn't* want you to come, *now* you hit him.

"And great job on the boards. The Suns have a 20–17 edge in rebounding. Every time we get it out, we run, every time we run, we score. Pretty simple game."

Then the point guard takes over. "The biggest thing is, they're in their locker room saying, 'This is the series right now,'" says Nash. "They're telling each other, 'We *can't* lose this game.' So they are going to come out with everything, and we have to match that. More energy, play harder than them. Then we're going to get calls instead of lose calls. When we play a little hesitantly, that's when we don't get anything. We come out with massive energy, we're gonna get calls, they're gonna get tight and this game will be ours."

Nash never says anything loudly or even emphatically, but you can sense his passion for beating his old team and the sense of urgency he feels about the game. *This is the one. Steal this, go up two to nothing and it's all but over.*

Then the strangest thing happens. Nash is the one who loses his aggressiveness. He takes zero shots in the third quarter and only one (a fadeaway jumper with the game almost over, which he makes) in the fourth. Meanwhile, Josh Howard takes over the game, driving, hitting jumpers, and disrupting the Suns' offense.

With 1:57 left, Dallas leads 96–91. Marion gets the ball and is almost immediately whistled for traveling. The call represents a new point of emphasis for the officials: If a player moves both feet when he starts his move, make the call. It makes some sense except for the fact that the more obvious traveling violations—those that occur when a player is going in for a wide-open dunk— are almost never made. Those are the ones that drive anti-NBA fans out of their minds.

Following the call on Marion, Nowitzki does a little foot shuffle at the other end and makes a layup to give Dallas a 98–91 lead. D'Antoni is beside himself on the sideline. He corners Joey Crawford, who did not make the call on Marion but was the official closest to the Nowitzki play and also the crew chief. Players and coaches have to be careful with Crawford, one of the league's best officials and one with a notoriously quick trigger.

"Joey, they call the walk on Shawn, and Dirk's was much more obvious," D'Antoni says during a break in the action.

"Dirk didn't walk," says Crawford.

"I got a house in Scottsdale I will give you if he didn't walk," says D'Antoni.

"Yeah?" says Crawford. "Good for you. I got a house, too."

"Good, I'll bet mine against yours," says D'Antoni. He is smiling by now. It's always best to have a smile on your face when you're talking to Crawford.

Still, the Suns have one more chance to win it. Trailing 101–96, D'Antoni designs a brilliant inbounds play that gets Tim Thomas a wide-open three-point look off of a screen by Barbosa. The shot appears on-line but misses, Phoenix's sixth misfire in its final seven three-point attempts. Live by the three, die by the three. And the Mavericks go on to win 105–98. Series tied.

"Let's put it all in perspective," D'Antoni says in the quiet locker room. "If we had lost the first game and won this, we'd be friggin' bouncing off the wall. We came down here, got the job done, like you did in Clipper Land. We had three or four shots to win the game near the end and they didn't go in. You know what? That's life. We're gonna go home and get them there. Let's go."

The coaches repair to watch the film. Marion's little jitterbug could conceivably be called a travel, but Nowitzki's is definitely a violation.

"Well, I got me a Joey Crawford house," says D'Antoni. "So why don't I feel better?"

Nash, meanwhile, tells the assembled press, "Mission somewhat accomplished." But, later, as he walks slowly to the bus for the flight home, he looks like a man who left something behind.

CHAPTER TWENTY-THREE

[*The Second Season*]

Phoenix, May 27 . . . .
SERIES TIED 1–1

"We lost, that's one thing, but we sit here and feel sorry for ourselves. The mood is not great. I can't put my finger on it, but it's just not great."

Everybody had a bad night after getting back from Dallas. Thoughts of the one that got away just wouldn't go away. But Alvin Gentry also had a terrible morning, as he reports when he arrives at the arena for the morning coaches meeting. The burglar alarm at his neighbors' Scottsdale home had gone off early, and Gentry dutifully climbed out of bed, put on a pair of shorts, and went over to investigate.

"So the Scottsdale police arrive and start asking me questions," says Gentry. "I tell them my neighbors are on a cruise in the Mediterranean, and I came over to check on the house when I heard the alarm.

"Now, this one policeman starts giving me the third degree. 'How long have you lived here?' 'Do you have any I.D.?' 'Do you know the name of the people who live in this house?' Guy's got a tight shirt on, belly sticking out. Now, what does he think? That I robbed the house in a pair of shorts, then waited for the police to arrive?

"The guy kept me there like twenty minutes. Finally, I said, 'Look, I live next door and I'm going home. If you don't believe me,

269

arrest me.' I go outside and another neighbor is driving by and he says, 'Alvin, anything wrong?' And I say, 'Nothing that not being black wouldn't cure.' "

Game 2 was a puzzler, replete with statistical anomalies. Dallas point guard Devin Harris, who had thirty points in the first game, had only nine; most of the pregame conversation about him had been a waste of time. Tim Thomas, who sometimes gets his hands on every defensive rebound that comes his way, finished the game with one. On the other hand, James Jones, who almost wasn't noticed, had six blocked shots, an extraordinary total for someone considered a smart defender but not a particularly athletic one. Leandro Barbosa had good looks the entire night but made only three of fifteen shots.

And then there was the Nash number: One shot taken in the second half. But as the coaches review the game film, the explanation for it seems painfully obvious: The Mavericks threw constant double-teams at him, sometimes triple-teams, and Nash almost never had an open perimeter shot or a clean path to drive. On the rare occasions when a big man had to defend Nash alone (last night it was usually DeSagana Diop), that defender did a good job and discouraged Nash from even attempting to break him down, or, as Kevin Tucker always shouts from the bench when Nash is isolated on a big, "walking the dog."

One school of thought holds that Nash could be faulted for not at least attempting to do more, for hurtling his body into the lane and trying to get to the foul line. But that isn't his game. Another school is that he could be praised for trying to play the correct way and not letting the offense devolve into one-on-one chaos. But sometimes that's what a leader has to do. The coaches choose not to take either school. The most frightening alternative isn't talked about either: That the Mavs are good enough and smart enough defensively to have seized upon a game plan that will throttle Nash the rest of the way.

A more familiar topic does evolve out of the film-watching, however: the spiritless play of Marion. Again, it is not what he does—

it's what he *doesn't* do. Make the extra effort to block a shot, for example, or stand around on offense while Nash dribbles instead of cutting to the basket and looking for a pass. "There are about six plays on defense in the second half," says D'Antoni, "when he doesn't even compete." Earlier in the season, before a 102–96 loss to the Mavericks, D'Antoni had shown a snippet from the first game of the year against Dallas, when the Suns had blown a seventeen-point lead and lost 111–108. "Shawn," said D'Antoni after Dirk Nowitzki took an unimpeded shot in the lane, "you might look at getting that from behind." Five months later, he is still trying to make the same point.

But, then as quickly as they castigate Marion, the coaches wonder if they're being a little hard on him, that old problem of expecting too much from someone so gifted. "Nobody in the history of the game got nineteen points and eleven rebounds," says Gentry, laughing, "and took more shit about it."

As D'Antoni paces the floor, which he often does when he's trying to figure out a game plan, he notices a strange sight out of the fourth-floor window. "You gotta see this," he says. And there is an African-American riding a horse down Jefferson Avenue, which passes in front of the arena. Nobody can believe it.

"Good thing that guy wasn't at your neighbor's house this morning," says Phil Weber.

"Now I just know that guy doesn't have his black cowboy card," says Gentry. "Hey, remember in *Blazing Saddles* when ..."

There ensues a few minutes of conversation about Mel Brooks's classic comedy that tells the story of a black sheriff; it is welcome respite from talking about the game.

May 28

Marc Iavaroni has written on the board in the coaches office: "Change schemes when nauceous." What does that mean? I ask.

"It means we change up our coverage when Mike gets sick of something," he says, "which in Game 2 took about one play."

I point out that *nauseous* is spelled wrong. "That's the first mistake I've seen on your board all year," I tell him. "Stan Van Gundy may give good board, but I'm guessing he doesn't spell as well as you."

The only major strategic change for Game 3 is that Marion will start on Josh Howard. D'Antoni almost never uses statistics to make a point, but he tells Marion before the game: "When Howard scores over twenty points, they're undefeated." Marion nods. He has already heard the stat from a dozen different sources. Iavaroni also reminds Marion: "We gotta have five players and be below the ball. Shawn, you have to be in on this." It's easy to sense that Marion believes he is being singled out for criticism that should be going to the whole team.

Right before the Suns trot out, Nash stops into the coaches' office and says to D'Antoni: "Maybe once in a while if I screen for Boris, instead of the other way around, it would be a different look."

"Good idea," says D'Antoni.

Nash is looking for something—anything—that will break down a Dallas defense that, for him, seemed nearly impenetrable in the second half of Game 2.

This one couldn't begin worse for Phoenix. Seven seconds into the game, Ed Rush, the ref who mistakenly called the technical on Diaw in Game 3 of the Laker series, overrules an out-of-bounds call and instead whistles Barbosa for a personal. D'Antoni goes absolutely ballistic. He hates ominous starts. Diaw continues to play well in the middle, and, when Nash and Tim Thomas heat up in the second period, the Suns grab a 52–47 halftime lead.

But while the same halftime score seemed hopeful in Game 2, it now seems shaky. It's a "bad lead." Too much stop-and-start-and-stop on offense. Too much standing around and not enough cutting to the basket. (Phoenix had just one first-quarter assist.) Too many squandered opportunities against a Dallas team that shot only 40 percent from the field. Too many times when a seemingly golden fast-break opportunity evaporates because not enough Suns ran downcourt. And the onus falls, again, on Marion.

"Shawn's gotta go to the hoop and dunk it!" Those are the words not of a coach but of Robert Sarver, who stops in the coaches office, plops down on the couch, and rips up his score sheet in anger.

There is a downcast feeling among the players, too. The Mavs have been mediocre in their execution, at best, yet still trail by only five in a game that the Suns desperately need to win. Plus, Dallas is clearly the aggressor. Josh Howard's flagrant foul on Tim Thomas in the second quarter should've fired up the Suns to retaliate in some small way, but they didn't. As was the case early in the Laker series, Phoenix seems to be getting bullied.

D'Antoni tries to ignite some fire. "All five guys have to be active on every possession," he says. "It can't be two guys or three guys—it has to be all five. Forty possessions means forty times everybody goes for the rebound, everybody goes for the loose ball. We do that, we win. That's mental fucking toughness."

Which the Suns don't have, whether it be caused by the no–Raja Bell effect, the Mavs' depth, or their own collective fatigue. As Howard, and, inevitably, Nowitzki heat up, the Mavs lead by four, then six, then eight. Diop, whose arms seem to extend the entire width of the court, contains Diaw, and no one else can catch fire. The Suns hang around but Thomas makes a careless pass that leads to a Howard layup and a six-point lead with 1:47 left. Game over. Dallas wins 95–88.

Right after the game, Gentry says what D'Antoni is thinking: "We had more shots tonight with five, four, or three seconds on the shot clock than I've ever seen us have. We had no movement." D'Antoni isn't sure what he's going to tell his team, but the decision is taken away from him by Nash, who is already lecturing when the coaches enter for their postgame recap.

"When we're really tough is when we kick and move it," Nash

is saying. "That's when we're hard to guard. They're not a great defensive team, but they become one when guys stop and go one-on-one. All right, something doesn't work, we dive, it's not there, okay go back to it." Nash's tone is reasonably calm but he moves his arms animatedly, similar to the motion that D'Antoni makes when he tells his team to rev it up. "We keep it moving, they are not a great defensive team," continues Nash. "But we can't score thirty-some points [they scored only thirty-six] in the second half. That's not us."

The players listen and some nod their heads. But it's a quiet room. Nash is obviously upset. What should happen now is that someone else stand in support, echo what Nash has to say, then call everyone together and turn it into a positive. Perhaps Bell would've been that second voice had he played in the game, but the timing is not right for an injured player to make a speech. James Jones had tried before and it didn't work. Brian Grant is a respected voice, but he hasn't played since God knows when. Tim Thomas is too new. Boris Diaw doesn't have the personality to address the team, nor does Barbosa. No, it should be Marion, the other cocaptain. But he stays seated, perhaps because he thinks that Nash is talking mostly to him.

D'Antoni takes over. "All right, real quick," says the coach, "just to repeat what Steve said, obviously we didn't watch the film yet, but my impression is: We didn't run. If we don't run, if we can't find the energy, then we can forget it." He stops. There is silence and a couple of coughs.

"And if we hang our heads, we're really fucked. We have to show some leadership here. Somebody's going to have to step up and show something. Guys, you get here about once, twice, maybe, three times in your career. We're here! So, first, enjoy it. Two, bust ass. Three, yell and scream like crazy people out here. Let's play! We lost, that's one thing, but we sit here and feel sorry for ourselves. The mood is not great. I can't put my finger on it, but it's just not great. These games are too important, guys, too important.

"What we do great, we just didn't do it. The ball didn't hop, we just didn't run."

Then D'Antoni remembers that the Suns are down by only 2–1. He must bring them back up. He can't lose them now. The seven-game experiences against the L.A. teams have to be presented as a positive.

"Hey, guys, we been through a lot," says D'Antoni. "We been at 2–1 before. We just have to come in, get the next one, and even this thing up, then see if they get tight in Dallas. Now let's go!" Marion's 1-2-3 SUNS chant is emphatic, but, clearly, there will have to be a mood swing before Game 4.

In the press room, Nash talks about "slumped shoulders" and "bad body language" and "giving in." He mentions no names but does add that, "We miss Raja's fighting spirit."

In the coaches office, meanwhile, Bell and D'Antoni are meeting behind closed doors. Bell has had enough of being a spectator.

CHAPTER TWENTY-FOUR

[The Second Season]

Phoenix, May 29 ....
MAVS LEAD SERIES 2–1

"Every time a second goes by, we get less productive."

In the morning, D'Antoni takes a call from Herb Rudoy, Raja Bell's agent. It pretty much makes official what the coach and player talked about last night after the game.

"I just wanted to let you know," says Rudoy, "that you'll have to kill Raja to keep him out of the lineup tomorrow night."

D'Antoni talks it over with Aaron Nelson. They're going to see how Bell does with movement drills at practice, but no one should so much as hint to the media that he is even thinking of coming back.

The coaches barely even discuss it among themselves. There are too many other problems, and a feeling of desperation permeates the morning meeting. A specific Dallas play—a high pick-and-roll involving Dirk Nowitzki and Jason Terry, D'Antoni's particular *bête noire*—is frozen on the plasma screen for at least fifteen minutes as they figure out how to defense it.

That's not even the Suns' biggest concern, which remains, as always, their offense. *Fix the offense and fix the game. Keep everyone moving and we can't be beat.* One frozen frame shows Nash surrounded by four Maverick defenders. Marion doesn't go to the corner, Diaw doesn't dive down the lane, Thomas doesn't come over to set a pick, and Nash, near the end of the shot clock, throws it away. It's a microcosm of what went wrong in Game 3. They talk about adding a couple more options for Diaw and Nash, but, as Iavaroni says, "I don't know how many more things we can give Steve and Boris to do."

At practice, though, D'Antoni conveys none of the wretched feeling that was in the coaches room. "The biggest thing is that it's only 2–1, guys," he tells the team. "They have to beat us two more times. And we've dominated them for the last two years, so I don't think they can do it."

As his teammates run through the Mavs' dummy offense, then work on their shooting, Bell goes through a series of drills under Nelson's direction. Nelson is looking for little things that others might miss, a lack of explosiveness, or maybe a look of pain on Bell's face when he cuts quickly. There is no question that Bell is retarding his recovery by trying to come back. Two weeks would be a normal healing time for anyone, and a less-dedicated player, which is almost anyone, might be out for as long as a month. But the governing medical thought is: Bell will probably not do permanent damage to the calf even if he tears it a little more, but if he doesn't get back on the court the season could be over. He'll have nothing *but* time to rehab it.

Nelson knows that Bell isn't 100 percent, but he looks pretty good. D'Antoni wonders if Bell "has some gene that kicks in during times of stress." It can be a bad thing, when it re-leases his temper, but perhaps now it is firing, pushing him to get better and beat the odds. Every once in a while a teammate will go over and say something to Bell, but it's not like he needs encouragement. "Plus," says Nelson, "he has this." The trainer pulls out a medal from under his shirt. "St. Rafael," he says, "the patron saint of healing."

When Bell is finished, he comes over for an energy drink.

"Something you should know, Raja," I tell him. "Willis Reed? Who made that amazing entry at the 1970 Finals when he was injured?"

"I've seen the video," says Bell.

"He wore number 19. Just like you."

Bell smiles widely. "I'm going to remember that," he says.

D'Antoni, Nelson, and Bell himself are still selling the idea that he won't return for Game 4. And, in truth, they don't know. They have to see how Bell responds to this workout and then gets additional treatment over the next twenty-four hours. But Dan D'Antoni has no doubts. "Raja will play," he says. "God heals warriors faster than mere mortals."

His brother overhears him. "Sorry, Danny," he says, "but I've got to steal that line for the media." He does, too.

D'Antoni has other business for the day—a meeting with Marion, just the two of them, in the coaches office, door closed. And it's not just because Marion had ten points, a playoff low, and zero assists in Game 3. The coach thinks it's time to get his feelings out, and he senses that Marion has something to say, too.

Marion complains, not unexpectedly, that D'Antoni never hollers at anyone except him.

"What you're really saying," says the coach, "is that I don't holler at Steve."

D'Antoni says that is not accurate because he hollers often at Boris and Leandro, but he does concur that he rarely directs criticism at Nash. He tells Marion there's a reason for that: "Because when Steve screws up, particularly on defense, it has nothing to do with lack of hustle. It has to do with him simply getting overpowered or out-quicked. But your mistakes, Shawn, can sometimes be tied to lack of hustle or desire."

D'Antoni also says that Nash, though being the MVP, is the one taking extra practice and working hard to expand the parameters of his game. That implies that Marion could use extra work, too, particularly on his ball-handling and outside shooting.

Marion still insists that the coaches judge him more harshly than they judge other players, that he's held to a different standard. And, if he's held to that standard, if he's the one who always has to adjust his game to everybody else, then he's the one who should be getting props from the franchise. But most of the marketing machinery, he complains, churns out for Nash and even Stoudemire.

D'Antoni hears him out, and, at the end of the meeting, he comes to the same conclusion he always comes to: *Shawn is a good guy and I wish we could get this straightened out.* Player and coach shake hands. Whatever each feels inside, there is nothing close to a schism. Marion says he will come out battling in Game 4.

May 30
GAME 4 TONIGHT

D'Antoni shows up at 7 a.m. only to find an empty coaches' office, which is highly unusual. At the very least, Iavaroni should be there, padding around in his stockinged feet, piles of Tylenol packets under his chair. But then he remembers: It's a 6 p.m. game and he himself has scheduled shootaround for two hours before game time, not at the normal 11 a.m. The coaches aren't due to come in until about 1 p.m. Before turning around and going home, D'Antoni calls his brother and wakes him. "I'm up, Danny, so you may as well be, too," he says.

At his home, Raja Bell picks up the morning edition of the *Arizona Republic* and reads a story about himself: "Raja Bell, who will not play in tonight's Game 4 at US Airways Center, is more optimistic about his availability for Thursday's Game 5 in Dallas."

Bell dashes off an e-mail to Aaron Nelson saying he is almost sure he can play. "What time will you be at the arena?" Bell writes.

"Three p.m," Nelson responds.

"Be prepared," Bell writes back.

Bell shows up at the appointed hour, Nelson puts him through some paces, and Nelson says, "Okay, you can go. I'll tell Mike."

At about the same time, Iavaroni is finishing up his board.

3rd MAJOR ACHIEVEMENT
Underdogs vs. lakers (4-3) ✓
Underdogs vs. clippers (4-3) ✓
Underdogs vs. mavericks TONIGHT IS THE NEXT STEP! SHOW WINNING SPIRIT!

About a half hour before tip-off, D'Antoni takes his position in front of the team. He looks to his right. There is Bell, lacing up his sneakers in front of his locker, where, a few minutes earlier, he had heard Charles Barkley weigh in with his observation that Bell shouldn't be playing and should've surrendered his spot to a healthy player. Magic Johnson, also part of the studio team, has more or less agreed with Barkley. The comments only serve as more motivation.

Nelson has fitted Bell with a half-sleeve directly over the partially torn calf and a longer second sleeve over the entire leg. The team already knows he's coming back, and D'Antoni doesn't even mention it except to note Bell's defensive assignment for the evening—he'll start on Jason Terry but will probably have to cover Josh Howard and Jerry Stackhouse at times. Bell didn't know whether he was going to start or come off the bench—that was purely the coach's decision.

Before D'Antoni sends them out, he again emphasizes the need for speed.

"Alvin," D'Antoni says to Gentry, "what was that offensive stat again?"

"We were seven of eleven when we shot within the first seven seconds of the shot clock," Gentry answers.

"Every time a second goes by," D'Antoni says, "we get less productive."

The Suns seem ready. But back in the office D'Antoni still isn't sure. "If we don't come out with energy," he says, "we're screwed."

The crowd greets Bell with a loud ovation. It's hard to say whether a heroic return from injury measures up to a mugging of

Kobe Bryant, but it's certainly in the same league. A minute into the game, Bell hits his first shot—a sixteen-foot jumper. Then he hits another a minute later. Marion is active, getting two dunks on hard dives down the middle, exactly the kind of play D'Antoni wants him to make.

But the Mavs weather the emotional start of the game and chip away at Phoenix's early eight-point lead. No matter how often Nash drives to the basket, he can't get a call, even though the Maverick guards ride him out of the lane by putting two hands on his waist. On one play in the second period, Tim Thomas is arguing with a referee when Nowitzki, his man, calls for the ball and takes a jump shot that Thomas barely even sees him get off. Fortunately for the Suns, it misses.

The Suns' halftime lead is 51–46, again that frightening five-point advantage. Bell gives a brief interview to TNT's Craig Sager, in which he said he felt "disrespected" by Barkley's and Johnson's comments. This leads Barkley to call Bell a "whiner." Somewhere along the line, Barkley has lost his sense of humor, at least in regard to himself. He is beginning to treat everything he says as scripture—disagree, and thunderbolts shoot from the sky.

On his way into the locker room, Nash stops by the family room to kiss his twins. He seems relaxed. He even picked up a lucky field goal when, on an intended lob to Marion, the ball went directly into the basket. Everyone is playing well, especially Barbosa, who has made six of seven shots and grabbed four rebounds off the bench.

But five points, as the Suns know, isn't nearly enough for security.

Again, Nash speaks in the locker room. As the postseason has gone on, he has increasingly made his voice heard.

"We've had the lead every game in this series," Nash says. "Let's get out there early and get prepared. Let's get off to a good start in this quarter."

He never stops dispensing that advice, and most of his team-mates never stop ignoring him. Marion is particularly late going ou for the third period. Still, the Matrix hits a big three-pointer midway through the period to put Phoenix up by six, then a dunk with thirty-two seconds left that puts the Suns up 79–67 after three. When Diaw dunks over Nowitzki early in the period, Marion claps his hands, raises his fist, and hugs Diaw, a rare expression of emotion.

Shortly after that, Bennett Salvatore, the Suns' old friend from the infamous Game 4 of the Lakers series, whistles Bell for a personal foul, and D'Antoni, convinced it was a charge on Nowitzki, leaps out of his seat to protest. Salvatore gives him a technical, and D'Antoni appears to be on his way after Salvatore when Iavaroni steps in front of him. As the lead assistant, Iavaroni considers it one of his duties to keep the head coach from getting ejected.

But the lead only climbs after that as the Mavs have no answer for Barbosa, who makes ten of thirteen shots. His performance so excites Ivete Barbosa that her blood pressure shoots up and she has to leave her seat to receive oxygen. Bell comes down awkwardly at one point early in the fourth when he drives along the baseline, and the bench lets out a collective groan. D'Antoni immediately signals Nash to substitute for him, but, true to form, Bell draws an offensive foul on Stackhouse before leaving with nine points, four rebounds, three assists, and three drawn offensive fouls. The ovation is thunderous.

At most, a nonsuperstar might have one big moment in the postseason. Bell has now had three: The flagrant foul on Bryant; the game-tying and series-saving three-pointer against the Clippers; and this throw-off-the-crutches return against the Mavs. The rage that Bell felt after the San Antonio game in early March seems like years ago.

Late in the game, with the Suns leading by 94–71, D'Antoni walks down to Kurt Thomas at the end of the bench.

"You want to try it, Kurt?" he says.

"Sure," says Thomas and checks in for the first time since February 22. Over the last two weeks there had been much speculation about Thomas's return, but, in truth, D'Antoni hasn't much considered it. All along, he saw Thomas as being more valuable in the Finals (against either the Heat or the Pistons, both of whom have big, physical centers) than he did against Dallas. And in any case he worried that Thomas would slow down the offense. But the cushion presents an excellent chance to at least give Thomas a look. Thomas looks rusty, picking up two quick fouls in his brief time.

The final is 106–86. Marion grabs a spray can of black paint and draws an X across the 10 that appears on the courtside numbers, indicating the Suns' tenth playoff victory. The last number all the way to the right is 16, which is how many playoff wins the champion will have when it's all over.

Barbosa finishes with twenty-four points but does not stick around to share his thoughts with the media—he has gotten the word about Mama and leaves immediately after showering. Nash and Diaw finish with twenty-one and twenty, respectively. But the most telling stat is what Nowitzki didn't do: He made only three shots and scored just eleven points.

Back in the locker room, where the mood is upbeat but not insanely joyous—everyone knows that a Game 5 in Dallas less than forty-eight hours away will probably decide the series—I ask Kurt Thomas if he saw the fan who was wearing his number 40 jersey.

"I didn't see it," says Thomas. "I wonder why someone would even bring it."

It's a shame for the Suns that Thomas got hurt and hasn't been a factor in the playoffs. His no-nonsense professionalism would've helped.

CHAPTER TWENTY-FIVE

[The Second Season]

May 31 . . . .
SERIES TIED 2–2

"We just got discombobulated in the fourth quarter."

Robert Sarver's morning begins with a phone call from Jerry Colangelo, who had heard Sarver's response to a question asked him by Dan Bickley on the columnist's radio show on KGME.

"If you guys win the title," Bickley asked, "should Bryan Colangelo get a ring?"

Sarver answered, "I don't think so."

Colangelo thought it was a classless comment and told Sarver so. Sarver didn't apologize or amend his opinion, but he did say that he was caught off-guard by the question and might've responded differently had he had time to think about it.

Both of them are present at the arena this afternoon as Janet Napolitano, the governor of Arizona, presides over a pep rally declaring "Phoenix Suns Week." All you need to know about the stylistic change at the top of the franchise is a split-screen visual of Colangelo and Sarver. Colangelo is dressed, as he almost always is in public, in blue blazer and conservative tie. He looks like he's going to a Rotary fund-raiser. Sarver is wearing a casual white shirt and a pair of black jeans with a small rip in one of the legs. He looks like he's going to catch folk night at Hava Java.

"I got caught without a change of clothes," says Sarver, who travels between Phoenix and San Diego (where he lives) by private plane. "I decided at the last minute to go to Dallas, and this is all I have." Jerry Colangelo, see, doesn't get caught.

The Suns coaches crowd onto the stage; it's one of those frozen-smile occasions, but, since Napolitano is a card-carrying Democrat, D'Antoni, Iavaroni, and Gentry are reasonably glad to be there. (For the record, Colangelo is a registered Republican, but he likes Napolitano, too.) Gradually, some of the players show up, in an order prescribed by their status or personal inclination for punctuality. Pat Burke, the injured Dijon Thompson, Tskitishvili, and Kurt Thomas arrive first. Then, surprisingly, Eddie House. Nash, Barbosa, James Jones, Bell, and Stoudemire beg off—"getting treatment" is a legit excuse—and Tim Thomas and Shawn Marion stroll in a little late, while the governor is speaking. Thomas, in fact, starts to sit in her seat but is quickly shooed away.

Governor Napolitano declares the Suns "an Arizona treasure," suggests they are going to thump the Mavericks in Dallas, and that's pretty much it.

"I've been around for Suns Days, Suns Weeks, and Suns Months," says Colangelo. "If we can win this whole thing, all that remains is Suns Millennium."

June 1
GAME 5 TONIGHT

Phoenix is clearly the media darling of this matchup. D'Antoni answers every question with a smile. Buttonhole a Suns' assistant and you'll get a friendly quip. Nash sometimes looks as if he's staring into a firing squad when he's put in front of a large press gathering (a "cattle call" as it's sometimes called, or a "clusterfuck" as the media knows it), but he always makes himself available and always until the last question is asked and answered. Same for Marion, Bell, Diaw, whoever.

The Mavs' shootaround, by contrast, is grim. Obviously, it has something to do with their loss in Game 4, but, to the press, Dallas unquestionably wears the blacker hat. The Mavericks are not an unpopular team; it's just that the Suns are so much *more* popular.

"Dirk left without talking to the media today," I tell Nash.

"He's like that when he's happy, too," says Nash of his buddy.

In many ways, the respective personalities of the team leaders, form the overall team personality. Early in the postseason, Dallas's Nowitzki made the drastic public relations misstep of revealing that, on occasion, he hums a David Hasselhoff tune ("Looking for Freedom," which had been popular in Nowitzki's native Germany when he was growing up) to relax himself at the free-throw line. He might as well have said: I dig Barry Manilow. Both at home and on the road, Nowitzki was subsequently greeted by Hasselhoff masks, Hasselhoff cheers, and, most frighteningly, Hasselhoff—never one to miss capitalizing on a public relations opportunity, the former *Baywatch* beefcake showed up in Dallas for Game 2.

Dirk's good buddy, meanwhile, was getting immortalized by Nelly Furtado, a certified out-of-the-mainstream singer/songwriter, a Canadian herself and cute to boot. In "Promiscuous," Furtado sings: "Is that the truth or are you talkin' trash/Is your game MVP like Steve Nash?" So, while the Mavs were defined by the musical tastes of a clueless Teuton, the Suns, through Nash, had cornered the market on indie legitimacy. Nash feels bad that his buddy is getting Hassel-trashed. But not that bad.

At the end of shootaround, I jokingly ask Tim Thomas if he can make another full-court shot, and soon a half dozen players are launching balls at the distant basket, most of them sailing wide right, landing in the seats with a loud crash or narrowly missing various TV technicians and maintenance personnel who are setting up for tonight's game.

"Let's get out of here before we kill someone," says D'Antoni with a trace of exasperation.

Eddie House decides to try one more shot, aiming for the water cooler at the extreme left side of the basket, having determined that the "motherfuckin' air current" will carry it right. It swishes.

"We need a ninety-four-footer tonight," says Dan D'Antoni, "we know who to go to."

As I munch on a sandwich at lunch, Robert Sarver suddenly looks over and says, "Do you mind if I do something with your eyebrows?"

"Excuse me?"

"They're too thick," he tells me. "Kind of frightening. We could go to the salon at the hotel and get it done. I'll pay."

The coaches are cracking up but apparently he's not kidding. "I'm busy this afternoon," I say, "but maybe, if there's a Game 7 back here, we can do it then."

The challenge for D'Antoni is to decide how much emphasis should be put on the game in his remarks. Everyone knows that, in a deadlocked seven-game series, Game 5 is the fulcrum. Call it a must win and get them all charged up? Or take the casual one-play-one-game-at-a-time approach? D'Antoni goes back and forth. He never plans his pregame remarks and what tumbles out is pretty much off the cuff.

"All right, guys, tonight is a matter of remembering this is Game 5," he says. "If there's eighty possessions, then we have to play eighty possessions. It's a matter of being active, it's a mind-set, that the most important thing going on for these two hours is knowing we're going to bust their ass.

"We have to treat it like a Game 7. We gotta go in and get at their ass. Energy and commitment on every play. Keep your mind on this fact—that Game 5 might be the most important game of your careers.

"We have only one player who's been in the finals—Raja. [Bell makes a small bow and a couple players bow back.] But this is the game we gotta get." Then he suddenly realizes that he shouldn't treat it as an absolute must-win. "Now, we also got Games 6 and 7, too. But try to get in your mind that these next three games, particularly this one, could set your whole life up. All right, Noel, whatta you got?"

As they quietly watch the menu of dunks, fast breaks, and three-pointers, D'Antoni says a version of what he's been saying since training camp: "They got no answer if we run."

The first quarter goes horribly for the Suns, but they make their move in the second behind Tim Thomas, who comes off down screens, finds his way to the perimeter, and gets good looks. The Mavericks are so intent on double- and triple-teaming Nash that they are willing to leave anyone else wide open. Near the end of the half, Thomas and Nowitzki get in each other's face and a double technical is called. Thomas looks at Nowitzki, puckers his lips, and blows him an air kiss. Thomas gives the Suns some attitude but, as with his facial hand-wave, the gesture carries the air of a taunt. It's not all-out punk, but it's punkish.

Dallas leads 58–55 at halftime, but, in contrast to the "bad leads" the Suns had in Games 2, 3, and 4, this is a "good deficit."

"It's ours," whispers Todd Quinter as he goes into the dressing room. "I can feel it."

Almost everyone, it seems, feels the same way. The coaches are a little concerned with Diaw, who has missed seven of his ten field goal attempts—"He's shot two air balls," says Iavaroni, "and he's a little screwed up right now"—but, other than that, the sense of confidence is palpable, particularly in Thomas. His now-he's-here-now-he's-gone ride through the postseason continues. There are games when he simply disappears, fails to get himself open, and ignores the boards. Then there are games when you can't imagine the Suns winning without him. He is almost as important as Nash. Tonight is one of those games. He finished the half with fourteen points, missing only one shot, and has hit all of his three three-pointers. No matter that his man, Nowitzki, has seventeen points. That is to be expected. The Suns can weather that. What they must do is continue to attack the Mavs offensively.

"I'm thinking that Howard on you, Tim, which he has been, I haven't seen him play defense in the post," says D'Antoni. "He just reaches and grabs. I think we can exploit that.

"Now, also, offensively—and, Steve, you tell me what you think—but we gotta put wood on these guys. [He means set hard screens; that is an area where Kurt Thomas is missed because Marion and Tim Thomas set weak screens.] We can't have a guy trailing the play because Steve can't see behind him. Steve has to have that assurance that we busted the guy who's tailing him.

"All right, anybody got anything?"

Nash does—his now familiar refrain: "We gotta be real tough at the beginning. We get these guys early in the third, they're gonna fade. Let's get out there and get ready to go."

For the Suns, a dream scenario unfolds almost immediately. Two minutes into the third period, Josh Howard collects his third foul, then almost immediately gets his fourth, and Avery Johnson sends him to the bench. That leaves them with either the smaller Jerry Stackhouse or the slow-footed Nowitzki on Thomas, and Thomas is feeling his touch. He makes a three-point shot, drives in for a dunk, draws a foul, and completes a three-point play. Then he hits two more threes in quick succession. Suddenly, the Suns lead 77–70 with 3:27 left in the third quarter. Suddenly, the whole complexion of the series has changed. Suddenly, the Suns are in charge. The obnoxious American Airlines Center P.A. announcer, "Humble" Bill Hayes as he calls himself, tries to get the crowd into it, but they are shocked. The Mavs, back on their heels, call time-out.

On their bench, the Suns seem to be celebrating a little too wildly, and Nash and the coaches try to calm them down. The

Mavericks storm out of their huddle, intent on turning the game around.

Nowitzki draws a foul and makes both free throws. Devin Harris, relatively quiet since the first game, converts a three-point play. Before D'Antoni can call a time-out, Nowitzki makes an eighteen-foot jump shot and the score is tied 77–77. Nowitzki makes another three-pointer and another jump shot before the end of the period, and now the Mavs seem in control 82–81.

Three minutes into the fourth period, Bell's reputation gets him again. Referee Kenny Mauer, a coconspirator from the infamous Game 4 of the Lakers series, calls a foul on Bell, then, after the play is over, he detects Bell pushing off on Josh Howard and adds on a technical. D'Antoni explodes off the bench, and Maurer T's him up, too. D'Antoni throws his clipboard onto the floor, shattering it.

Whatever else was going through Bell's mind, he is clearly frustrated by his inability to move freely because of his calf. He had pulled off one minor miracle with his return in Game 4, but, as the medical staff expected, the injury isn't going to get better with strenuous use; it's going to get worse. Also, the Suns had by this point detected on game film several instances when they believed that Howard was deliberately tripping them. Howard got under Bell's skin, and D'Antoni exacerbated the situation by losing control.

Nowitzki makes both technicals, then converts a jump shot, and, suddenly, a one-point Dallas lead is a five-point lead, 93–88. Barbosa makes a jump shot to cut it to three, but the Suns, clearly shaken, get no closer than that. Whether or not it is his fault, Thomas does one of his disappearing acts and doesn't score in the fourth quarter, takes only one shot, in fact. The Suns panic on offense and rush their shots. When Barbosa misses a floater in the lane, Dan D'Antoni says, "In November, you can take that shot, but in June you can't."

Nowitzki, meanwhile, doesn't miss down the stretch and scores twenty-two points in the fourth period alone to finish with an even fifty. Whatever message Thomas was sending with his air kiss, it served only to motivate Nowitzki. As in the previous series, when the home fans chanted for Kobe Bryant and Elton Brand, Nash had to endure the chants of "M-V-P! M-V-P!" for Nowitzki. They were intended not only as support for their own player but also as a commentary on the selection of Nash. Avery Johnson gets the luxury of taking out Nowitzki with 1:12 remaining, and the ovation lasts for almost a minute.

The final is 117–101. From the point that Bell and D'Antoni got their technicals, the Suns were outscored 28–13. The stretch run, which so often belongs to Phoenix, was all Dallas. It is an excruciating loss that puts the Suns down 3–2 in the series.

"It's not gonna matter," says Gentry as the Suns enter the locker room, "because we're gonna bust their ass the next two games." But it sounds hollow. This was opportunity squandered.

"All right, we had a shot at them," says D'Antoni to the team. "We didn't get it done tonight, but we will get it done on Saturday. All right? Everybody cool?" They come together enthusiastically, but, on this night, no one says anything else after the coach, not even Nash.

Back in the coaches room, the replay is on. D'Antoni looks surprised when they show a replay of the two technicals.

"The score was 88–89 then?" he says. "We were only down one?" The realization hits him like a punch. If Bell hadn't gotten called for the T and if he hadn't added to it with his own technical . . .

"That's where the game went," says Weber, "right there."

For a change, Marion put it best: "We just got discombobulated in the fourth quarter," he says.

On his way out of the arena, Sarver confronts Terdema Ussery, the Mavericks' president and CEO. Before Game 4 in Phoenix, Cassandra Johnson, Avery Johnson's wife, had gotten involved in a heated exchange with two Suns fans. Owner Mark Cuban and little-used Maverick reserve center DJ Mbenga both went up to investigate, the latter unthinkingly since it earned him an automatic league suspension. Sarver still isn't sure what happened in Phoenix, but he tells Ussery that, with all the provocative video that plays on the scoreboard in Dallas, the Mavericks have no justification to complain.

"Your scoreboard taunts the opponents, you inflame your fans, and you have a negative atmosphere here," says Sarver. "Then you go crazy when something happens in another arena." That is an exaggeration since the Mavs did not "go crazy" about the Cassandra Johnson incident. But Sarver did what he thought was correct, and he did it without going to the media.

Mark Cuban, meanwhile, is planning to complain to the league office about an elbow that was thrown by that notorious enforcer, Shawn Marion.

CHAPTER TWENTY-SIX

[The Second Season]

June 2 . . . .
PHOENIX, MAVS LEAD SERIES 3–2

"Our guys fought as hard as they could. They just ran out of steam."

Discussions of next season, subconscious or not, have started to dominate the conversation in the morning meetings. How could they not? Analyzing weaknesses that have been exposed during the Dallas series inevitably lead to discussions about how to solve those weaknesses. The assistant coaches have been regularly working out prospects after practice, and Dave Griffin and Vinny Del Negro talk about little else except the upcoming draft.

Then, too, the coaches desperately need another topic besides Dallas. Talking about next year leavens the burden of strategizing for tomorrow's Game 6. Hours of that lie ahead anyway. There have been so many defensive theories propounded over the last two weeks—since the playoffs began forty days ago, in fact—that the coaches are becoming confused themselves. "I'll be honest with you guys," says Gentry, "if you asked me right now what we're supposed to do if Jason Terry and somebody screen-and-roll, I wouldn't know if we're doubling, trapping, or doing nothing. I just think we're getting too may things going on."

Gentry blows his nose. "Plus, I'm miserable with this damn summer cold."

Unless the Suns manage to trade up, their draft picks at twenty-one and twenty-four won't furnish much help. In essence, the Suns' "draft" could amount to trading away the picks for money and getting back a (hopefully) healthy and motivated Stoudemire, re-signing Tim Thomas, extending Diaw and Barbosa, and maybe picking up one other stray piece. The Suns' brass had gone back and forth on pursuing Thomas. A few weeks before the end of the regular season, D'Antoni said that he was going to have a conversation with Thomas, urge him to give everything he had the rest of the way so he could "fool somebody and get another big contract. It just won't be from us." But, given his big-game heroics and the fact that he is easygoing in the locker room, Thomas does now figure in their plans, provided he can be locked up for somewhere around $4 million a year. The Suns' prevailing philosophy is, he'll break your heart if you pay him any more than that.

The idea of a stand-pat scenario make sense, the reasoning being: *Look how far we got without Stoudemire, so imagine him coming back to join Marion, Nash, and an improved Boris Diaw, and if Kurt Thomas is healthy and Tim Thomas can keep hitting big shots . . .* But putting together an NBA team is like building a sand castle at the beach. Add something here, but over there, where you can't see it, something else is crumbling.

The essential question is: Can Marion, Diaw, and Stoudemire coexist at the frontcourt positions? And who plays where? Nomenclature isn't that important—list either Diaw or Stoudemire as the center and the other as the power forward—but they both like to post up at the left block. Plus, neither of them is adept at guarding big people, Diaw because of his limited size, Stoudemire because he's an execrable fundamental defender. One answer would be to start a (hopefully) healthy Kurt Thomas, but then who would go to the bench? Diaw is the likely answer, but he's played so well that cutting his minutes is an undesirable option.

Also, with Stoudemire and Diaw in the starting lineup, that puts

Marion at small forward, and the coaches are insistent—even if Marion believes otherwise—that he is better off at power forward, where his superior quickness turns him from mediocre to Matrix. "When you move him from 4 to 3," says Gentry, repeating a point on which all of the coaches agree, "he becomes a much more average player." (Were Marion present, he would say, "You guys are crazy.")

The coaches muse, as they often do, about players on other teams who would be a good fit for their system. Everyone likes Orlando's Hedo Turkoglu, a big and athletic forward. Dan D'Antoni likes another Magic player, Darko Milicic, the much-maligned Yugoslav who in the 2003 draft was picked ahead of Carmelo Anthony, Chris Bosh, and Dwyane Wade. (Dan takes no end of grief for this.) Gentry likes Eric Piatkowski (whom he coached when he was with the Clippers), a role player for most of his career but a deadly outside shooter and a good team guy.

"Well, I guess we can't sign anybody before tomorrow," says D'Antoni. "So let's get to work."

Despite the pressure, practice looks pretty much the same, as always. Not a lot of video, not a lot of strategizing. That will come tomorrow. The fact that this could be the last full practice session of the year isn't mentioned. And when it's over, it could be a post-practice scene before a meaningless game in February. D'Antoni, backed against the wall with a sea of reporters in front of him, is cracking jokes. Asked about the report that Cuban has contacted the league about Marion's allegedly throwing an elbow, D'Antoni says, "Jeez, get the guy a desk in New York. Enough's enough." Tim Thomas describes the poker game that took place on the plane ride back home after the agonizing Game 5 loss. Burke, Grant, Stoudemire, Kurt Thomas, and Tskitishvili engage in a spirited three-point shooting game.

"On how many teams would you see the practice before a Game

6, conference finals ending with seven-footers in a three-point shooting contest?" says Del Negro.

Iavaroni is down there conducting it, sweating profusely as he throws back the balls to five players who won't even be getting in tomorrow night's game.

"It's therapy," says Iavaroni. "I'd only be up looking at more video."

In the locker room, meanwhile, Raja Bell is exercising his role as trip coordinator. He approaches Eddie House and asks, *"Quisieras llevar las esposas en el viaje?"* A Miamian, Bell is almost as likely to be heard speaking Spanish as English. He and Dave Griffin, who latched on to the speech patterns of Yamil Benitez, an Arizona Diamondback outfielder from Puerto Rico, communicate almost totally in a kind of pidgin English-Spanish with a thick Cubano accent.

House looks blankly at him for a moment, then says, "You want to know if I'm taking my wife to Dallas, right?"

"You're the man, Eddie," says Bell. "You're picking up this shit."

"I don't care," House says. "Whatever you guys think." Nash has come over to join the conversation.

"Well, we're just trying to get an idea of what everyone wants," says Bell.

"I'd say yes, because I just want my little one [his son, Jaelen, 4] to experience it," says House.

"That's a very nice thought, Eddie," says Nash, "especially since he won't remember a damn thing about it."

"Fuck you, Nash," says House.

"It's agreed, then," says Bell.

The word *if* is never spoken. There *will* be a Game 7 back in Dallas and the families *will* go on the trip.

June 3
GAME 6 TONIGHT

Review of game films has revealed, according to the coaches, at least a half dozen occasions when Josh Howard has deliberately stuck out his foot and tripped a Suns' player. D'Antoni had called Stu Jackson yesterday to complain, and Jackson said, "We're looking at it." Today Jackson called back and said, "We did call it once. And we'll keep looking for it."

"I guess we should be happy with that," says D'Antoni.

If there is one consistent criticism of D'Antoni, it's that he complains too much to the referees. On his influential ESPN.com blog, Bill Simmons writes this morning that "nobody works themselves into a foot-stomping, squinting, aghast frenzy like the Suns' coach." D'Antoni frequently masks it with a quip, as he does sometimes with Violet Palmer, the NBA's only female ref.

"Violet," D'Antoni will say, "I can't believe some of that stuff that's being called out there."

"We're doing our best, Mike," she'll answer.

"Oh, I'm not talking about you," D'Antoni will say with a smile. "You're fine. It's those other two knuckleheads."

"Come on now, Mike," she'll say.

But those sitting near courtside know that D'Antoni does make his grievances heard. The *Arizona Republic*'s Paul Coro has a theory that D'Antoni would get many more technical fouls except that before and after the game he's such a nice guy that referees don't always take his griping seriously. His protests are mostly, of course, partisan-based, as are those of every coach. (And every player, GM, owner, and fan.) But often they are about overly physical play, to which he has a legitimate aversion. D'Antoni's teams are not constructed to play a banger's game—especially not with Kurt Thomas on the shelf—and it's not the kind of style he likes.

D'Antoni does not suggest that Avery Johnson is coaching hard fouls. But the Dallas series fits seamlessly into the pattern of the two that preceded it—the opposition does most of the attacking, and Phoenix, except for Bell, does most of the recoiling.

"I think Raja ought to go up to Howard before the game and say, 'If you trip one guy, we're coming after your ass,'" suggests Dan D'Antoni, half-seriously.

"Well, it would be better if we could do it with three guys," says Mike, "Kurt Thomas being one of them."

The loop of Nowitzki getting fifty on them plays endlessly. It's like a horror film, and there is nothing to do except watch it, wince, and rewind. Over and over. Watch, wince, rewind. On a switch, they see Bell all over Nowitzki, "getting into his legs," as Iavaroni puts it, forcing Nowitzki to take a horrible off-balance shot. Which goes in.

"You know what?" says Iavaroni. "There's no defense in the world that can keep a seven-footer from fading away and making a shot."

"But is there a defense out there that keeps Nowitzki from *getting* that shot and we just haven't figured it out yet," wonders D'Antoni. (It really isn't a question because he knows what the answer is—probably not.) "Maybe we run at him. I don't know if I'm comfortable having Steve Nash right there at the foul line with Dirk Nowitzki shooting a jump shot at the end of the game."

"We'll figure it out," says Iavaroni. "And you know what? If we don't, they're a better fucking team than we are."

"It'll come down to that look in our eye when we walk out," says Dan. "Do we have it or not?" This is the older D'Antoni's default position: Don't worry so much about the technical part of the game—work on the mental and the motivational.

On the screen, Nowitzki makes another seemingly impossible fallaway. Gentry lets out a powerful sneeze.

"Bless you," says Weber.

"I know you don't mean it," says Gentry, "but thanks."

The tape rolls on. No answers, only endless questions.

"I know what we have to do," Gentry says finally. "We have to get them to keep Keith Van Horn in the game."

"I'll make a call to Avery," says D'Antoni.

There seems to be no sense of urgency in the dressing room, no sign that this is anything but a normal game. Barbosa gets his shots in early with Dan—REMEMBER THE BACKYARD is the last item on Dan's tip sheet. Nash warms up in the practice gym with Jay Gaspar. Bell and House trade quips, as they normally do. Stoudemire, in street clothes, drifts in, drifts out, drifts back in. The bigs meet, the wings meet, then D'Antoni takes over.

"Even in Game 5," he says, "they only shot forty-seven percent, so we did pretty good, guys. It's still about second-chance points. It's still about closing out and not putting people on the foul line. Don't panic. Don't overreact. The keys are activity, energy, keeping them off-balance. We just have to go forty-eight minutes.

"And one last thing—this team has a lot of fake tough guys, and they're starting to piss everybody off. All the shit they do, the tripping and stuff. You know what? Get in their face and bust the horseshit out of them. I don't want you to disrespect them, but there are some punks on that team. They want to win it here. Let's just be sure it doesn't happen."

D'Antoni sends them out. Back in the coaches office, I ask Dan, "Well, do they have that look in their eye?"

He considers it. "I'm not sure," he says.

The Howard-tripping story has been widely circulated, and TNT did a pregame piece on it. Sarver, wearing a Shawn Marion jersey, approaches Howard during the pregame warm-ups and makes a comment about it.

"I don't know what you're talking about," Howard tells the owner, "but in two hours we're going to be celebrating on your court."

Howard's confidence notwithstanding, the Mavericks come out as if they are content with playing a Game 7 back at home. Devin Harris and Jason Terry get in early foul trouble, and Nowitzki has come back to Earth. The Suns are in position to get ahead by as much as twenty-five points, and would have if everyone were playing like Boris Diaw. Over the last forty-eight hours the coaches had been concerned about Diaw's play, particularly his tendency to force shots, which is out of character for him. "He just wants to win so badly," says Gentry. They debated on whether to show him video of instances when he should've passed instead of shot, but D'Antoni ultimately decided against it. "Sometimes you try to coach more out of a guy— make the right play, take shots at the right time, all that—and you get less," D'Antoni said. "Boris's frame of mind is much more important than anything we can teach him on the fly."

The decision was a wise one, for Diaw is playing with a computer-perfect mind. He finishes the first half with twenty points and eight rebounds and the Suns lead 51–39.

The cloud on the horizon is foul trouble—Diaw, Bell, and Barbosa, who played only nine minutes—all have three. "All in all, though, I'll take whistles like this," says D'Antoni. He means that a game that isn't rough-and-tumble favors the Suns. The flip side of that is that a lot of fouls exploits Phoenix's lack of depth and also slows down the tempo of the game.

"Okay, guys, we stay out of foul trouble and move our feet, we're going to be fine," D'Antoni tells the team. "Also, contest jump shots, but pack it in, and know that you can take some more liberties on certain guys, like [Devin] Harris and [Darrell] Armstrong.

"You're doing a helluva job on Nowitzki [who has missed seven of nine shots], keeping him in front. Now, you know they're going to come in and try to make a push the first five or six minutes. So we gotta come out of this dressing room fired up and ready to go. Anybody got anything?"

Nash adds his warning: "Let's get out there early."

The inevitable Dallas push doesn't come early. But it comes midway through the third quarter after Phoenix takes a 60–45 lead. Nowitzki gets hot, then Terry, then Nowitzki again. Thomas commits a turnover, Bell misses a three-pointer, Marion loses the ball, Nash misses a short jumper. The Phoenix lead is cut to ten, then eight, then six, then four at the end of the period.

Is there collective weight, one wonders, in all of those struggles the Suns have been through? Does the sheer burden of overcoming so much—the injuries, the intrigue, the suspension, the enervating seven-game series that preceded this one—inevitably take its toll? As the lead slips away, do the Suns, unconsciously, start to think about the others that got away (Games 3 and 4 of the Laker series, or this last game in the Maverick series) or even the ones that *almost* got away, like Game 6 of the Laker series and Game 5 of the Clipper series?

The Mavs tie the game on a Josh Howard layup, then take their first lead since the opening seconds on a dunk by seven-footer Diop, who is left wide-open. Nash gets Diaw a dunk to tie it back up, but now Stackhouse is into it and Josh Howard is all over the court.

Nash can't get free. Has the burden of carrying the team through a hundred games—dribbling and probing, dribbling and probing—simply caught up to him? Tim Thomas misses a couple of shots. Has the Rental, who had saved the season a month ago in Game 6 against the Lakers, run out of gas? Marion can't get open for a good shot. Has he been missed too often on cuts and has stopped cutting? Or has the smorgasbord of defenders the Mavs have to throw at him—Howard, Stackhouse, Griffin—simply worn him down?

The Dallas lead reaches seven points, 84–77, after Howard makes two free throws with 3:46 left. Over the next minute and a half, Nash makes a driving layup, loses the ball, makes another driving layup, then loses the ball again. He is playing himself into exhaustion and that's what happens when you do that—one frantic moment up, one frantic moment down. Nowitzki makes two free throws with 2:45 remaining. Nash makes another driving layup with 1:49 left, but Howard more than matches it with a three-pointer that puts the lead back to ten. Tim Thomas fouls out, followed by Barbosa. It's all but over.

Even in the final seconds, D'Antoni keeps coaching.

"Who can we foul?" he asks.

"They're all pretty good shooters," answers Gentry.

In short, there are no more good answers.

Nash and Nowitzki, who back in 1998 were introduced to-gether at a Maverick press conference—Nash having arrived from Phoenix by trade, Nowitzki by the draft—happen to be together near the Suns' basket as the final seconds tick away. They embrace just as Adrian Griffin dunks at the other end, finalizing a 102–93 victory that sends the Mavericks to their first-ever championship series and puts an end to the Suns' semi-miracle of a season. Nash and Nowitzki talk for a few seconds, Nash wishing his buddy good luck as he goes on to play the Miami Heat in the Finals, and then they part company. D'Antoni waves to the crowd as he walks off. Diaw does the same, tears dotting the corner of his eyes. Marion, too, is crying. Barbosa is wide-eyed, as if in shock.

Dave Griffin is right inside the locker room door, as always, slap-ping hands with every coach and every player as they go by. Only when he goes into the coaches office does he roll up his box score and heave it at the wall.

"Well, we moved a step closer with a couple of guys standing over there in suits," says Gentry, alluding to Stoudemire and Kurt Thomas. But he knows he can't put a good face on it. "It's the first time I saw us back on our heels a little bit," he adds. "We missed a couple of shots and we kind of hung our heads."

"We scored fifteen points in the third period," says D'Antoni.

"And L.B. getting in foul trouble hurt us." His voice sounds hoarse, choked with fatigue and emotion.

Gentry stares at his possession chart. "And then we got in a lot of half-court stuff," he says. He begins counting. "We were two for fifteen at one point from the end of the third into early in the fourth."

D'Antoni has other concerns—tomorrow's individual exit meetings with the players—and confers with Griffin on the schedule. Sarver comes in, his Marion jersey dotted with sweat.

"I'm not going to be around tomorrow," he says, "so I'd like to talk to them now."

"Let's go in," says D'Antoni.

The locker room is quiet as D'Antoni speaks, then Sarver, then Marion. Then the coach turns to his cocaptain.

Steve? You got anything?

An hour after the game, the benedictions have been pronounced.

"I'm hurting inside right now," Marion said. "It was a helluva year. It was great playing with these guys. To see us go out here and do what we did was amazing. I got no words for it now. I wish it wasn't over. All we overcame, all the injuries, everything, I'm proud to be a part of this."

"Never once did I think about one of these elimination games being the final game," said Bell. "It just always felt like we had a team that was going to get it done."

"Our guys fought as hard as they could," said D'Antoni. "They just ran out of steam."

"The Suns had an incredible year," said Avery Johnson. "Nash is such a special player. I had to change my pick-and-roll coverage every time down the court. It was a special run for them, especially without Stoudemire."

Dustin Krugel of the Suns' public relations staff announces, "It was two hundred and fourteen days ago that we began the season by blowing a seventeen-point lead to Dallas. We led by eighteen at one point tonight."

Ninety minutes later, Nash walks out alone. Even most of the fans have left their posts along what the players call "the gauntlet," a long table behind which season ticket-holders can get autographs. Nash is walking slowly. He stops and signs a few times, shakes some hands, flashes a weary smile. His family has gone home ahead of him. As he heads toward the players' parking lot, I stop him. Other duties require me to ask him about Nowitzki for a story I'm writing for *Sports Illustrated*.

"This isn't the best timing," I say, "but I want to ask you something about Dirk."

"Sure," he says.

From behind me, I hear a voice say, "Give it up, Jack. Book's over."

"Who's that?" I ask.

"Raja," says Nash.

"Tell him 'Not quite.' "

CHAPTER TWENTY-SEVEN

Phoenix, June 4 . . . .

"You know, the perception is: Amare' comes back and we win a championship. We all know it's not that simple. I'm not afraid to make a move, but I don't want to do something . . . rash."

Today is the thirtieth anniversary of the most famous game in Suns' history, one of the most famous games in NBA history, in fact. On June 4, 1976, in Boston Garden, Game 5 of the Finals, the Suns, who came into the postseason not even favored to advance one round, extended the Boston Celtics to three overtimes before losing 128–126. They then lost the series in Game 6, which is as far as the franchise got in 1993 when the Bulls beat them at home in a Game 6. Last night's loss to Dallas ended the farthest incursion a Suns team had made into the postseason since that Barkley-led '93 squad. If anyone who shows up for the send-off series of meetings has taken note of the day, he doesn't say anything. Ancient history is not a valued commodity to pro athletes.

The locker room has a last-day-of-school feel to it. Jay Gaspar has placed a couple of huge bins in the middle, into which dozens of stray sneakers, T-shirts, and other warmup gear have been tossed. The assistant coaches rummage through it, picking up isolated pieces of equipment they will donate to local middle schools and high schools. "It'll all pretty much have to go to really big kids," says Gentry.

The players pack up their assorted belongings and receive their 2005–06 season books, a modest document put together by the marketing department. "Eddie," Nash says with mock shyness to House, "would you be the first to sign my yearbook?"

Each of the players has a fifteen-minute exit meeting with D'Antoni, Griffin, and Del Negro, who next season will take over officially as director of player personnel. Griffin is vice president of basketball operations answering to D'Antoni, who became, after Colangelo's departure, executive vice president of basketball operations and general manager as well as head coach. "Mike's got a business card problem," says his brother. D'Antoni is now one of the most powerful men in the NBA.

The exit meetings are designed to be air-clearing sessions during which the player is supposed to present gripes, and the coach and personnel men are supposed to give an honest evaluation of where the player does or does not fit in next year's plans. After the exit meetings are over, the players will meet in private to divvy up the playoff shares. It's a fitting symbolic end to the season: It's all about the Benjamins.

As the meetings go on behind closed doors, the assistant coaches cluster outside of the office, enjoying time with each other that, mercifully, doesn't include devising defenses to stop Dirk Nowitzki or Elton Brand or Kobe Bryant. Phil Weber is compiling a list of viable night spots for Dan D'Antoni's bachelor sons who are coming for a visit. "I'm the fun counselor," says Weber.

There is almost no talk of the upcoming Finals between Dallas and Miami. They need a break from basketball, though it will be short-lived. The sessions to be spent discussing the draft and trade scenarios will sometimes be longer than the ones spent discussing playoff strategy. And those meetings start tomorrow.

Inside the office, D'Antoni is talking to Boris Diaw. If there is one player who exceeded preseason expectations, it is Diaw. D'Antoni's training camp comment—"Boris might get us all fired"—has been amended to "We have to have this guy." The same thing has happened to the franchise that happened to Thomas Jefferson: It has been utterly and absolutely seduced by France.

"Boris, real quick, I'll tell you what I told you last night," begins D'Antoni. "In the biggest game of the season you gave us thirty and eleven. You were the league's Most Improved Player. I just appreciate everything you've done. You're fun. You helped make the locker room great. Other than kissing your ass, I don't have much to say.

"The main thing is that there is no reason your goal should not be to be one of the best players in the league. That's how good you can be. I think you could do a little more in terms of getting with these guys [the trainers] and work on your body. You don't want to break down, you don't want to get old. Because you could play next year a little more on the perimeter, use your quickness.

"I think we're close to winning a championship. Now, the next step is getting Amare' back. You've never experienced that. It's like throwing a big boulder into a pond. There is going to be some waves and there will be some impact. Maybe you can't get on the left elbow as much as you'd want and you have to get on the right elbow, stuff like that we just have to figure out."

Diaw mostly nods, ever the pleasant fellow. He can't even find much to debate about. They talk briefly about the upcoming world championships at which France, led by Diaw and his close friend, San Antonio point guard Tony Parker, should be extremely competitive.

"This summer is good for me because I will be playing a lot of guard," says Boris. "I look forward to seeing you there." He smiles at D'Antoni, who will be an assistant for the U.S. team.

"Good luck, Boris," says Griffin, "and enjoy carrying Tony Parker's ass."

The meetings have gone well, as D'Antoni reports to Nash when he comes in for his session. Pat Burke didn't seem happy over the final six weeks of the season, yet, in his exit interview, he expressed a desire to remain with the team. "Part of what happened with Pat was my fault," D'Antoni tells Nash. "I had my reasons but, as a coach, they just weren't good enough. But you know what? As long as he's good with you guys, that's all that counts."

"I love all the guys who don't play," Nash tells D'Antoni, Griffin, and Del Negro. "Off the court, when we travel, they all give a lot. I believe in all that stuff about the importance of the group and how it functions. I believe it's important."

"Somehow we have to keep it fun for you, Steve," says D'Antoni. "The only thing that will wear you down over the next five years will be mental. Your body will hold up fine. We'll try to cut your minutes down a little, but even playing thirty-four minutes . . . it's the *kind* of minutes."

"Was it harder for you this year, the way we had to play?" asks Griffin.

"It was a little harder, yeah," says Nash. "Without Amare', it seemed like I was fighting every play."

"You know, the perception is: Amare' comes back and we win a championship," says D'Antoni. "We all know it's not that simple. I'm not afraid to make a move, but I don't want to do something . . . rash."

"That's what Dallas did for two straight years," says Nash, speaking from experience. "They thought they were close so they brought in Antoine Walker and Raef LaFrentz. Next thing we knew, we were worse."

"But, again, Steve, man, what you've done here, two-time MVP, all the . . ."

"You can only say 'He makes everybody better so many times,'" says Griffin.

"Why don't you ask about renegotiating?" I say.

"You're supposed to be keeping quiet," Griffin says.

"Make sure you're telling me how you're feeling, Steve," says D'Antoni, laughing, "because I'm retiring when you are."

"I'm planning on playing next year at least," says Nash with a smile.

D'Antoni gets up, somewhat sheepishly, and pulls a basketball out of a plastic shopping bag. "One thing . . . could you sign this?" The whole year has gone by and he has never asked Nash to autograph anything.

Nash signs and gives it to D'Antoni, and they exchange one of those awkward man-hugs. Griffin and Del Negro get up and Nash man-hugs with them, too.

"I should stay out of this," I say.

Nash reaches out and gives me a man-hug, too.

"Jack," he says, "now you can fuck off."

EPILOGUE

On June 28, the morning of the 2006 NBA draft, Chris Bianco of Pizzeria Bianco brought in a few dozen of his celebrated basil-and-mozzarella sandwiches to the coaches office on the fourth floor of US Airways Center. He hung around for a few hours as the Suns tried to move up from their twenty-first and twenty-seventh draft positions.

Robert Sarver popped in and out. At one point he called me in to Mike D'Antoni's office, grabbed a pair of scissors, and thinned out my eyebrows.

Dave Griffin worked the phones all day, D'Antoni having pretty much turned the seed work of the draft over to him. The Suns doubted they could move up high enough to snag one of the big-name players, but perhaps they could make a deal to get in the mid-teens and select Thabo Sefolosha, a six-foot-six-inch forward/guard from Switzerland who was the consensus favorite of the coaches and personnel people.

But the Suns couldn't get anything done, and Philadelphia snagged Sefolosha with the thirteenth pick. So the Suns traded away both of their picks, enabling them to save about $9 million through various means.

Some of that was targeted to re-signing Tim Thomas. Instead, the Rental signed a four-year $24.2 million deal with the Los Angeles Clippers. The Suns thought that too much money to pay for Thomas but aren't thrilled he'll be going to a Pacific Division rival.

Phoenix successfully extended the contract of Leandro Barbosa, giving the Brazilian Blur a five-year deal worth about $33 million. An extension could not be worked out for Boris Diaw, who will become a restricted free agent at the end of next season.

Eddie House opted out of the final year of his contract and signed with the New Jersey Nets. Kurt Thomas and James Jones will be back unless the Suns move one or both—that had not happened as of August 30. Pat Burke is also expected to be back with the team, but the Suns did not pick up the option on Nikoloz Tskitishvili, who will likely be playing the 2006–07 season in Europe.

Brian Grant took a medical retirement. He will still be paid more than $15 million from the Lakers.

As of early August, the Suns made one major roster move—signing free-agent point guard Marcus Banks to a five-year deal worth about $21 million. He is an open-court player and, most of all, a pit-bull defender, an ideal backup for Nash, which the Suns considered their most pressing need. Phoenix also picked up Eric Piatkowski, a Gentry favorite who has three-point range, and Sean Marks, an all-purpose big man with whom Burke will be competing for bench minutes.

Amare' Stoudemire, Shawn Marion, Mike D'Antoni, and Jerry Colangelo all went to camp in Las Vegas with the U.S. Olympic team. When the team left for the Far East and the FIBA world championships, however, only D'Antoni, the assistant coach, and Colangelo, the head of USA Basketball, went along. Stoudemire was one of the final three players cut, and it wasn't a major surprise. He had also played for the Suns' summer league team in Las Vegas and pronounced himself improving every day from his knee surgery. Others still worry about his lost "pop."

Marion eventually begged off the Olympic team because of concerns about tendinitis in his knee. He was widely believed, however, to be suffering from "tired-itis."

It is expected that Colangelo will have a diminished role in the affairs of the Suns and, increasingly, is looking for a gold medal in 2008 as the final part of his basketball legacy.

In that competition, the United States saw both Barbosa, who played for Brazil, and Diaw, who was named captain of the French team.

With a considerably higher profile, Raja Bell made several personal appearances here and abroad. "The Raja Bell World Tour," Griffin called it. He and Steve Nash were scheduled to go with the NBA on its Basketball Without Borders mission to South Africa in September.

While walking his twins one hot July day in New York City, Nash was beseiged by autograph seekers. He impulsively ducked into a salon and got his long locks shorn. "I just felt like taking it off," he said by way of explanation. As of August, he had what in the 1950s was known as a crew cut. D'Antoni was ready with a wisecrack: "All those people who were always telling Steve that he should cut his hair," said the coach, "may want to rethink their position."

As for the empty space on the wall outside of the coaches office, once filled by the photo of Charles Barkley and Michael Jordan, there is now a team shot of the Suns linking arms in their pregame ritual. It adorns the cover of this book.

ACKNOWLEDGMENTS

My bosses at *Sports Illustrated* gave me their blessing to do this project, and I thank them for it: managing editor Terry McDonell, deputy managing editor David Bauer, and executive editors Rob Fleder and Mike Bevans. The editor with whom I worked most closely during the NBA season, Chris Stone, showed me an incredible amount of leeway, as well as an astounding knowledge of, and interest in, the Phoenix Suns for someone based in New York City.

Editorial guidance was provided by four other *SI* types: senior editors Mark Bechtel and Hank Hersch, writer-reporter Chris Mannix, and my literary coconspirator, senior writer L. Jon Wertheim. Also, one non-*SI* type, Donna Kisselbach, who didn't let the fact that she is my wife deter her from proffering opinions.

Special thanks to my agent, Scott Waxman, and my editor, Brett Valley at Touchstone, both of whom had the vision to see a book emerging from a magazine article.

The project would never have gotten off the ground without Julie Fie, the Suns' vice president of communications, who is so good at her job that she can be forgiven for sipping that green vitamin concoction that goes everywhere with her. Her assistants, DC Headley, Dustin Krugel, and Sue Laschowsky, were of great assistance, too.

I appreciate the help extended me by all those people who had to push buttons, make calls, or open doors to afford me entrance to the arena or a particular office: Debbie Villa, Ceola Coaston, Kym Hornbeak, Dave Bassoni, and Tom Guy. Jill Mueske, the Suns' travel chief, never failed to help me reach my desired destination.

I enjoyed flying with, busing with, dining with, and just talking to the Suns' extraordinarily down-to-earth broadcasters, in particular, Al McCoy, a legend in the Valley of the Sun and points beyond. Vinny Del Negro (whose considerable acumen will now be used in the front office), Eddie Johnson, Tim Kempton, Gary Bender, Tom Leander, and Dan Majerle couldn't have been more cooperative even as they had to wonder from time to time: What exactly is this guy doing?

Many members of the Phoenix media became friends or acquaintances, including KSAZ TV 10 anchorman Jude LaCava and *Arizona Republic* columnist Dan Bickley. And I have nothing but admiration for the Suns' beat writers, Paul Coro of the *Arizona Republic* and Jerry Brown of the *East Valley/Scottsdale Tribune,* who watched as an interloper entered the dressing room they covered and always accepted it with the right spirit. Their stories were well-written and insightful, too. Marc Stein of ESPN.com provided encouragement and a constant reminder that he is a tough man to beat in the info-gathering game.

The Suns' big guns were friendly and open, starting with chairman and CEO Jerry Colangelo, one of the most important team execs in the history of the NBA. Managing partner Robert Sarver didn't know me at all when I started hanging around, and he may have even gotten used to me, and my eyebrows, by June. I owe a considerable debt to Bryan Colangelo, who left his position as general manager in February and went to Toronto. Thanks also to five other members of the franchise hierarchy: Rick Welts, Dick Van Arsdale, Mark West, Jim Pittman, and Harvey Shank.

Every day I was with the team I saw four friendly faces in the training room: head athletic trainer Aaron Nelson, strength and conditioning coach Erik Phillips, assistant trainer Mike "Cowboy" Elliot, and assistant equipment manager Jay Gaspar, who, in an emergency, washed a couple of my shirts and gave me a couple pairs of logo-ed socks. Please forward bill. Another friendly face in the video room was that of Jason March, and a friendly face outside the locker room was that of Laurel D'Antoni. Thanks to all of them for their help and guidance.

The team's ace doctors, Thomas Carter and Craig Phelps, were not only knowledgeable and helpful but also good traveling companions. I thank Doc Carter in particular for answering an early-morning call. Something about a kidney stone.

Dave Griffin, who got promoted to vice president of basketball operations during the season, had a steady supply of wry observations and seemingly unlimited knowledge about the league. Noel Gillespie, the team's outstanding video coordinator, is young enough to be my son, so why does he know more about basketball than I do?

It is extremely difficult not to like this Suns team, and that is an opinion held not just by those who see it on a daily basis but by almost every reporter with whom I came into contact this season. For sharing their thoughts with me and being unfailingly friendly and cooperative, I thank, in alphabetical order: Leandro Barbosa, Raja Bell, Pat Burke, Boris Diaw, Brian Grant, Eddie House, Jimmy Jackson, James Jones, Shawn Marion, Steve Nash, Amare' Stoudemire, Kurt Thomas, Tim Thomas, Dijon Thompson, and Nikoloz Tskitishvili.

Finally, one of the nicest things you can do for someone is to make them feel at home, and, so, my loudest shout-out goes to the Phoenix Suns' coaching staff: Mike D'Antoni, Alvin Gentry, Marc Iavaroni, Phil Weber, Dan D'Antoni, and Todd Quinter. Before hanging out with the Flying Geniuses (as Dan jokingly calls them), I wouldn't have thought it possible to have this much fun doing a job. Writing about someone generally precludes having a friendship with them, and all I can say is that I hope I stayed on the correct side of that very thin line.

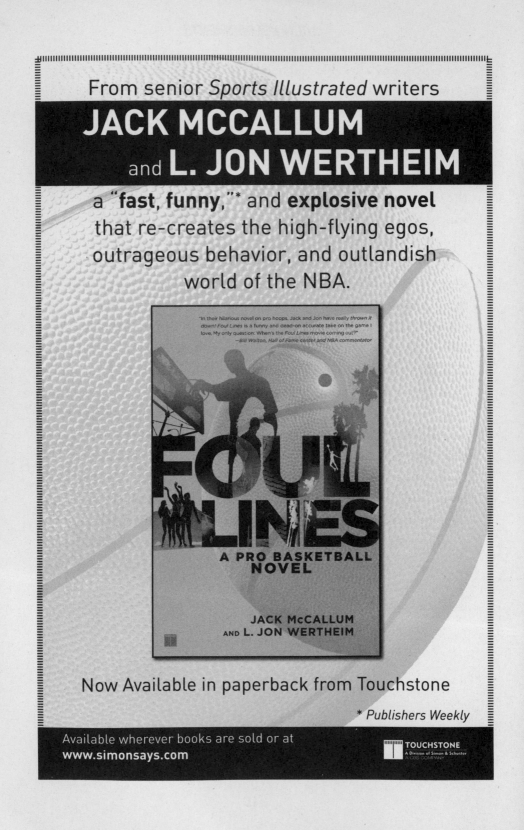